ENVIRONMENTAL PROTECTION

WHAT EVERYONE NEEDS TO KNOW®

ENVIRONMENTAL PROTECTION

WHAT EVERYONE NEEDS TO KNOW®

PAMELA HILL

OXFORD
UNIVERSITY PRESS

OXFORD
UNIVERSITY PRESS

Oxford University Press is a department of the University of Oxford. It furthers
the University's objective of excellence in research, scholarship, and education
by publishing worldwide. Oxford is a registered trade mark of Oxford University
Press in the UK and certain other countries.

"What Everyone Needs to Know" is a registered trademark of
Oxford University Press.

Published in the United States of America by Oxford University Press
198 Madison Avenue, New York, NY 10016, United States of America.

Library of Congress Cataloging-in-Publication Data
Names: Hill, Pamela, 1949– author.
Title: Environmental protection : what everyone needs to know / Pamela Hill.
Description: Oxford ; New York, NY : Oxford University Press, 2017. | Series:
What everyone needs to know | Includes bibliographical references and index.
Identifiers: LCCN 2016033953| ISBN 9780190223076 (pbk.) |
ISBN 9780190223069 (hardcover) | ISBN 9780190223083 (Ebook updf) |
ISBN 9780190223090 (Ebook epub)
Subjects: LCSH: Environmental policy. | Environmental protection. |
Environmental law—United States. | Environmental degradation—Prevention.
Classification: LCC GE170 .H56 2017 | DDC 363.7—dc23
LC record available at https://lccn.loc.gov/2016033953

1 3 5 7 9 8 6 4 2

Paperback printed by LSC Communications, United States of America
Hardback printed by Bridgeport National Bindery, Inc., United States of America

For Michael and our children Daniel, Elizabeth, and Matthew

CONTENTS

3 Environmental Laws   24

4 Environmental Protection and the Global Community   34

5 Water   44

6 Air   76

7 Ecosystems   101

8 Climate Change   123

9 Waste   147

10 The Built Environment   165

PREFACE

This book provides an overview of environmental protection for readers who are curious about the subject and want to learn more about it, or who are seeking more information on particular aspects of it. The intended audience is the general public and policymakers, students, academics, environmentalists, and public interest and business personnel. I raise a number of questions in the book that have no obvious answers, but are meant to help the reader actively engage in the challenges this important subject presents. The book covers environmental protection globally, but its main focus is the United States. This is the country from which I take many examples and whose environmental conditions and practices I draw upon most heavily. I am an environmental lawyer. Most of my professional career was at the US Environmental Protection Agency, and I teach US environmental law, so my orientation makes sense from this perspective. Furthermore, the United States is the source of many important environmental laws and policies, as well as a contributor to many global environmental problems. It is, then, an appropriate lens through which to consider environmental protection more broadly.

Before I wrote this book, when people assumed I was an "environmentalist" I often corrected them: if being an environmentalist meant just protecting the environment, that was not who I was. I was also interested in the relationship of environmental protection to economics and politics, and to other societal concerns competing for the public's tax dollars. However, after researching and writing this book I have come to understand better how at risk our global environment is, and how protecting it is not just important (as I always thought it was) but absolutely critical to our economic and social well-being. It is no exaggeration to say that protecting the environment from the harms it currently suffers is directly related to the very survival of our species. So I have become an environmentalist, and I hope that readers of *Environmental Protection: What Everyone Needs to Know* will share, if they do not do so already, the sense of urgency that I now realize is appropriate.

A note on how to use this book. When acronyms and abbreviations first appear (environmental law, science, and policy use many), I provide the words they stand for. They are also included in the index so the reader can find their full form. The endnotes are not exhaustive. Rather, they identify sources of direct quotes and studies directly referenced in the text. Occasionally, they provide the source of data or an opinion I think the reader may simply be curious about. Suggestions for further reading at the end of the book provide additional sources, both print and online.

Many people helped me write this book, starting with the academics, lawyers, government personnel, business people, and public interest professionals I have been fortunate to work with throughout my career. A few people, however, provided detailed and specific ideas, editing, and support, and I owe them special acknowledgment. My heartfelt thanks to these colleagues in the environmental field: Carl Dierker, Veronica Eady, Nancy Marvel, Eric Schaaf, and Ann Williams; to these experts in specific subjects: Dawn Andrews, Gail Feenstra, Daniel Steinberg, Rama Subba Rao Velamuri, and Robert Tinker; and to these members of my family: my children Daniel, Elizabeth, and Matthew Coogan, and my sister Elizabeth Hill. Thanks to my research assistant, Chloe Noonan, who provided consistent and excellent advice, editing, researching, and fact-checking. Thanks to Boston University School of Law for funding this assistance, and to Stephanie Weigmann of the Boston University School of Law Library for her useful suggestions. Thanks also to Elizabeth Walker for formatting help.

I am deeply grateful for the support and wise advice of Nancy Toff, my editor at Oxford University Press.

This book would not be what it is, indeed it would not have been written, without the ideas, patient and insightful editing, and day-to-day encouragement of my husband, Michael Coogan.

ENVIRONMENTAL PROTECTION

WHAT EVERYONE NEEDS TO KNOW®

1

ENVIRONMENTAL PROTECTION

AN INTRODUCTION

What is the environment?

Various materials and conditions, some natural and some made by humans, affect life on earth. Taken together, they form the environment. Sunlight is part of the environment as is an ocean bed deep beneath the surface, or groundwater flowing through and under cracks in subterranean rocks and sand. The environment extends to the very end of the earth's atmosphere. It includes the corner of Broadway and Forty-Second Street in New York City, as well as your living room and the furniture in it. In this book living things are part of the environment, but the insides of living things are not, although they might be in a book about the microbes that inhabit our bodies. Clearly, however, parts of the environment enter living things all the time—carried in the food humans and animals eat, the air we breathe, and the water we drink; plants similarly take them in as they incorporate water, air, light, and soil for their growth and survival.

What is environmental protection?

Environmental protection is a relatively new idea. Fifty years ago colleges did not offer degrees in environmental science. Newspapers did not have columns on the environment. Lawyers did not practice environmental law. The branch of philosophy called environmental ethics did not exist. Corporations did not have environmental policies. Today all of these are common because environmental protection, however one defines it, has taken root around the world.

There is no universally agreed upon view of what constitutes environmental protection, however. Many different economic interests, philosophical perspectives, and cultural values come into play when considering it. Notions of environmental protection are debated vigorously in the United Nations, the US Congress, and other national assemblies; in the boardrooms of corporations and environmental public interest groups; and among individuals. Environmental protection can mean very different things to different people.

To many environmental policymakers environmental protection has meant keeping pollution levels down, and much attention—governmental, academic, individual—has been devoted to this important goal. Indeed, much of this book explores pollution, because it is a basic cause of our environmental problems. Now, however, many thinkers recognize the limitations of pollution control as it is usually handled, which is by limiting pollutant discharges into water and emissions into air from large industrial and municipal sources, by "permitting" (issuing permits for) only a fixed quantity of them. Rather, environmental protection is increasingly about sustainability, a much broader concept. It embraces concerns about entire ecosystems and about cumulative impacts that require assessing all the contributors to the environmental harms occurring in a particular location (or the entire world in the case of climate change) and reducing pollution from all of them. Applying this approach, a polluted urban river would be cleaned up not just by prohibiting factories and sewage treatment plants from discharging wastewater into it from pipes, but also by reducing runoff from nearby streets and agricultural runoff upstream, by prohibiting dumping used motor oil down storm drains that release their contents into the river, by disallowing dog feces in parks along the shore, and so forth. Cumulative health impacts might also be considered in setting environmental priorities and taking action. A population already burdened by pollution and low socioeconomic status might be a more appropriate candidate for better air pollution controls than a more advantaged population, and the more advantaged population might be a more appropriate candidate for a new waste incinerator than the already burdened one.

So environmental protection means—or should mean—reducing pollution, making sustainable choices, seeking holistic solutions, and distributing the burdens and benefits of industrialization fairly among all populations, considering their current situations, their contribution to the harms being addressed, and the resources available to them.

Why does the environment need protection?

The most obvious, if not the most self-serving, reason is that the human species needs the environment. This in some respects is a new concept because until less than one hundred years ago, the environment was thought to be by and large self-healing and simply too big, too venerable, too basic to be seriously undermined, especially by creatures such as humans—a progressive, adaptive, and essentially well-meaning species. Children need protection; property needs protection; countries need protection. But the environment?

From our vantage point in the twenty-first century such thinking is preposterous. Globally, it is now generally recognized that the environment needs protection. In the last hundred years there has been an exponential increase in the types and quantity of pollutants, some of which are synthetics we have created—newcomers to the planet whose long-term consequences we do not yet know. There has been explosive population growth, bringing increased demands for natural resources and competition for clean water and food in many parts of the world. A different phenomenon is also occurring in some places: affluence expressed by an excessive and unprecedented rate of consumption, and a remarkable indifference to wastes from that consumption, which clog our oceans and poison our groundwater. Climate change and its consequences, though particularly daunting, are just the latest entries in a long list of human-caused harms to the environment, from deforestation to smog, that have increasingly been the subject of policy debate and attempts at regulatory control worldwide.

Facing such assaults, the environment cannot be its own advocate—it needs human voices and human action.

How did protecting the environment become a societal concern?

For most of our history, humans have had a complex relationship with the environment. We have feared its storms and volcanoes, and its creatures, from lions to locusts. We have deified it with thunder and rain gods. We have manipulated it for millennia, rechanneling rivers for irrigation and burning forests to make way for crops. We have at the same time simply enjoyed and revered it, as our paintings, literature, music (such as Beethoven's great Pastoral Symphony), and leisure activities demonstrate. Starting in the eighteenth century with the Industrial Revolution, we have increasingly plundered and polluted it. After World War II, as a result of technological advances and related commercial profits, we have continually altered it with new and poorly understood chemicals. Rarely, however, did people spend much effort protecting it. To be sure, there were isolated environmental protections. Kings fenced in the game they hunted, and ancient civilizations guarded water supplies from contamination. As early as 300 BCE, an Indian treatise, *Arthashastra*, addressed at length human-made hazards to the environment. Broad awareness of the environment and its importance began to develop in the modern era during the late nineteenth and early twentieth centuries when, in the United States, not-for-profit organizations such as the National Audubon Society and federal agencies such as the Fish and Wildlife Service were established, and people such as John Muir and Theodore Roosevelt began to articulate environmental values.

But it was not until the second half of the twentieth century that environmental protection on a global scale became an important social value. That shift was quick and dramatic, and a good thing. Not often can one point to a single source of a shift like this. But here we can: it is Rachel Carson's *Silent Spring*. Writing in the introduction to a reprint of the book, then Vice President Al Gore put it this way: "*Silent Spring* came as a cry in the wilderness, a deeply felt, thoroughly researched, and brilliantly written argument that changed the course of history. . . . The publication of *Silent Spring* can properly be seen as the beginning of the modern environmental movement."[1] In *Silent Spring* Carson brought into focus for the first time the effects of chemicals primarily used to kill harmful insects. Such chemicals had become ubiquitous in the environment from spraying, but were also unwittingly poisoning birds, fish, and people. The silent spring alludes to lines from a poem by John Keats in which "the sedge is wither'd from the lake,/And no birds sing."[2] Many of the chemicals she described are now restricted or banned, including DDT, aldrin, dieldrin, and parathion.

Carson was attacked as an extremist, especially by the chemical companies profiting from the pollution she warned against. They heavily financed scientific research to rebut her findings (which have never been seriously disproven) and tried to suppress the book after excerpts appeared in the *New Yorker*. Carson died of breast cancer in 1964, two years after the book's publication. In the final stages of her disease, her testimony in Congress paved the way for a decade of congressional action on environmental protection. Internationally, such organizations as the World Wildlife Fund emerged, and the United Nations commenced its long engagement with the environment starting with the first Conference on the Human Environment in Stockholm in 1972.

Carson's work was not only a David and Goliath story; it was a clarion call that coalesced nicely with two other developments. One was an increasingly affluent and literate postwar population, which was not only reading the news but for the first time was watching it nightly on television. The other was some unmistakable signs from the environment itself that, to quote Miss Clavel in *Madeline*, "something is not right."

One such sign was the Cuyahoga River Fire of 1969. The Cuyahoga runs through Cleveland, Ohio and for years had been the repository of local industrial waste, sewage, and debris. The river was so permeated with these materials that it had caught fire several times, starting in 1936 when oil and garbage on the surface burst into flames because of a blowtorch spark. The largest, most costly fire on the river was actually in 1952, but it was a lesser one in 1969 that caught national attention when it was reported in many periodicals, including *Time* magazine, and televised on the evening news. It did not really matter that the riveting photograph *Time* used was from the 1952 fire. The point was made and the essence of the news story was true: rivers actually were burning and had been for a long time, directly as a result of pollution. The dramatic and counterintuitive picture of a river on fire grabbed national attention, including that of Congress. This image has remained in the annals of environmental protection ever since.

Another example is the *Torrey Canyon*, a supertanker that went aground in 1967 off the southwest coast of England. The tanker spilled about 120,000 tons of crude oil into the Atlantic and onto Cornwall, contaminating 120 miles of its shores and 50 miles of those of Brittany across the English Channel. The ecological, aesthetic, and economic effects were enormous. The only positive outcome was that like the Cuyahoga River fire, the *Torrey Canyon* became a symbol and wake-up call about the power of pollution as well as the unique dangers of oil spills, and the inadequacy of science and law to address them. It also became the paradigm for a recurring tragedy. The same results—ecological, aesthetic, economic—have followed in subsequent spills, such as the *Exxon Valdez* oil tanker in Alaska in 1989 and the British Petroleum *Deepwater Horizon* oil rig in the Gulf of Mexico in 2010.

By the 1960s the press was harvesting many stories of environmental problems amid growing public interest. Starting in the 1970s, environmental protection became an abiding value particularly in the United States, spawning a unique, bipartisan set of powerful environmental laws still in force. Richard Nixon, the president at the time, put it this way at the beginning of the decade in his State of the Union Address: "The great question of the 70s is, shall we surrender to our surroundings, or shall we make our peace with nature and begin to make reparations for the damage we have done to our air, to our land, and to our water?"[3] In 1970 he established the Environmental Protection Agency and gave it the responsibility to implement the new laws. After this promising beginning the United States has had a mixed environmental record. Fortunately, though, also in the 1970s, environmental values began to be the subject of significant concern and action globally, with leadership from the United Nations. This is especially so now as the entire world puzzles over climate change.

What is the Environmental Protection Agency?

The US Environmental Protection Agency (the EPA) is the main government agency charged with administering the federal environmental laws in the United States. The EPA's job boils down to the difficult task of converting the broad mandates in laws passed by Congress into regulations and programs that can be understood by the public and by those who need to follow them, mostly industries. In addition, the EPA distributes large sums of money to states and other entities for specific purposes described in the environmental laws, such as money to run state environmental programs or to build sewage treatment plants. These funds make possible much of the environmental protection that the EPA oversees and the United States enjoys.

President Nixon created the EPA by an executive order, bringing together pieces of federal departments that previously had elements of environmental protection responsibility among their larger mandates. It is an independent regulatory agency and part of the executive branch of government. The president appoints its administrator with Senate approval. The EPA has a headquarters in Washington, DC in charge of policy and regulatory development, more than a dozen labs, and ten regional offices responsible for enforcement and for working with the states on program implementation. The EPA employs about 17,000 people, including scientists, engineers, policy analysts, lawyers, and economists.

The EPA's independent status, notwithstanding its connection to the executive branch, is intended to protect its objectivity and the scientific basis of its programs and policies; both are highly valued within the agency. However, the agency is often buffeted by politics. An extreme example occurred during the Ronald Reagan administration when career staff clashed repeatedly with high-level political appointees. Similarly, during the George W. Bush administration the views of policymakers in the White House and political appointees within the agency especially concerning climate change created serious problems for some career staff.

Do most countries have environmental agencies similar to the EPA?

Yes. For example, China's Ministry of Environmental Protection performs functions similar to the EPA and has collaborated with the EPA for over three decades, as have many other governments' environmental agencies. The Umweltbundesamt has been Germany's main environmental protection agency since 1974. The Ministry of Natural Resources and Environment of the Russian Federation is Russia's EPA equivalent. Although many countries have high-level governmental agencies whose missions broadly concern environmental protection, they vary in focus, structure, and efficacy.

What values drive environmental policy?

Environmental protection has been embedded as a value in our global social fabric at least since the 1970s. The question becomes, then, what values to apply when solving specific environmental issues. Consider this oversimplified scenario: a proposed railway line would run through a wetland on its way from one major city to another, reducing the number of cars and pollution on the road and getting passengers to and from the cities much faster. Should the railway line be approved? Those who take a human-centered (anthropocentric) view value the human benefits from the railway line and would say yes. Those who value the nonhuman benefits of the wetland (such as wildlife habitat) and want to protect it would say no (unless saving it helps humans, as well it might). This is a fundamental values divide in environmental policymaking: human interests versus broader ecological interests. It raises the moral question of whether the human species can do whatever it wants to the environment to advance its own interests, or whether it is only one among many living things and has no right to destroy parts of the planet and deplete its resources for its own benefit at the expense of other species—whether, in fact, it has an obligation to protect these other living things.

At least in western moral philosophy, the human-centered perspective tends to win out: Aristotle himself said that "nature has made all . . . things for the sake of humans."[4] The divine command to the first humans in the Bible is to "fill the earth, and subdue it; and have dominion over the fish of the sea and over the birds in the air, and over every living thing that moves upon the earth" (Gen. 1:28). Moreover, the dominance of the economic lens in deciding environmental issues tends to promote human-centered environmental values. But there is significant counterbalance. Some biblical scholars, for example, point to stewardship concepts in the Bible. Many indigenous peoples such as American Indian tribes manifest a strong and abiding spiritual attachment to and respect for nature. The ecological values of the nineteenth century American transcendentalists Emerson and Thoreau linked nature directly with divinity, and are still influential, as is the environmental ethic of thinkers like Carson and Aldo Leopold, famous for his land ethic. In 2015, in his encyclical *Laudato Si'*,

Pope Francis reiterated remarks of his immediate predecessors and other Christian leaders that degradation of the environment is a sin.

The relationship between human-centered interests and ecological ones finds its way into jurisprudence. Mineral King Valley in 1969 was a beautiful area and game refuge in the Sierra Nevada mountains when the Disney Company proposed to build a resort there. Environmental groups tried to block it using a now famous legal argument: trees and other living creatures threatened with harm should have standing to sue in court, much like an orphaned child, with lawyers representing their interests. The legal theory did not win the day, but it received much attention in the US Supreme Court where the case ended up. The notion that "trees have standing" appeared in the dissent penned by Justice William O. Douglas and joined by Justices Brennan and Blackmun,[5] and remains a provocative reminder of the fragility of a natural environment that has no voice, as well as of the stark conflict between economic and ecological values.

Environmental values and their role in environmental problem solving are much more complex than the human-centered versus natural world dichotomy described above. Consider another scenario: Cape Wind was an ambitious project that would have generated energy from many giant wind turbines off Cape Cod, Massachusetts in Nantucket Sound. The debates about Cape Wind swirled with disparate sets of values: habitat values (birds and whales); religious and cultural values (Native American burial grounds); aesthetic values (the view from the shore); economic values (jobs); and sustainability values (renewable energy).

What is sustainability?

This concept, often associated with development, arrived very late to the environmental protection lexicon. But it has become a core, and challenging, environmental value. A foundational definition appears in the 1987 report to the United Nations from the World Commission on Environment and Development: development is sustainable when it "meets the needs of the present without compromising the ability of future generations to meet their own needs."[6] Sustainability, then, is about the future, and that is what makes it such an elusive and difficult goal. Long-term planning for humans does not extend more than a few years; a long-range business strategic plan, for instance, rarely looks beyond ten. Sustainable development, agriculture, and energy policy, and any other sustainable environmental practices, necessarily extend beyond the lifetimes of the people considering them. Sustainability is not just making sure a particular marine food source is not fished out of existence and lost as a profitable market, although it includes this small goal.

While retaining its original intergenerational aspect, policymakers now are adding additional features to the concept of sustainability. The Plan of Implementation of the 2002 United Nations World Summit on Sustainable Development states that it will "promote the integration of the three components of sustainable development—economic development, social development and environmental protection—as interdependent and mutually reinforcing pillars."[7] These three pillars of sustainability have become important elements for environmental policymakers who are trying to implement it.

As a practical matter, sustainability means improving economic conditions, reducing poverty, adhering to fundamental fairness, and achieving a healthy environment—all on a global scale and far into the future. If pollution control was the central concern of environmental policymakers in the late twentieth century, sustainability is the central concern now.

Why is environmental protection so hard to achieve?

We can take many straightforward (if not easily accomplished) steps collectively and individually that would help reverse the environmental degradation of the last few hundred years, such as energy conservation, lifestyle changes, aggressive pollution controls, consumption reduction, and innovative technologies. Still, we have a very hard time taking these steps. Given the risks and the payoffs, one wonders why. Here are six reasons.

First, people have few natural economic incentives to protect the environment because environmental resources often are free, or seem to be. The classic parable "The Tragedy of the Commons," written by Garrett Hardin in 1968 and widely recognized as instructive by environmental economists, lays out the problem. Hardin's commons is a pasture open to all. For years it offers enough space and grass for all herders to easily graze their animals. Because of the success of the herders, however, the time comes when the number of animals exceeds the commons' capacity. Yet because the commons' resources are free, the herders gain nothing individually by reducing their herds. So each herder decides to keep adding animals. In Hardin's words, "therein is the tragedy. Each man is locked into a system that compels him to increase his herd without limit—in a world that is limited. Ruin is the destination toward which all men rush, each pursuing his own best interest in a society that believes in the freedom of the commons. Freedom in a commons brings ruin to all."[8] Hardin's commons is a metaphor for our oceans, air, wildlife, and soils, all seemingly so abundant. The message is that environmental protection requires collective action and control of self-interest, both very hard to achieve.

Even if incentives such as taxes, values, or coercive laws succeed in changing behavior in an environmentally protective way—a way protective of the commons—a second problem creates additional challenges. It is the gap in time that frequently exists between when environmental degradation starts and when people become alarmed by it: environmental problems typically sneak up on us— they do not normally jump out and bite us. This lag time has often been expressed through the famous boiled frog allegory. If you put a frog in boiling water it will jump out and save itself, but if you slowly warm up the water the frog will remain there and boil to death. Whether or not this is accurate scientifically, it is on point as a metaphor for the phenomenon of climate change as well as almost all other human-made environmental problems. It demonstrates that to protect the environment people must perceive and act upon dangers that seem speculative and distant. Unfortunately, our species is not wired for this sort of action. With the fight or flight mentality we inherited from our hunter-gatherer ancestors, our instincts are to react to present danger, not the insidious, incremental, often imperceptible threats to the environment from our own activity. The environment is hard to protect because its degradation is so stealthy that humans are not usually fearful enough to act, as we would if our homes were on fire.

A third problem is that many actions with a negative impact on the environment are simply not felt by those who create them. When they do become apparent, often the people harmed are in no position to prevent the impacts. The people benefitting, experiencing no harm and often far away, have no incentive to reduce the harm. Dioxin is a toxic waste byproduct of the process at paper mills that makes paper white, a feature of paper that people all over the world enjoy. For years dioxin was discharged into rivers, such as the Penobscot River in Maine, and ended up in the fish people ate there. Most directly affected were members of the Penobscot Indian Nation, whose reservation is composed of islands on the river, and who for centuries have fished for food there, ingesting dioxin as a result. The consumers of white paper, on the other hand—the vast majority of whom do not eat much if any fish from the Penobscot River, who live nowhere near the paper mills, and who know very little about how paper is made—are unaware of the water-quality issues imbedded in the product they use.

Fourth, environmental problems and solutions are not obvious. In most instances uncertainty is uncomfortably present as we work on them: when, in fact, will the planet's climate get too warm to support life as we know it? Is it really too dangerous to swim in water with high levels of bacteria, and if so, how high do the levels need to be to close a major beach on a hot Sunday in August? Should cancer-causing substances contained in products we enjoy be prohibited altogether even though the exact nature of their risks is unclear?

Fifth, in the United States at least, environmental issues have become increasingly partisan and political, in stark contrast to the bipartisanship they enjoyed in the 1970s. It is very hard these days to get the US Congress to rally behind them: practically every environmental issue in the twenty-first century has become snarled in political wrangling, from the Keystone pipeline to the future of coal.

Sixth, the successes of the early years of the environmental movement were of the low-hanging fruit kind. Reducing pollution from large factories, although by no means easy to achieve, is much less difficult than grappling with global climate change or groundwater pollution from thousands of small sources. Yet these and similar issues are what confront us today.

At bottom, though, the environment is hard to protect because it requires setting aside self-interest, seeing beyond the present, thinking and acting globally, and understanding the deep connection between a healthy environment and human progress, even human survival. It also tends to elude solutions, as evidenced in the answer to the next question.

What does the idea of unintended consequences have to do with environmental protection?

The idea of unintended consequences describes an outcome different from what was planned, expected, or wanted—something that happens all the time. Although the outcome can be beneficial, it can also be detrimental; this unfortunately is how the notion usually arises in the context of environmental protection. The environment is a very complicated place, and trying to correct injuries to it can also be complicated. Indeed, the environmental protection movement is the response not to planned assaults on the environment—no ordinary person or industry sets out to pollute the air or water—but to the unintended consequences of human activities that had benign goals. Who could have intended climate change to be the consequence of industrialization? Or water pollution to be the consequence of chemical fertilizers?

The unintended consequences of the particular responses to such harms themselves are also telling. They demonstrate just how difficult environmental protection is, and how important it is to develop answers to environmental problems holistically, because it is the linear responses that have often produced additional problems. No one, for example, intends to send cancer-causing dioxin into the air from municipal incinerators designed to get rid of garbage, but many of them do. The US Congress did not intend to create pollution by enacting the early federal environmental protection laws. However, as Congress observed in the findings section of the 1976 Resource Conservation and Recovery Act (the federal law addressing solid and hazardous waste), "as a result of the Clean Air Act, the Water Pollution Control Act [the Clean Water Act] and other Federal and State laws respecting public health and the environment, greater amounts of solid waste (in the form of sludge and other pollution treatment residues) have been created."[9] What this means is that air and water pollution controls often create byproducts that cause a land pollution problem big enough to require additional federal attention.

As forward-looking and flexible as environmental laws have proven to be, they do not normally embrace the idea that everything actually is connected to everything else and so should be regulated that way. To correct this defect, some environmental thinkers have proposed that these laws should be recast into one big environmental protection statute that better anticipates such things as unintended consequences, cumulative risks, and synergistic effects.

2

POLLUTION

What is pollution?

Pollution is the presence of anything in the environment that produces undesired effects. Substances that may be entirely innocuous in one location may cause pollution in another. Salt is a key component of ocean water, but when salt water finds its way to fresh water, especially drinking water, as it did during Hurricane Katrina, it causes pollution. Similarly, pharmaceuticals are important medical tools with many uses from controlling pain to curing infections, but when disposed of down the drain they cause pollution.

Pollution is usually associated with humans, such as the pollution from synthetic chemicals or from factories. It may, however, be caused by naturally occurring substances such as arsenic, radon, and soil sediments, which can appear in the environment without human involvement. And some pollution is the result of natural events, such as air pollution from erupting volcanoes. Most of it, however, comes from human activity and can be controlled.

Pollution is sometimes easy to detect. Any pedestrian walking near the tailpipe of a diesel bus knows the exhaust she is breathing is pollution. Much pollution, however, is very hard to detect. You cannot detect harmful levels of lead in soil, food, and paint chips (all often ingested by children). You cannot taste harmful levels of bacteria in your drinking water. You usually cannot smell ozone in the air. Yet these are all forms of pollution.

What are pollutants?

Pollutants are emissions of matter or energy (such as heat, sound, and radiation) that cause pollution. Whether something actually is a pollutant, however, is not always straightforward. Whether it should be regulated is a further complication. These determinations require first assessing the risk the suspected pollutant poses. A second step involves determining whether the risk is great enough to warrant concern and, ultimately, regulation (risk management). Noise and light, for example, can be pollutants but in general they are not regulated, even though there are very good reasons to do so. Moreover, scientists and policymakers may, and often do, disagree about what quantity or level is needed to justify regulation of a pollutant, a determination that can depend on its location. Small amounts of bacteria in a remote forest stream might not cause harm, but in Walden Pond or Loch Lomond where people swim or in drinking water sources, they very well could be harmful. Finally, once something is designated a regulated pollutant, the controls required can appear to be costly and impractical, especially to business. Are there feasible technologies to control particular pollutants? Is there a cost threshold for regulating pollutants? Should there be? Such questions concerning how to identify and regulate pollutants are answered using a mix of science and policy. The result is a collection of substances called "pollutants" that is in some respects limited in scope and undercontrolled.

What are persistent organic pollutants?

Persistent organic pollutants (POPs) are synthetic chemicals produced either intentionally (DDT, polychlorinated biphenyls or PCBs, and dieldrin, for example) or unintentionally as industrial or combustion byproducts (dioxins and furans, for example). They are of tremendous concern globally and enjoy an unusual amount of regulatory attention because of the grave, proven risks they present, including their role as endocrine disruptors. These risks are based on four troubling characteristics. First, POPs persist in the environment, sometimes for centuries. Second, they travel over great distances carried in different environmental media. They have been found, for example, in the Artic, thousands of miles from any known sources. Third, they collect in fatty tissue, so small exposures may aggregate into harmful health effects. Fourth, they bioaccumulate up the food chain.

PCBs, dioxin-like substances used for a long time and extensively in the electrical industry, are notorious POPs. They collect in sediments (as do others because of their chemical characteristics) and have degraded many river bottoms, including the Hudson in New York, which has been the subject of extensive cleanup measures over many years.

POPs are among the few specific environmental pollutants to be subject to focused international attention. The Stockholm Convention on Persistent Organic Chemicals is a United Nations-sponsored international treaty, in force since 2004. Among the convention's aims are to eliminate POPs, starting with the twelve worst (known as the "dirty dozen") and to clean up old POPs stockpiles and equipment containing them. These goals have not yet been met, but substantial progress is being made globally.

Some of the dirty dozen were named above. Here is the complete list: aldrin, chlordane, DDT, dieldrin, endrin, heptachlor, hexachlorobenzene, mirex, toxaphene, PCBs, dioxins, and furans.

What are endocrine disruptors?

Endocrine disruptors are substances that interfere with the endocrine system, the system responsible for regulating hormones throughout the body. They are associated with reproductive and developmental problems (particularly during the prenatal phase), some cancers, and neurological effects, including cognitive impairment. Substances that cause endocrine disruption include many synthetic chemicals, several of which are practically ubiquitous, appearing in such common consumer products as plastic bottles, toys, cosmetics, metal food containers, and pharmaceuticals. Such substances also appear in drinking water sources. Perchlorate, an ingredient in rocket fuel, for example, has been found in water supplies and is of concern because of its potential effects on thyroid function.

What are bioaccumulation and biomagnification?

Bioaccumulation is the uptake of substances by living things from water or food in amounts greater than can be removed by these organisms. Chemicals in polluted water often bioaccumulate in protozoa, small fish, and larger fish; on land they bioaccumulate in plant matter. The concentrations of these chemicals increase in intensity as they move higher up the food chain—that is, when larger predators eat smaller prey; this is biomagnification. A 1997 study found that levels of PCBs in northern Canadian caribou were as much as ten times higher than the levels in the lichen they ate; the PCBs levels in their predators, wolves, were six times greater than that.[1] Bioaccumulation and biomagnification are important phenomena that exacerbate the impacts of chemicals in the environment for humans and other species when these chemicals find their way into the fish, animals, and vegetables we eat.

How do we know what a safe level of pollution is?

We don't. Some would say that no level of pollution from, say, a known carcinogen or other toxic substance is safe and so that substance should be prohibited. Although this happens on rare occasions—DDT is a banned carcinogen—the idea broadly applied is perceived as completely impractical by most policymakers. A more common approach is to try to determine how much exposure to a pollutant is required to produce harm and, based on that information, to regulate it. That is why in the United States, for example, the EPA has set national maximum contaminant levels for specific pollutants in drinking water, recommended water quality criteria for specific pollutants in lakes and rivers, and national emission standards for hazardous pollutants in the air. Other countries have similar standards. These pollution limits assume that although the pollutants can be harmful, the risks they present at these established levels are acceptable.

There are many pollutants for which safe levels have not yet been established. Either we know too little about them, such as nanopollutants, or we have simply not yet established a reliable safety threshold. For instance, in the United States, 62,000 chemicals remained on the market without testing when the Toxic Substances Control Act was passed in 1976. By 2011 the EPA had required testing of only about three hundred of them, and only five are now regulated under the act. In fact, the law had for years been recognized to be inadequate and out of date. At last, in 2016, important bipartisan reforms were passed in the US Congress and signed into law by President Obama.

What is noise pollution?

Noise is unwanted, unpleasant, or disturbing sound. It can, among other effects, disturb sleep, disrupt conversation, contribute to stress-related illness, and induce hearing loss. The US Congress recognized noise pollution in 1972 with the passage of the Noise Control Act and in 1978 with the passage of the Quiet Communities Act. However, in the United States, noise pollution control at the federal level has not been robust. During the Reagan administration, Congress stopped funding federal noise-abatement activities and responsibilities shifted to state and local governments. The EPA retains a limited role in reducing noise pollution, principally by disseminating information and engaging in studies. Other governments have addressed noise pollution, including the European Union, which has an environmental noise directive. Although noise laws exist, often the problem is addressed simply through informal negotiation (for example, between noisy neighbor and bothered neighbor).

What is light pollution?

Sky glow is a familiar kind of light pollution resulting from the many sources of artificial light emanating from cities and suburban sprawl. Caltech's Palomar Observatory is the home of the famous Hale Telescope and of many key astronomical discoveries about our universe. Scientists in the 1930s selected rural Palomar Mountain to site the observatory in part because its dark skies, far from city lights, enabled observation of distant galaxies. Today, Caltech and Palomar fear that the continued rapid urbanization of southern California will so increase sky glow that it will significantly reduce the effectiveness of the observatory for research. They are working with nearby city, county, and tribal governments to reduce sky glow impacts. In the early twentieth century on a clear night it was often easy to see the Milky Way galaxy dramatically dominating the night sky. This is no longer possible for most of the planet's people, over 50 percent of whom now live in cities where light blots out the stars. The "Starry Night" that inspired van Gogh is lost to many of us. Indeed, the US National Forest Service identifies starry night skies as important components of the places it protects, like an endangered species.

Other common forms of light pollution are glare, which is unshielded artificial light that can have a blinding effect, and light trespass, which is unwanted artificial light entering someone else's property, like the flood of nearby commercial lighting into one's bedroom.

Light pollution creates problems not only for astronomers and nature lovers. It also seriously disrupts the diurnal rhythm of life for wildlife and humans—confusing the migratory patterns of birds, for example, and inducing sleep disorders and related medical problems in people. Because artificial lighting consumes roughly one quarter of all energy worldwide it is also a major contributor to the energy challenges, closely tied to climate change, now of global concern.

Unlike many forms of pollution, light pollution is relatively easy to reduce. Although lights are important for safety and for the pleasure and primal comfort they provide, humans tend to overilluminate and to illuminate inefficiently. If lights are properly shielded (with downward facing streetlights, for example), used only when necessary, and fitted with energy-efficient bulbs, dramatic reductions in light pollution can be enjoyed without sacrificing the many, many benefits that lights provide.

What is nanopollution?

Perhaps it is better to start with the question "what is nanotechnology?" because nanopollution is its byproduct. Nanotechnology is the science and engineering of particles in the nano-scale range, between 1 and 100 nanometers. (A nanometer is one-billionth of a meter; for comparison, a strand of human hair is about 2.5 nanometers in diameter.) It is a fast-developing, promising, and lucrative field with upward of eight hundred nanotechnology-containing commercial products on the market. Most readers of this book have likely encountered one or more of them in such products as spill-resistant fabric, cosmetics, sports equipment, food, and medical devices. It has promising applications in pollution control. Nanotechnology is potentially revolutionary, akin in its possible benefits to computer technology.

The problem is that we know very little about the potentially harmful effects of nanopollutants, although it is reasonable to assume that these extremely small particles can reach deep inside the human body and other organisms and do bad things. They have ready access through inhalation and ingestion. Another pathway is absorption into the skin, for example, from nanoparticle-containing sunscreens we apply. Scientists believe that these particles may damage important internal mechanisms such as DNA. Notwithstanding serious issues, their manufacture and use are not meaningfully regulated. As is often the case in environmental protection, here we seem to be exacting a high degree of certainty that harm will occur before we intervene with regulation. Similarly, asbestos was not regulated until after it had been associated with mesothelioma; DDT was not regulated until after it had been associated with toxicological effects; and climate change is only now starting to command the attention it needs after its impacts have actually been observed.

Whether and when to regulate a pollutant or pollution are major questions of environmental policy. Should we wait until we clearly detect harm? Or should we act when we only suspect a substance or activity may harm us in the future, recognizing that risk assessment is too crude a tool to anticipate many harms? Without sufficient information, historically at least, we often have given substances the benefit of the doubt and let them into the market and into our environment until something bad happens. The results of this approach are exactly what Rachel Carson reported in *Silent Spring*. The environmental laws that followed *Silent Spring* were a legislative reaction to the bad things that had happened. Indeed, most environmental laws are reactionary: they usually respond to, rather than anticipate or prevent, the effects of pollution. Recently, though, a countervailing environmental policy perspective is emerging known as the precautionary principle. Nanopollution is a problem to which that principle could be applied.

What is the precautionary principle?

The precautionary principle is the idea that even without sufficient scientific certainty, some potential harms to the environment require action. Conversely, lack of clear evidence of harm should not be an excuse for refusing to minimize risk. In other words, rather than giving certain substances the benefit of the doubt, the precautionary principle "sounds like common sense: better safe than sorry; look before you leap."[2] The idea has taken hold as a policy framework in many countries and appears in many international environmental agreements. The important 1992 Rio Declaration from the United Nations Conference on Environment and Development, for example, states as one of its principles that "in order to protect the environment, the precautionary approach shall be widely applied by States according to their capabilities. Where there are threats of serious irreversible damage, lack of full scientific certainty shall not be used as a reason for postponing cost-effective measures to prevent environmental degradation."[3] The precautionary principle has less currency in the United States. Applied to nanopollution, given its potential for harm, precaution would encourage more investment in research and regulatory measures that would prevent surprising health and environmental detriments. Were we to apply precaution to activities contributing to climate change, we would perhaps be facing less dire global climate conditions.

Critics of the precautionary principle argue among other things that it stifles innovation and cramps lucrative markets without a firm basis for concern. This would be the case, perhaps, if the principle were applied across the board for every potentially harmful chemical. But it is not. Rather, it encourages seeking cost-effective alternatives and preventative measures in appropriate circumstances rather than seeking the shortest path from the point of production to the point of profit.

Consider biphenyl A (BPA), a chemical, thought to be an endocrine disruptor, with many applications, including in the production of many plastic bottles such as those containing water and infant formula. In the 2003–2004 National Health and Nutrition Examination Survey, the US Centers for Disease Control found detectable levels of BPA in 93 percent of 2517 urine samples from people six years old and up.[4] Whether it is harmful, and how harmful it is, is the subject of considerable global research, regulatory confusion, and debate. Should regulators give BPA the benefit of the doubt, an approach generally taken in the United States, or apply the precautionary principle as appears to be the trend in some European countries?

What are the most dangerous pollutants?

Given our lack of understanding of many of the pollutants all around us, it is impossible to answer this question. Are nanopollutants among the most dangerous? Who knows? In addition to the POPs, some of the most dangerous ones we do know about are photochemical smog, chemical fertilizers, known carcinogens and other toxic chemicals, and especially the greenhouse gases responsible for climate change.

3

ENVIRONMENTAL LAWS

What is environmental law in the United States?

In the United States environmental law consists of laws enacted by Congress and by state legislatures to address environmental issues, and the written legal decisions of judges resolving environmental disputes arising from these laws. Both are now voluminous. Local laws also influence environmental protection. Although they have a smaller geographic scope, they can have enormous impacts on municipalities and beyond. For example, zoning ordinances determine development patterns, which influence vehicular use and, by extension, fossil fuel emissions. Environmental law covers subjects one would expect, such as water and air pollution, but it also addresses other issues such as the siting of airport runways and bottle recycling.

Environmental law is relatively new, the first major legislation having been enacted in the 1970s. At about the same time, American law schools started offering courses on the subject, major law firms developed special environmental law departments, and judges began to grapple with disputes concerning the environment in state and federal courts, including the US Supreme Court.

Environmental law is unusual. Unlike virtually every other legal area, it deals primarily not with individuals, property rights, or society, but with human impacts on the natural world. Although the impetus of environmental law often is to protect humans from pollution, its main object is not the human species. Rather it is wetlands, wildlife, trees, soil, oceans, streams, and air. This strange orientation creates new problems for lawmakers and judges, forcing some hard questions. For example, what is the monetary value of a shoreline degraded by an oil spill? Can saving an endangered species prevent building a lucrative housing development? Who can represent in court the interests of future generations destined to suffer the consequences of climate change?

What does the US Constitution say about protecting the environment?

Nothing, explicitly. Like many other basic values, rights, and privileges that laws protect and many Americans embrace (civil rights, for example), the environment is not mentioned there. This creates a challenge because all federal laws, including the federal environmental laws, need a basis in the Constitution to be legal, implementable, and enforceable. The courts strike down laws that have no such basis. Fortunately, a few specific powers given to Congress in the Constitution, especially the power to regulate interstate commerce, provide this support. For years, the Commerce Clause as it is known, has been used, and upheld by the Supreme Court, as the constitutional basis for environmental law.[1] Through the Commerce Clause Congress can regulate not only goods that move from state to state, but also matters that affect interstate commerce. So entirely intrastate matters that have impacts on other states, even if the effect appears to be small, can be regulated. For example, this empowers the EPA to regulate intrastate, onsite hazardous waste as part of Congress's broader objective to protect interstate commerce from pollution; and the Fish and Wildlife Service to regulate endangered species whose habitat may be only in one small area because the species affects biodiversity and similar values that cross state lines. The reach of the Commerce Clause presents complex and evolving legal questions that have come into play with respect to important national issues such as federal gun control laws and the Affordable Care Act. With respect to environmental laws, it remains a solid constitutional basis. Other constitutional provisions relied on to support environmental laws include the power to tax and spend, to enter treaties, and to regulate public lands.

State constitutions often contain provisions different from the US Constitution. In keeping with this valuable element of US law, environmental protection provisions appear in several state constitutions, including Illinois, Montana, Hawaii, and Pennsylvania. Pennsylvania, for example, provides that the state's "public natural resources are the common property of all the people, including generations yet to come. As trustee of these resources, the Commonwealth shall conserve and maintain them for the benefit of all the people."[2]

Why did Congress enact environmental laws?

In his State of the Union address in January 1970, President Richard Nixon said: "We still think of air as free. But clean air is not free, and neither is clean water. The price tag on pollution control is high. Through our years of past carelessness we incurred a debt to nature, and now that debt is being called."[3] Nixon was not an environmentalist, but he was an astute politician. His words reflected values being articulated by environmental thinkers and politicians, embraced by an enfranchised, increasingly affluent middle class, and fueled by dramatic environmental disasters reported on the nightly news. They also synchronized with the mood of a country skeptical of the military-industrial complex that Nixon's predecessor, Dwight Eisenhower, had warned about, and the big business interests bemoaned by progressives like Ralph Nader in his book *Unsafe at Any Speed*. This context powered unprecedented congressional action for the next decade, ushered in by the first Earth Day on April 22, 1970. Impressive bipartisanship produced many major environmental laws in the United States, especially when compared with the congressional gridlock in the twenty-first century's second decade on globally significant environmental problems.

On a practical level, as Nixon and members of Congress understood, the environment was not primarily a local issue. The problems it presented crossed state boundaries, in the air and water, and even in products like the car. They required a level economic playing field across the states that only Congress could provide: otherwise, how could the economy work if New Jersey regulated water discharges from factories one way and New York another, and how could Michigan try to harness its air pollution with expensive requirements for its industries while Alabama offered the same industries a regulatory pass to attract them? These were not simple questions, but the environmental laws went a great distance in addressing them. They moved environmental protection from haphazard local and national attention at the beginning of the decade to comprehensive federal control by the end of it.

What are the most important US environmental laws?

The most important federal environmental laws are the National Environmental Policy Act, the Clean Air Act, the Clean Water Act, the Resource Conservation and Recovery Act, the Safe Drinking Water Act, the Endangered Species Act, and the Comprehensive Environmental Response, Compensation, and Liability Act, although others help protect the environment in important ways. The EPA maintains an excellent online database of US environmental laws and related information.

Most of these laws apply a "command and control" approach. It has three elements: enforceable regulations issued by the EPA (or a state); compliance by industries, municipalities, other large entities, and sometimes individuals; and penalties for noncompliance. They also generally assume that pollution is a fact of life that is to be managed, not eliminated. The Clean Air and Clean Water Acts, for example, do not prevent pollution; they "permit" it. The premise of these laws is that pollution will occur; that government's job is to find safe levels of it and issue permits to industries (primarily) and others allowing them to pollute up to that level. Similarly, the federal hazardous waste law is titled "Hazardous Waste Management," not "Hazardous Waste Prevention" or something along those lines. These are policy directions that signal certain outcomes, importantly the continued presence and acceptability of large amounts of pollution. The presumption could have been reversed with a pollution-free or pollution-minimizing set of statutory requirements that permitted pollution and management of waste as fallbacks when the presumptive goal could not reasonably be met. That, however, was not the choice Congress made, although it occasionally has codified these alternative presumptions, often tracking emerging sustainability principles. An example is the 1990 Pollution Prevention Act. This law and similar ones, however, include very few enforceable requirements.

Three other themes run through the laws. One is federalism: Congress intended that the federal government would establish pollution control programs, but that states sooner or later would take them over. So there is a close federal–state relationship that lies at the foundation of these laws. As a result, most states now have primary responsibility for implementing and enforcing federal air, water, and waste programs. In these circumstances the EPA remains in the background providing oversight and occasionally stepping in with enforcement actions against noncompliers in the state if appropriate.

The second theme is public participation: all the major environmental laws contain strong requirements for comments by citizens, including industries and public interest groups, before programs, regulations, and other major federal actions affecting the environment become final. On the one hand, honoring citizen participation has promoted public engagement and improved the quality of many federal actions; it has also increased the public's acceptance of them. On the other hand, honoring it has required public comment periods and responses to comments that have slowed action on important environmental problems. On balance, though, robust public participation has proved to be a very positive feature of these laws. "Citizen suit" provisions in virtually all the environmental laws offer another important avenue for citizen involvement. These provisions enable citizens in essence to stand in the shoes of government enforcers and bring actions against violators of environmental laws. They also enable citizens to bring suits against government agencies when they fail to take actions mandated in a statute. Examples of this are "schedule suits" to compel the EPA to issue regulations it has failed to issue in the timeframe required by Congress by putting the agency on a schedule overseen by a court.

A third theme is the frequent focus of these laws not just on the environment but on "human health and the environment," a recurring phrase in environmental statutes, regulations, and policies that indicates the importance of protecting human health in the context of protecting the environment.

What is the National Environmental Policy Act?

The National Environmental Policy Act (NEPA) does not directly control any major pollutants as does, for example, the Clean Air Act. Rather, it sets up a decision-making process that requires a comprehensive look at the environmental impacts of major federal actions.

This is a broad category covering not just actions taken directly by the government such as building a military base, but also actions licensed, funded, or permitted by it, such as highway projects, power transmission lines, and airport construction and expansion. As one scholar has put it, NEPA "legitimized public participation in environmental policy making."[4] The main vehicle for this is preparation of an environmental impact statement (EIS) early enough in the development of such actions to allow for the consideration of alternatives and for public input. A well-known project that was subject to the EIS process was the Keystone oil pipeline proposed to run from Canada to Texas and required to receive a presidential permit (denied by President Barack Obama in November, 2015). Most states have NEPA equivalents. Further attesting to NEPA's efficacy, more than a hundred countries have followed it with some form of EIS requirement.

There are additional reasons for NEPA's prominence. First, it is the original environmental statute, signed by President Nixon on January 1, 1970. As such, it is widely recognized as ushering in "the environmental decade" and setting a lofty tone for the laws that followed. It starts with a statement of purpose: "to declare a national policy which will encourage productive and enjoyable harmony between man and his environment; to promote efforts which will prevent or eliminate damage to the environment and biosphere and stimulate the health and welfare of man; [and] to enrich the understanding of the ecological systems and natural resources important to the Nation."[5] This policy includes fulfilling "the social, economic, and other requirements of present and future generations of Americans,"[6] an important acknowledgment of the responsibility to protect future as well as current generations from environmental degradation, which is particularly relevant in the context of climate change.

Second, it requires consideration of all environmental impacts as opposed to a media-by-media, pollutant-by-pollutant approach. This is a significant perspective that unfortunately is not sustained in most other environmental laws. The freestanding, disconnected nature of most of them undermines a fundamental fact about the environment: everything is connected to everything else. Fully effective environmental protection needs to address environmental problems comprehensively, not one by one. NEPA recognized this, at least to a degree.

Do environmental laws protect Native American lands and populations?

About 56 million acres of land in the United States (roughly the size of Michigan) are held for various Indian tribes and individuals. Much of this land is reservations, of which the largest is the 16 million-acre Navajo Nation in Arizona, Utah, and New Mexico. It is an understatement to say that the legal relationship between American Indians and the US government is complex and evolving, and its history often tragic. Native American law is similarly complex. What follows should be read with that understanding.

Tribes in the United States are sovereign with nationhood status. They are self-governing, but within limits set by Congress. So unlike foreign nations, their sovereignty is not complete. Rather, as described by the US Supreme Court in 1831 in *Cherokee Nation v. Georgia*, they are "domestic dependent nations" subject to the authority of the federal government,[7] with limitations expressed, for example, in treaties, and more recently in congressional acts and orders. An important feature of this relationship is the federal Indian trust responsibility, which is viewed as a legally enforceable duty on the part of the United States to protect tribal rights and property. Over the years this responsibility has been exercised very unevenly. Indeed, federal policy has evolved from seeking subjugation of Native Americans to, by the 1970s, a government-to-government relationship aiming at partnership and support. This government-to-government relationship is increasingly reflected in environmental law.

To the extent that Indian tribes retain legal authority, they may enforce their own environmental laws on tribal territory. Most federal environmental laws, such as the Clean Water Act and Clean Air Act, treat federally recognized tribes "in a similar manner as a state" and they can assume responsibility for federal environmental programs as a state would, upon a showing of adequate authority.[8] Moreover, the federal government provides some limited funding for tribal environmental programs. Generally speaking, tribes are not subject to local and state environmental laws unless Congress specifically provides otherwise.

This framework presents opportunities for tribes to exert control over natural resources that are important to them economically, religiously, and culturally. However, many Native Americans live in conditions of poverty and deprivation, making it difficult for tribal governments to implement and enforce environmental protections even with grants of some federal funds for this purpose. Moreover, it is sometimes attractive for businesses to engage in economically valuable but environmentally questionable enterprises on financially strapped reservations. For example, solid and hazardous waste disposal on tribal lands by off-reservation waste management companies may bring in money for the tribe, but along with it likely environmental problems. It appeals to the companies because they may face less stringent environmental restrictions there than they would in a particular state, and they are in a location far from resistant cities and towns where the waste was generated. Thus tribal lands can become dumping grounds.

Is US environmental law out of date?

The short answer is yes. Congress has not seriously touched the subject in almost twenty years (with the exception of recent amendments to the Toxic Substances Control Act, a moderately important federal environmental law). Several significant environmental concerns have arisen since the major laws were passed in the 1970s. Climate change, hydraulic fracturing for extraction of natural gas, nanopollution, nonpoint source pollution, and a host of other issues that press upon the nation and the planet now were not on the agenda then. Like an old rowboat that still plies the water these laws deliver much that is needed, but they are badly in need of upgrading. Fortunately, they were written with flexibility and so they enable actions that address many current problems. A prime example is climate change. Congress has no major pending climate-change legislation. The Obama administration, recognizing the urgent need for the United States—a main contributor to the problem—to act, used existing authority under the Clean Air Act to reduce pollutants known to influence climate change. Regulations have been promulgated to reduce tailpipe and power plant emissions, for instance.

Courts can also help. For example, the Resource Conservation and Recovery Act (the federal hazardous waste statute) authorizes the EPA to take actions to address, in the words of the statute, an "imminent and substantial endangerment."[9] Judges have interpreted this language to mean endangerments that can occur in the future, not just screaming emergencies such as a toxic spill into a river. This judicial interpretation has enabled the cleanup of many hazardous waste sites that pose not an immediate threat in the everyday sense, but an insidious threat from the slow leaking of old drums of hazardous wastes into drinking-water wells. The progressive interpretation of statutory language is important, and the courts have often—but not always—stepped up to the task. Clearly, however, courts cannot be looked upon to solve all the weaknesses in the framework of environmental law. Congress needs to act if the United States is to continue to make progress protecting the environment.

What are the environmental laws of other countries?

In addition to the extensive array of international environmental treaties, conventions, and the like, many countries have adopted a variety of environmental laws, some extensive, concerning, for example, air pollution, water pollution, and the disposal of waste. These laws vary in scope, objective, and allocation of regulatory power. Moreover, many environmental laws in other countries are in flux, and the extent of their implementation and enforcement varies widely. Some countries, unlike the United States, explicitly include rights to environmental quality in their constitutions. But this does not necessarily translate into progressive legislation.

Although the United States became the main global leader in environmental law in the 1970s, other countries have since moved to the forefront. For example, in Europe, Germany's Green Party emerged in the 1980s as a progressive environmental presence in the German Bundestag (the equivalent of Parliament) and soon joined with other political groups to create a consistent policy presence there and to urge strict environmental regulation through federal law. Other European countries, notably the Netherlands and Denmark, have a history of environmental progressivism. Countries such as Sweden and Finland have demonstrated similar leadership. The European Union itself has created important legislation including specific air-quality standards for specific pollutants. Member states are encouraged to develop plans to ensure compliance with these standards. Through its executive, the European Commission, the European

Union has also produced Environmental Action Programmes, the most recent of which (the seventh) is intended to guide EU environmental policy through 2020.

In Asia, Japan since the late 1960s has had comprehensive environmental legislation. Its 1993 Basic Environmental Law imposed stronger controls to address complex environmental problems such as urban pollution and mass production and consumption, with attention to sustainability and future generations. In 1994 Japan drew up a Basic Environmental Plan, which includes long-term objectives to implement the law. India enacted Water and Air Acts in 1974 and 1981 respectively, and an Environmental Protection Act in 1986. In 2010 it established the National Green Tribunal to dispose expeditiously of environmental cases. China substantially revised and strengthened its 1989 Environmental Protection Law (EPL) in 2014, largely in response to the dramatic increase in pollution resulting from the rapid economic growth China has experienced over the last several years. Among the upgrades to the EPL are much stricter penalties for violations, provisions for raising public awareness, and allowance for nongovernmental organizations to go to court against polluters. Such changes are consistent with the announcement of China's premier "to declare war on pollution."[10]

These are just a few examples of significant governmental activity around the world addressing environmental challenges. Much depends on the ability of particular countries to enforce laws that may appear to be strong, but which may operate in an overall governmental context where, for example, funds and staff for oversight are lacking, where fundamental constitutional rights and citizens' involvement are not cultivated, or where the administrative infrastructure—such as a robust and independent judiciary—has not been fully established.

National efforts, some more successful than others, in addition to providing environmental protection country-by-country, are crucial underpinnings to international environmental agreements, which would be ineffective without them.

4

ENVIRONMENTAL PROTECTION AND THE GLOBAL COMMUNITY

Is protecting the environment a global concern?

Yes, and this is a relatively recent development, roughly tracking the modern environmental movement of the late twentieth century. The 1945 Charter of the United Nations does not mention protecting the environment, although it lists other important social values. Until the 1970s, international attention to environmental problems was sporadic at best. Much of it went to protecting such things as fishing rights and valuable birds and mammals. But since then, at an accelerating pace, the international community has coalesced around global environmental concerns, just as have many individual nations. The reasons for this include the strains on the planet from population growth, interdependence of countries economically, some dramatic environmental disasters and scientific discoveries, and greater awareness of the global nature of environmental problems themselves.

Is there international environmental law?

Yes, in fact today international environmental law is one of the most dynamic branches of the broader subject of international law (the rules and norms governing relations between nations). It is rapidly growing with a sometimes confusing proliferation of agreements, declarations, protocols, treaties, conventions, and frameworks. Treaties are the most common means by which countries respond to international environmental problems; they are like contracts and impose specific responsibilities on the parties. Negotiators, however, often face obstacles when trying to fashion binding agreements that will be hard to sell back home. This has given rise to what people in the field call "soft law," agreements that are more guidance than law. Soft laws, such as declarations and charters, rest on norms shared by the global community, and while not enforceable in international courts, they can be important guides to global environmental values and to the practices expected from individual nations by other ones, as well as a way to maintain flexibility and to maneuver around impasses at the negotiating table. Today the international community is awash in various kinds of international environmental law. Given how difficult it is to get nations to agree on complex environmental matters, however, too much has proven to be far better than too little.

What is the role of the United Nations in global environmental protection?

The United Nations plays a vital role, in part because it is the only international organization that even begins to offer a forum where countries can engage on the subject. That is not to say that the United Nations is exactly right for the task, because it is not. However, through relevant parts of its extensive system, the United Nations has taken the initiative over and over again to promote cooperation among nations on international environmental issues as these issues have become more and more urgent. This is consistent with its Charter, which includes as one of its purposes "to achieve international co-operation in solving international problems of an economic, social, cultural, or humanitarian character."[1]

This began in 1972 in Stockholm with the UN Conference on the Human Environment, which set the direction for much of the activity that followed. Stockholm for the first time placed environmental issues squarely into the world of international law and policy. The Conference is responsible for establishment of the United Nations Environment Programme (UNEP), whose mission is "to provide leadership and encourage partnership in caring for the environment by inspiring, informing, and enabling nations and peoples to improve their quality of life without compromising that of future generations."[2]

UNEP's Headquarters is in Nairobi, reflecting the prominence of developing countries in the international environmental arena. It was here that a follow-up conference occurred in 1982, followed in 1992 by the United Nations Conference on Environment and Development in Rio de Janeiro. The important Rio Conference, also called the Earth Summit, was a mammoth event and undertaking, attended by 178 countries and producing agreements on such emerging critical issues as biodiversity and climate. It also produced the Rio Declaration with 27 principles, including one on sustainability, and a forward-looking action plan called Agenda 21. The Johannesburg South Africa World Summit on Sustainable Development followed in 2002, to review progress since Rio. Then again, in Rio in 2012, the United Nations convened Rio+20 to continue the global conversation and reaffirm the commitment of the international community to international environmental problem solving.

It is important to recognize that this necklace of conferences, conventions, and treaties is much larger than the few parts of it just summarized. It includes other well-known efforts such as the Montreal and Kyoto Protocols, and the more recent Paris Agreement on climate change. It is held together by an immense and continuous thought process begun in 1972 and continuing into the present, with the engagement of thousands of people from all over the world including in all phases world leaders, scientists, nongovernmental organizations, and the private sector. Much of it is recorded in pages and pages of rigorous documents—from highly technical ones to overviews at 30,000 feet.

What are the main obstacles to achieving global environmental agreements?

Global environmental issues are addressed by countries with competing interests, differences in power, and diverse perspectives. There are many challenges, not the least of which is trying to get two hundred countries to agree on anything, let alone on solutions to problems as confounding as those affecting the global environment. Domestic politics of participating countries also are important and inevitably complicate the road to international agreements. Three other obstacles stand out: national sovereignty, incentives, and differences between developing and developed countries.

Today it is well understood that environmental problems are at bottom international, requiring international solutions. More true, though, is the idea tenaciously held by practically everyone (except perhaps some nomadic indigenous peoples) that nationhood—national sovereignty—is paramount, almost sacred. Nations are free—that is, entitled—to do just about whatever they please, including exploiting, conserving, or destroying the natural resources inside their borders (as well as the air and water around them). So national interests—economic, military, cultural, security, environmental—and the closely guarded prerogative of nations not to be policed or regulated by other nations, often eclipse global ones. This can work well unless the interest at stake involves interdependency among nations. Such is the situation the world faces with environmental protection. For example, it is in everyone's interest to reduce carbon, a main cause of climate change. But if it involves the imposition of controls (and enforcement) by foreign nations on others with some negative economic consequences to particular nations—that is, when sovereignty is undermined—agreements can falter. The Rio Declaration on Environment and Development exemplifies this tension. It starts globally by "recognizing the integral and interdependent nature of the earth, our home," but continues with the seemingly contradictory statement that "States have, in accordance with the Charter of the United Nations and the principles of international law, the sovereign right to exploit their own resources pursuant to their own environmental and developmental policies, and the responsibility to ensure that activities within their jurisdiction or control do not cause damage to the environment of other States or of areas beyond the limits of national jurisdiction."[3] The responsibility not to "cause damage to the environments of other States or of areas beyond the limits of national jurisdiction" is a helpful qualification. It asks countries in essence to be good neighbors. But a sovereign right is far more powerful than a responsibility. This clear imperative to protect sovereignty is repeated, sometimes word for word, over and over again in many of the most important global environmental agreements.

A second, related obstacle is incentives. Why, hypothetically, should the United States reduce its carbon emissions if India will not do it to the same degree? What incentive does an impoverished and elephant-rich country have to stop exporting ivory, a major export product? Why should the local population support a ban on such sales when elephants trample their crops?

Finally, there is the disconnect between developed and developing countries. This has plagued international environmental problem solving for as long as the international community has been grappling with it. It comes down to the very hard question of how much developing countries should sacrifice their own advancement to protect the environment, and how much, if at all, developed countries should help them out.

Should developing countries be asked to help solve environmental problems?

It may appear obvious that the answer is yes: we are all in it together, and so it is not fair to make some countries do more than others to clean up the environmental messes we have made and continue to make. It was on this basis that George W. Bush refused to sign the Kyoto Protocol, which put developed countries on a schedule to limit greenhouse gas emissions, but not developing ones. Beneath the surface, however, things get much more complicated, and that is why the position of Bush and the United States on Kyoto was met with such dismay by many, at home and abroad. The 2016 Paris climate change agreement addressed some of this more skillfully than did Kyoto.

The first complication is the universal recognition that developed countries are the ones primarily responsible for the world's environmental problems. In 2000, the developed countries had about one-fifth of the global population but they generated about four-fifths of the world's pollution and used about four-fifths of the planet's energy and mineral resources to do it. Fairness suggests that the polluters should pay a greater share to fix, or to compensate others for, the pollution they have caused.

Second is the problem of poverty, suffered disproportionately by developing countries, and exacerbated, many would argue, by the postcolonial weakened condition of these countries and by the continued depletion of their resources and well-being by the acts, direct and indirect, of the developed world. It took, for example, a major international treaty, the Basel Convention, adopted in 1989, to address with limited success the transboundary disposal of hazardous waste by developed countries in developing ones. A treaty was necessary because poor countries badly in need of the revenue they received for hazardous waste disposal lacked the infrastructure to handle this unsafe material properly. In the face of great poverty, and often lacking a strong fabric of environmental laws and their enforcement while offering a cheap labor force, developing countries are easily exploited with negative environmental consequences. Although some economists have questioned the empirical basis for this "pollution haven hypothesis," much evidence points to its soundness. Moreover, in the face of other pressing needs, such as food and clean drinking water, poorer countries simply cannot afford to protect the environment, a secondary goal. To an affluent, environmentally conscious American, burning down parts of a biologically diverse rain forest by the local population may seem irresponsible, as would also, one hopes, the exploitation by a US corporation of rainforests for their natural resources. But in a country where an expanding population needs agricultural land, clearing for crops may be an immediate necessity. Indira Ghandi in a speech at the 1972 Stockholm United Nations Conference on the Human Environment stated the problem this way:

> Are not poverty and need the greatest polluters? For instance, unless we are in a position to provide employment and purchasing power for the daily necessities of the tribal people and those who live around our jungles, we cannot prevent them from combing the forest for wood and livelihood; from poaching and from despoiling the vegetation. When they themselves feel deprived, how can we urge the preservation of animals? How can we speak to those who live in villages and slums about keeping the oceans, the rivers and the air clean when their own lives are contaminated at the source? The environment cannot be improved in conditions of poverty.[4]

Third is the related question of development. Fairness indicates that developing countries should be able to develop, and their industrialized neighbors should help attend to the environmental consequences of that development because they bear so much responsibility for the mess we are in now. Since the Stockholm Conference, the international community has recognized this uncomfortable dynamic between developed and developing countries. Maurice Strong, Secretary General for both the Stockholm Conference and the Rio Earth Summit, addressed it as follows in 1991:

> At the 1972 Stockholm Conference on the Human Environment, developing countries were deeply concerned that their own overriding need for development and the alleviation of poverty might be prejudiced or constrained by the industrial countries' growing preoccupation with pollution and other forms of environmental deterioration—dilemmas resulting from the same processes of economic growth that have produced such unprecedented progress and prosperity for the industrial world. Some participants from the developing world said that they would welcome pollution if it was a necessary accompaniment to the economic growth that they urgently needed.[5]

These three interlocking issues—fairness, poverty, and the legitimate development goals of countries that are not yet fully industrialized—suggest that it is reasonable for wealthier nations to support poorer ones with resources and funding in light of the central role wealthier nations have historically played in global environmental degradation. They also point to the need to help developing countries advance not only using the approaches employed in the past, but using new approaches informed by principles of sustainable development, a concept present in many international environmental agreements.

What is the connection between international trade and the environment?

The Burmese python made *New York Times* headlines in 2015 in an article titled "The Snake That's Eating Florida."[6] It reported that the python, reaching up to twenty feet and two hundred and fifty pounds, is wreaking havoc on the Florida Everglades, eating its way through entire species and changing this rich, important ecosystem. The snake is perhaps remembered, however, for the news it made in 2009 when an eight-foot-long python pet strangled a twelve-year-old to death. The Burmese python is an invasive species, brought to the United States through the pet trade. The Obama administration eventually banned imports of pythons for obvious reasons.

The introduction of invasive species—from bugs in fruits to the Burmese python—is one of many direct connections between international trade and environmental protection. Other direct connections include pollution from ships and planes transporting goods across the oceans. Still others involve the movement of hazardous wastes from one country to another where they may be accepted as a useful material; and recently, the shipment of dangerous electronic waste (mobile phones, laptops, and tablets, for example) from richer countries to poorer ones.

It is the indirect connections, however, that have perhaps a greater impact. It is cheaper to produce goods in countries that don't have strict environmental controls and where labor is cheap. A multinational corporation might locate there, creating pollution from the production process and enjoying a work force commanding lower wages than the one at home.

Free-trade agreements have been criticized for driving up pollution and causing other negative social consequences, although they have enjoyed general support from many economists. Environmental groups, for example, have slammed the North American Free Trade Agreement (NAFTA) repeatedly. It is blamed, among other things, for increased air pollution in Mexico as industry locates and is booming there, and for disadvantaging Mexico's local farmers as they fail to compete with foreign agribusiness heavily reliant on environmentally harmful pesticides and chemical fertilizers. NAFTA has also been derided for relegating environmental cooperation to nonbinding appendixes. Of course, there is another side to this story: NAFTA proponents see it as making countries richer and therefore, ultimately, less polluting. They see NAFTA's "carrot" and partnership approach to environmental responsibility as more effective than the "stick" of enforceable sanctions, and point out that the process NAFTA sets up under the Commission for Environmental Cooperation is a sufficient enforcement mechanism. The recent Trans-Pacific Partnership free trade agreement has also been criticized by environmental advocates while being defended by its proponents.

Which countries are best at protecting the environment?

The relative environmental performance of a country depends on many factors, not the least of which is its economic condition. Moreover, some important indicators of environmental performance are not yet readily available. One well-known resource for those who are interested in rankings is the highly regarded, though imperfect, Environmental Performance Index (EPI), which uses nine issue categories: air quality, water and sanitation, water resources, agriculture, forests, fisheries, biodiversity and habitat, climate and energy, and health impacts. The categories fit under one of two objectives: environmental health and ecosystem vitality. Using this method, with the EPI caveat that presently available data is insufficient and better measurement systems are needed, the EPI lists the 2016 top ten best-performing countries overall in this order: Finland, Iceland, Sweden, Denmark, Slovenia, Spain, Portugal, Estonia, Malta, and France.[7]

Sweden offers an example of progressive environmental policy. Sweden is notable, for example, for its allocation of public funds for research and development of environmental technology, getting energy from renewable resources, and recycling of not just items such as cans and bottles but even clothing. Sweden has also shown leadership in global climate change negotiations.

Is the United States a global leader in environmental protection?

The EPI ranks the United States twenty-sixth overall among countries. Today it is not a clear global leader, which is unfortunate since it is an economic dynamo, a leading polluter of the environment, and often called the most powerful nation in the world. The United States, however, once was not just a leader, but also the global leader in environmental protection. The modern environmental movement took shape in the United States: it was the home of trailblazers like Rachel Carson, and its Congress enacted the first modern national environmental laws, laws that became

models for the rest of the world. President Nixon was a big sup-
porter of the efforts of the United Nations to bring the environment to international attention. Fast forward to 1992: George H.
W. Bush needed the prodding of the US Congress to appear at
the important Rio Earth Summit, attended by more heads of state
than any other UN conference ever, and he did not sign the enor-
mously important Biodiversity Convention that emerged from
Rio. Under Bill Clinton, the United States stepped up once again,
signing the Kyoto Protocol: but then under George W. Bush the
country retreated almost entirely from environmental protection,
both domestically and internationally. For example, he refused to
ratify Kyoto (ratify means consent to be bound by; signing does
not include this commitment) and refused throughout his presidency to acknowledge climate change or its causes as a major
issue. The United States (joined only by Haiti) is still not a party to
the 1989 Basel Convention on the control of transboundary movement of hazardous waste, although the United States is a major
generator of hazardous waste. And although the George W. Bush
administration signed the Stockholm Convention on Persistent
Organic Chemicals in 2001 along with 149 other countries, the
United States is not among the 179 countries that have ratified it.
The Obama administration had an uphill battle addressing climate change because of a balky US Senate. Indeed, the recent Paris
Agreement on climate change was structured to avoid the need
for US Senate ratification because negotiators understood that ratification in that forum would be impossible. There are exceptions
to this record, however. In 2013, The United States became the first
party to the important Minamata Convention on Mercury. This
global treaty seeks to phase out mercury pollution in air, water,
and soil because of its many adverse effects.

5

WATER

Why is clean water important?

Water covers 70 percent of the surface of the earth in all three forms of matter, solid (ice), liquid (flowing water), and gas (water vapor such as clouds). The human body is over 60 percent water. Of all the earth's water, more than 97 percent is saline; another 2 percent is locked up in ice, leaving roughly a scant 1 percent fresh water, much of which is underground. When water is clean it is life sustaining, indeed essential. When polluted, however, it can be the opposite: life threatening to individuals, communities, and entire species.

Humans need to take in roughly two to three quarts of water a day to survive, depending on their age, their gender, and where they live. Most of this comes from drinking water, but some comes from food, which itself requires significant amounts of water to grow. To thrive, the earth's ecosystems need vast quantities of it from the oceans, lakes, rivers, and groundwater. Water moderates climate, circulates nutrients, and removes and dilutes wastes.

Water is widely known as "the universal solvent" because it dissolves more substances than any other liquid. It is also a fabulous mode of transportation not only for people, but also for pollutants. Thus it can dissolve pollutants, move them great distances from their source, and disperse them over vast areas. Once in a living thing, such as the human body, water, a significant component of blood and other bodily fluids, operates the same way and can efficiently distribute both nutrients and pollutants.

Usually we think of water as being found in oceans, rivers, lakes, and streams. Many wetlands are also included in this list. But there are other important categories such as watersheds, groundwater, and aquifers.

What is a watershed?

A watershed is not a water body. It is a drainage basin, and a crucial place to protect because it is the land area that carries rainfall and other water sources into a particular water body. A watershed can be small and drain into a single stream, or can be very large, serving a lake, river, or ocean. And small watersheds can drain into larger ones. The biggest in the world is the Amazon River basin, covering about 2,700,000 square miles. The biggest in the continental United States (and the fourth largest in the world) is the Mississippi River watershed, covering about 1,200,000 square miles extending from the Alleghenies to the Rockies.

The influence of a watershed on the water bodies it drains into can be huge. Moreover, each of us lives in a watershed, so what we do affects them, from putting herbicides on our lawns to disposing of sewage from our summer cottages into a nearby lake. For these reasons, in the United States, increasingly, holistic watershed management is being used to protect the watersheds of nationally prominent waters like the Mississippi, the Chesapeake Bay in the mid-Atlantic region, and Lake Champlain, whose drainage basin straddles Vermont, New York, and Quebec. Internationally, as in the United States, watershed protection has taken various forms. For example, to protect the watershed that supplies the water to 2.5 million people in Quito, Ecuador, a fund has been established that supports local communities and helps them engage in watershed protection practices there.

What is groundwater?

Groundwater is water underneath the earth's surface. It is practically everywhere. It is the freshwater that collects in the soils, sands, and rocks underground, sometimes at great depths, such as desert groundwater hundreds of feet below the surface, and sometimes close to the surface, such as the water that you sense as you walk in a boggy area. Very deep below the surface groundwater does not collect much at all because the weight of the earth becomes great enough to make the bedrock too dense to receive it. But there are huge quantities of it—much more than the water in the planet's rivers and lakes—and so it is a major water resource. It also is a transport vehicle for water pollutants that seep into the soil. As such it is a very important aspect of water pollution and protection. Groundwater can become polluted especially by nonpoint source pollution that at first settles on the surface of the earth and then moves beneath the surface. Because groundwater is the sole source of water for about 2.5 billion people worldwide and is a major source of drinking water (almost half of the world's population and half of the US population rely on it), groundwater pollution is of particular concern.

What are aquifers?

Aquifers are areas that hold groundwater. These natural storage containers can be large or small cavities or they can be more like sponges depending on the kind of rock or sand they are made of. Because they can be precisely located and can hold very clean groundwater—and lots of it—they have been central throughout human history, including the present, influencing where people live and how successful their agricultural activities will be.

The city of Beirut, for instance, was named for its limestone aquifers: its name means wells in Phoenician, the language of ancient Lebanon, and refers to the underground water that still sustains the city. Indeed, much of the original settlement of the Middle East was determined by the location of its underground water supplies. Its future well-being, too, may hinge on its deep sandstone and limestone aquifers, such as the ancient Nubian sandstone aquifer system underlying Chad, Egypt, Libya, and Sudan. This is the world's largest fossil aquifer, so named because its geological origins are Precambrian (the era ending about 570 million years ago) and it is nonrenewable. Water-poor countries are tapping the Nubian aquifer aggressively, in much the same way as resources such as oil are mined. It is slowly draining with low recharge rates in some areas and none in others.

The Ogallala Aquifer in the United States underlies eight western states and covers about 174,000 square miles. It took thousands of years for the Ogallala to fill with water and we are depleting it much faster than it can recharge. The Ogallala supplies almost all the water for the high plains (a very important agricultural area), mostly for irrigation. Yet another is the Edwards Aquifer in central Texas covering about 4,000 square miles, which is the main water supply for about two million people.

Clearly aquifers need to recharge faster than they are drawn down if they are to continue to provide groundwater for drinking and irrigation. What is not generally known is the role a depleted aquifer plays in salt water intrusion, the incursion of saltwater into groundwater, making it unusable. This happens when the natural flow of groundwater to the ocean is reversed, as large amounts of it are taken out of a coastal aquifer, letting salt water in. In the United States the Upper Floridan Aquifer, which underlies coastal South Carolina, Georgia, and northern Florida, is a major drinking water source. The US Geological Survey (USGS) reports saltwater contamination over an area of two square miles in Brunswick, Georgia, caused by saltwater intrusion into the aquifer resulting from the growing demands for water.[1] Likewise, the USGS reports that saltwater intrusion in southern Los Angeles County is endangering nearby aquifers that provide about 60 percent of the drinking water for about 2 million people.[2] Saltwater intrusion is a global problem, threatening aquifers as they are tapped to meet the needs of growing populations. In Manila, the Philippines, to give just one example, saltwater intrusion into an aquifer from nearby Manila Bay has been of increasing concern.

What is water pollution?

Water pollution is anything that enters water and causes harm to humans, other species, or the ecosystems the water supports. Whether a particular water body is considered polluted depends on its intended use, the amount of a harmful substance in the water, how much harm the substance causes, and how long the substance stays there. A spill of chemical waste into a fast-moving river has consequences different from the same spill in a reservoir. Although human activity is overwhelmingly the main cause of water pollution, water quality can be altered by natural occurrences such as earthquakes or by the presence of naturally occurring chemicals such as arsenic. Classic signs of water pollution are sudden fish kills in a river, or statistically significant reports of diarrhea from a community using the same drinking water well.

Extremely small amounts of a substance may cause water pollution. In fact, the presence of a water pollutant is normally measured in concentrations of parts per million (ppm) or parts per billion (ppb), or even parts per quadrillion (ppq). Salt, which can cause pollution, is measured in ppm. Fresh water is less than 1,000 ppm salt (that is, less than one tenth of one percent of it is dissolved salts). Ocean water is roughly 35,000 ppm salt. In the United States dioxin, a highly toxic chemical, is regulated at 30 ppq in drinking water (although no level greater than zero is actually considered safe). Some substances are dangerous at levels that cannot even be detected using conventional monitoring techniques.

Surface waters, such as lakes, rivers, and oceans, receive water pollution from pipes, ditches, and other stationary conduits discharging waste that often comes from industrial facilities or sewage treatment plants. These conduits are referred to as "point sources" and have been the primary focus of pollution control measures over the last half-century. Increasingly, however, concerns are rising about pollution from many diffuse sources, often those that are picked up by rain or snow and carried as runoff into surface water bodies and groundwater. These diffuse sources are called "nonpoint sources" and include agricultural waste, excess fertilizers, herbicides, pesticides, and oil and grease from roads, parking lots, airport runways, gas station pavements, and the like. Atmospheric deposition, such as acid rain, although often categorized as an air pollutant, is also considered a nonpoint source water pollutant because it catches airborne noxious gases and particulates in raindrops or snow flakes and deposits them into water.

Why is water pollution a problem?

The main reasons are that water pollution can threaten species living in polluted water, can contaminate human drinking water and irrigation supplies, can load the food chain with bioaccumulated toxins, and can carry disease. It is also often unsafe to bathe, swim, and enjoy other recreation in polluted water. Rio de Janeiro, host of the 2016 summer Olympic games, received major complaints from the sailors planning to compete in the city's polluted bay, who feared they would be contending not only with other sailors, but also with sewage and floating garbage (and the health consequences if they capsized and gulped some of the water down).[3] The World Health Organization estimates that two million diarrheal deaths occur annually because of unsafe water and related poor sanitation.[4] Water pollution is also a major contributor to water scarcity, an increasingly urgent global problem, especially in developing countries. Finally, water pollution affects the world's ecosystems, as dramatically evidenced by the harm to flora and fauna photographed in the aftermath of major oil spills, although effects on the natural world from continuous industrial and other discharges are at least as significant.

What are the main kinds of water pollutants?

There are many ways to categorize water pollutants. Here are seven main groups, described in the answers to the following questions: nutrients, pathogens, sediments, toxic chemicals, plastics, heat, and contaminants of emerging concern. Some of them overlap.

How can nutrients cause water pollution?

Nutrients are substances that promote growth. They are an essential part of the aquatic environment until they appear there in excess, a condition called eutrophication. When that occurs, as it often does, the nutrients are water pollutants. Nitrogen and phosphorus are the main nutrients contributing to eutrophication, with properties that also make these chemicals key ingredients in commercial fertilizers. In water they normally appear in low concentrations. In high concentrations they cause the rapid growth of certain plant species, especially algae. Eutrophication caused by humans is one of the principal sources of water pollution both globally and in the United States, and will likely increase as climate change warms water bodies. It also occurs naturally with benign effects as water bodies such as lakes and ponds age over very long periods of time.

What are algal blooms?

Algae are key members of healthy ecosystems. But thick mats of algae, algal blooms, can wreak havoc on the freshwater or marine ecosystem they occupy by blocking sunlight the other resident species need and by suffocating aquatic creatures. And they can disrupt navigational and recreational uses. When algal blooms rot and die, the decay process can deplete oxygen in the water (a condition called hypoxia) that resident species also need, sometimes creating massive dead zones, which can be found in many marine environments throughout the world. For example, the Gulf of Mexico is home to a huge dead zone currently threatening the fishing and recreational industries there. It is the largest such zone in North America and second largest in the world, about 5,000 square miles as measured by the National Oceanic and Atmospheric Administration in 2014.[5] On the other side of the globe, Australia offers a long history of very large algal blooms, one in 2009 that extended hundreds of miles along the Murray River. China's Yellow Sea is often blanketed with them. In Europe, major algal blooms have frequently occurred in the Baltic Sea.

Algal blooms also may create extremely dangerous toxins such as cyanobacteria that can sicken or even kill people and animals. These are referred to as toxic algal blooms. Like other algal blooms, they are associated closely with excessive nutrient loading. In July 2014, for example, about 400,000 residents of Toledo, Ohio were told their water was unsafe to drink because it had been contaminated by a toxin released from algal blooms in Lake Erie, where the city gets its water. The Vermont Department of Health maintains an interactive website on algal blooms in magnificent Lake Champlain where swimming has occasionally been prohibited because of them. The infamous red tide is another example of harmful algal blooms. It occurs regularly along the Florida coast and farther north on the coast of Maine and for years has caused many fish kills, as well as unpleasant symptoms for swimmers. It is not unique to the United States. Southern Chile, for example, has experienced recent serious outbreaks. Algal blooms can be blue, bright green, or brown, as well as red, and can look like paint on the water's surface. They can also be colorless.

How do excess nutrients get into the aquatic environment?

The main source, no doubt, is fertilizers and animal waste from intense, large-scale agriculture. Enormous quantities of manure, pesticides, insecticides, and fertilizer consolidated in these industrial-scale agricultural operations either go directly or indirectly into surface water or groundwater. Concentrated animal feeding operations (CAFOs) usually produce high concentrations of nitrogen and phosphorus, which are the main causes of eutrophication. The manure also contains growth hormones, antibiotics, and other synthetic chemicals fed to the livestock (in feed produced off-site) as well as disease-carrying pathogens. The impacts are reflected in the sheer size of these operations: the US General Accounting Office reports that a large feeding operation with 800,000 pigs can produce 1.6 million tons of manure annually, which is one and one-half times more than the sanitary waste the City of Philadelphia produces in the same amount of time.[6] Oddly, Philadelphia is required to treat its sewage, and this pig farm is not because treatment is not required for livestock waste, although some nutrient and other management requirements do apply to CAFOs.

Agricultural pollutants are carried as runoff from rain and erosion into streams and groundwater, and finally into larger water bodies. For example, the Gulf of Mexico is the ultimate receptacle of much of the agricultural waste from the huge Mississippi watershed, which covers 41 percent of the continental United States in the nation's agricultural heartland, as shown in Figure 5.1. Such waste from many states is washed into rivers, streams, rivulets, and gullies, where it adds pollution to these water bodies; they all head to the Mississippi, where downstream lie the receiving waters of the Gulf. Actually, 70 percent of the nitrogen found in the Gulf comes from above the point where the Ohio River meets the Mississippi.

But big agriculture is not the only contributor. The Mississippi watershed also collects nutrient-rich runoff and groundwater from urban and suburban places, which offer up such pollutants as fertilizer from lawns, dog feces, and water from septic tanks.

What are pathogens?

Pathogens are microorganisms that, in water, carry disease. They can be bacteria, viruses, or tiny water creatures such as protozoa, and come mostly from untreated sewage and other fecal material. They appear practically everywhere: in drinking water, swimming

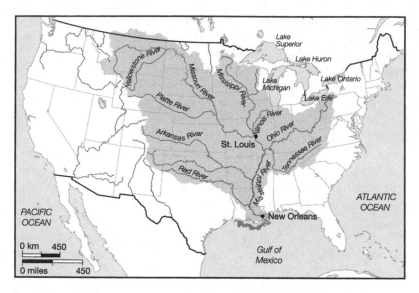

Figure 5.1 Relationship between the Mississippi watershed and the Gulf of Mexico. The dark area south of New Orleans represents a large dead, or hypoxic, zone fed by nutrient pollutants from the Mississippi watershed.

Source: United States Environmental Protection Agency Office of Water. https://www.epa.gov/ms-htf/mississippiatchafalaya-river-basin-marb.

pools, and streams, and at day care centers on the hands of toddlers and the toys they hold. In addition to diarrhea and other manageable symptoms, pathogens cause many serious illnesses, among them cholera, dysentery, typhoid fever, and hepatitis. In developing countries especially, pathogens account for a significant number of childhood deaths yearly. Despite regulatory controls in developed countries, outbreaks of disease-carrying pathogens are also fairly common. There are occasional giardia and cryptosporidium outbreaks in the United States, for instance, which cause symptoms including intestinal cramps and diarrhea. These infections can be acquired in seemingly benign circumstances—even when one is submersed in a babbling brook or a hot tub.

Here are two recent examples of major disease outbreaks from pathogens. In 2010, already ravaged by a massive earthquake, Haiti experienced a cholera outbreak that in one year killed about 6,500 Haitians and sickened more than 470,000, the worst in recent history, and the first in Haiti in a century. Cholera kills about 100,000 people each year worldwide. In February 2015, the government of Uganda announced an outbreak of typhoid fever centered on the capital city of Kampala. By March almost 2,000 suspected cases were reported. Typhoid fever affects about 21.5 million people each year in the developing world. In both Haiti and Uganda contaminated drinking water has been identified as a likely key contributor. Disease outbreaks are not limited to the developing world. About 5,700 people are estimated to be affected by cholera yearly in the United States. In 1993 Milwaukee, Wisconsin suffered a water-borne cryptosporidium outbreak that sickened at least 400,000 people and disrupted the daily lives of people, services, and activities in and near the city.

Why are sediments water pollutants?

Sediments are particles of dirt and other material, which are suspended in, travelling through, or settled at the bottom of water bodies. They are pollutants for three main reasons. First, too much of them can darken the water they enter (turbidity), thus blocking the sun from aquatic plants that need sunlight for photosynthesis, often killing them. Second, they can suffocate aquatic creatures: imagine fish gills clogged with sediments. Third, and probably most important, they often enter waters already contaminated by pollutants they have picked up along the way. Contaminated sediments at the bottom of water bodies, the homes of many aquatic creatures—such as clams, mussels, and crabs—can be lethal to them. If contaminants in these sediments bioaccumulate, as many do, they also may harm the animals higher up the food chain, such as trout, bass, and salmon that eat smaller species. Farther along the food chain, wildlife that eat contaminated fish, such as seagulls and bald eagles, can be harmed, too. At the top of the food chain, humans get their turn to be harmed by these bioaccumulated (and often biomagnified) pollutants in the fish they eat. Although dirt naturally gets into water, especially from the eroding banks of fast-running streams, much of it results from human activity. Prime examples are farm plowing, construction bulldozing, and deforestation from logging. Sediments also sometimes arrive from the air. Air deposition as a nonpoint source of pollution is particularly difficult to control.

Which chemicals are the most harmful water pollutants?

Any chemical in high enough quantities in the wrong location can be a harmful water pollutant. Some are synthetic. A subset of these synthetics is the particularly insidious group of compounds known as persistent organic pollutants. Some can occur naturally, like mercury, lead, and arsenic, a favorite poison in murder mysteries. But these pollutants are found primarily in industrial waste, as tragically demonstrated in the Minamata Bay mercury disaster. This was the slow mercury poisoning over many years in the mid-twentieth century of the residents of Minamata, Japan from waste dumped into Minamata Bay by Chisso Corporation, a local petrochemical and plastics company. It is considered one of the biggest water pollution disasters ever, and among the most instructive.

Minamata is a fishing village; the residents were sickened by the toxic methyl mercury that had bioaccumulated in the fish they ate. Chisso dumped mercury compounds into the Bay from 1932 to 1968. By the 1950s, the severe neurological effects and birth defects that it causes, including paralysis, speech impairment, and convulsions, had emerged; they continued to be felt in the 1970s and beyond. Thousands of people were diagnosed with mercury poisoning, now called Minamata disease, and many people died. The Minamata disaster brings home three important facts: first, mercury is a dangerous neurotoxin with increasing intensity as it bioaccumulates and biomagnifies in living things; second, humans are exposed to mercury contamination from the fish we eat; and third, this can affect developing fetuses, even in asymptomatic mothers. The world community has responded to Minamata and its lessons with the Minamata Convention on Mercury, a global treaty adopted in 2013.

The EPA has a Priority Pollutant List of 126 water pollutants, chemicals that are regulated when discharged into water, which is a resource for identifying harmful water pollutants.[7] But the list includes only chemicals for which the EPA has reliable test methods, leaving out a large number of potentially dangerous chemicals of increasing interest. This group has acquired the ominous descriptor "contaminants of emerging concern." Other lists are available, such as the European Union's list of thirty-three priority substances.[8]

What are contaminants of emerging concern?

Humans are developing new chemicals at an impressive rate: to color hair and fingernails, to wash dishes and clothes, to brush teeth, to kill pain, to fight infection, and on and on. Very little is known about the environmental effects of many of them. Similarly, many chemicals while not new remain poorly understood; we nevertheless have let them be discharged into the earth's water bodies, including drinking water supplies. For these groups, both new and old, we have simply too little information to know their effects (thus we have a convenient rationale not to regulate them), although we suspect they may be serious. Moreover, conventional treatment systems cannot be relied on to catch them because normally these systems are not designed with such chemicals in mind.

An example is polybrominated diphenyl ethers (PBDEs) used as flame retardants in furniture, rugs, electrical equipment, cars, and many other applications. They do not biodegrade easily and therefore they persist in the environment, they bioaccumulate, and they are practically ubiquitous in developed countries. In fact, they are persistent organic pollutants, as are some other contaminants of emerging concern. They can be carried in air and dust, as well as water. PBDEs are presumed to be endocrine disruptors and are associated with various toxicological effects, but the evidence is inconclusive because research is thin. One thing is established: they have been found in the blood serum of humans and in breast milk, and some studies show that levels have been increasing. These levels appear to be 3 to 10 times higher in United States than in Europe. Different countries have different approaches to PBDEs. For example, the Swedish government has banned them (with resulting decreases in levels), followed by the European Union; the United States, on the other hand, does not even list them as priority pollutants, and provides weak regulatory protection, although several states have bans in place. The US Centers for Disease Control and Prevention has reported that the "human health effects from PBDEs and PBBs [polybrominated biphenyls] at low environmental exposures are unknown. In animal studies, these chemicals have shown some effects on the thyroid and liver, as well as on brain development. More research is needed to assess the human health effects of exposure to PBDEs and PBBs."[9] If the precautionary principle were applied, more research and stricter regulation of PBDEs would occur in the United States.

Are plastics in water a serious problem?

Yes. Plastic debris in water is a major problem that is getting more serious every year. As humans use more and more plastic products such as bags and bottles, many of them end up as garbage on beaches and then in ocean water—somewhere between 4.8 to 12.7 metric tons each year and rapidly increasing (unless something is done about it worldwide). Some plastics are tossed from boats, or are the remains of fishing nets and lines. Because they are not easily biodegradable, once in the ocean plastics stay there indefinitely. Because they are very light, they float and bob along or just below the surface carried by currents. When they get caught in systems of rotating currents, called gyres, they can accumulate in a single large spot. The North Pacific Gyre—site of the Great Pacific Garbage Patch, as it is called— is mostly plastic debris and more than twice the size of France.

The main problem with plastics in water, especially the oceans, is that they are eaten by marine life. Many fish, sea turtles, and sea- birds have been found with plastic in their stomachs or with inter- nal bleeding or other harm from ingested plastic. Another problem is grisly entanglements in plastic debris that have also been lethal for marine mammals like seals and whales.

Plastic debris represents only the most dramatic and ubiquitous of the refuse that is tossed into water. Our oceans, beaches, rivers, and lakes receive everything from cigarette butts to tires. The good news is that aquatic debris can be reduced by relatively straight- forward waste management practices and recycling. This has had some success, for example in the United States, which generates large quantities of it.

Why is heat a water pollutant?

Mount Hope Bay is a shallow estuary (a place where fresh water, usually a river, meets salt water, usually an ocean bay) that is an arm of southern New England's larger Narragansett Bay. It enjoys the distinction of being one of twenty-eight congressionally designated "estuaries of national significance" in part because it is home to a rich and varied fish population important commercially and recreationally. It is also home to the Brayton Point power plant, the largest coal-fired plant in New England. The plant for many years ingested large amounts of the bay's water to cool its equipment, then disgorged the significantly hotter water back into the bay, raising the overall water temperature by several degrees. In the process it also slammed thousands of fish onto intake screens and sucked millions of larvae into the plant itself. In the context of an EPA determination whether to issue a permit for thermal discharges from the plant, scientists concluded that the bay's fish population had significantly declined largely as a result of this.[10] Brayton Point's heat, or thermal, discharge is pollution because it changes the water temperature enough to significantly reduce the water quality. The Clean Water Act, which includes heat in its definition of "pollutant," requires regulation of these impacts. The plant is scheduled to shut down permanently in 2017, like many other coal-fired electricity generating plants, because of the competition it faces from cheaper energy sources, and because of operation costs driven by appropriately tough regulations.

Heat that pollutes water often comes from power plants like Brayton Point. Another well-known source is nuclear power plants. These are point source discharges and relatively easy to control. Less well-known and harder to control nonpoint sources of heat are hard surfaces, like streets and rooftops, where water collects, gets hot, then drains off in various ways. Deforestation and urbanization near water bodies also contribute as they reduce shading. Thermal pollution causes harm not only to fish (rainbow trout, for instance, are very temperature sensitive), but also to vegetation such as sensitive sea grasses, and it can reconfigure ecosystems by encouraging alien species and discouraging native ones. Artificially lowered temperatures can undermine water bodies as well as heat. This cold-water pollution may happen, for example, when a dam discharges cold water into warmer water downstream disrupting the river's ecosystem.

How does noise cause water pollution?

In 1956, Jacques Cousteau's film *The Silent World* won the Oscar for best documentary. With Louis Malle, Cousteau had made the teeming and beautiful place under the oceans visible to the public. As the title suggests, it was a relatively quiet world filled with the delicate sounds of whales and dolphins. A half-century later, human activity has caused the noise levels in water to increase dramatically, polluting it with noises that damage and confuse aquatic species relying on sounds to communicate, to set directions, and to mate. Because of the properties of water and sound waves, sound travels faster and farther through water, and is much louder. Unlike a radio blaring next to you on a beach, however, blaring underwater noises do not register with humans much at all, and certainly not as harmful things.

Many of the sources of noise that pollute water, like jet skis and motorboats, can bother humans, too, at the surface. Others, like oil-rigs and ocean-tanker traffic, are usually out of range and so not bothersome. Still others are completely covert, like the sonar emitted from navy ships. A famous result of this sonar activity occurred in 2000 when four species of whales beached themselves in the Bahamas. After investigation, it became clear they stranded themselves in reaction to it. Taken together, aquatic noises create a dangerous cacophony that has worried marine scientists for decades but which has received little regulatory attention. In effect, then, noise is a contaminant of emerging concern.

What are the main sources of water pollution?

Water pollution comes from thousands of sources. At the top of the list are agricultural operations and industrial activities. Others of particular importance are sewage, stormwater, and all the chemicals people daily send down the drain into surface waters or groundwater. Motor vehicles, the source of so many environmental problems, are also a significant source of water pollution.

Is sewage treated before it gets into water?

In the United States, thanks to strong federal and state laws, much of the sewage from cities is now treated before it is discharged into rivers, lakes, and the oceans, usually in publically owned treatment works (POTWs), as is generally true of cities in most of the developed world. This treated sewage, however, is not simply the domestic refuse we normally think of. Often POTWs receive industrial wastewater containing not sewage, but pollutants such as toxic metals. This waste is often required to be pretreated before it enters a POTW, but sometimes it is not, or not treated well. As a result, the treated waste discharged from POTWs can still contain a variety of pollutants. Many city sewer systems, moreover, combine domestic sewage, rainwater runoff (with its oil, grease, and other pollutants), and industrial wastewater in one pipe for treatment at a sewage treatment plant, which presents serious problems when heavy rain or snow is too great for the pipes to handle. To deal with this, these systems are designed to overflow (called combined sewer overflows or CSOs), carrying raw human waste, industrial chemicals, and debris directly into nearby water bodies untreated. In the United States over seven hundred cities, with a total population of over 40 million people, have these combined sewer systems and their periodic overflows. CSOs are major water pollution sources sending pathogens, toxics, and debris into water. After heavy rain, local rivers and streams are often considered dangerous to public health because of them. New York City has 460 CSOs that discharge almost 30 billion gallons of raw sewage and polluted stormwater into New York Harbor every year. Other countries share this problem. For example, at least 20,000 CSOs discharge into the waters of the United Kingdom.

Some sewage in water comes from domestic sources that are not hooked up to a municipal sewage system at all but rely on individual septic systems connected to rural and suburban homes in small towns where inspections are limited. This sewage often seeps into groundwater when the system fails or breaks down. Finally, some sewage is discharged directly into lakes, rivers, and the ocean, as from seasonal cottages beside a rural lake or from boats far out at sea. Indeed, ships, ferries, and recreational boats are a major source of sewage. In the United States it is illegal to discharge untreated sewage from such vessels only up to three miles from shore—beyond that, no restrictions apply. There are some specific requirements for discharges within the three-mile limit for large commercial vessels, but recreational vessels are required only to follow best management practices developed by the EPA, with recreational boaters responsible for applying them. Some coastal areas are designated no discharge zones where not only untreated sewage from boats, but also treated sewage, cannot be discharged. This is a very good thing given the limited effectiveness of on-board treatment on recreational vessels (caused, for example, by improper methods, illegal practices at marinas, and poor boater education).

Sewage problems in the United States dwarf in comparison to the global picture in developing countries. According to United Nations statistics, about a third of the world's population lives without any kind of sewers, septic tanks, or latrines.[11] Inevitably, most human waste in these circumstances ends up polluting surface and groundwater and is a public health crisis in some of the neediest parts of the world.

What is stormwater pollution?

Stormwater pollution is rain and snowmelt that flows over land and, especially, over impervious surfaces such as rooftops, roads, and sidewalks, picking up debris, contaminants, and other pollutants along the way. Stormwater runoff usually ends up in water bodies. It is a leading cause of water impairment because it carries many harmful pollutants in high volumes of runoff into important water bodies such as urban rivers, major lakes, and marine bays, and is very often untreated.

Which industries pollute the water most?

Industrial scale agriculture is a big contributor of many water pollutants. Mining is another, carrying metals to water bodies, especially in runoff. Power plants send thermal pollution into rivers and bays from cooling operations. There are thousands of other industrial point sources from a variety of industries, including paper mills, pharmaceutical factories, steel mills, smelters, and electroplating operations. These are regulated to one degree or another in the United States and around the world. Together they are responsible for a large percentage of the pollution that enters surface and groundwater. In developed countries, much of the effluent from point sources associated with these activities is controlled. But inevitably significant amounts escape through spills, faulty pollution-control operations, noncompliance with regulatory requirements, or through the imperfections of the regulatory system itself. Nonpoint source pollution from these and other sources is an even more intractable problem.

Why are oil spills so bad?

One of the reasons water is a great conveyor of pollution is its property as a solvent. This is not true of its relationship to oil: oil does not dissolve in water, and it is lighter than water, presenting special problems. After it spills, it tends to spread out and form a thin slick or sheen. One does not need to be a marine biologist to detect oil slicks: they are readily apparent on the surfaces of water in marinas and the puddles in a parking lot. Oil slicks can occasionally get more viscous and tar-like as they sit on the water surface, partially evaporate, and slowly decompose creating opaque nasty floating sludge. When oil gets onto the fur of marine animals like sea otters it destroys insulating benefits; similarly, on the feathers of birds it destroys water repellency. When these animals try to clean themselves they ingest the oil and are poisoned by it. As contaminants in oil mix down into the water column, fish and shellfish come in contact with and ingest them producing harms to organs, larvae, and eggs.

Experience with oil spills shows that the consequences can be long-term and hidden: after the *Exxon Valdez* spill in Alaska, it took three years for the herring fishery to collapse; and salmon embryos exposed to the spilled oil eventually revealed hormonal disruption.

Oil spills are considered so bad that they motivated the US Congress to pass the Oil Pollution Act after *Exxon Valdez*. Spills are dramatic and consequential, but they are by no means the only source of oil in the aquatic environment. Other important human sources include road runoff (dripped from motor vehicles), used motor oil, and the many oil discharges associated with recreational boating. Natural seeps of oil from underground also account for significant quantities of oil in water.

What was the BP Deepwater Horizon oil spill?

The *Deepwater Horizon* oil spill has been described as the worst marine oil spill in US history. British Petroleum's (BP) *Deepwater*

Horizon oil rig in the Gulf of Mexico, about 50 miles southeast of the Mississippi delta, exploded on April 20, 2010, killing eleven people and gushing five million barrels of crude oil over eighty-seven days until it was capped. The damage to wildlife, habitat, and coastal ecosystems was massive, and continues. Impacts on the economy of the Gulf, primarily its fishing and recreational industries, have been substantial. The response effort was huge. Thousands of government workers and volunteers travelled to the Gulf to clean it up so visible signs of oil are mostly gone. But the slick covered an area the size of Ireland, spread to the shores of several states, has been found on the ocean floor, and persists in the sands and grasses of the coast and in the bodies of millions of sea and shore creatures. So total cleanup is elusive, and the real extent of the ecological and economic impacts will likely never be known.

How can cars pollute water?

Cars run on gasoline, a fossil fuel. When combusted, fossil fuels emit large quantities of carbon dioxide, a major cause of climate change and of a related problem, ocean acidification. In addition, fossil fuels emit nitrogen oxides and sulfur dioxide into the air, which mix with other chemicals causing harmful acid deposition into surface waters such as lakes, rivers, and streams. Although there are many sources of acidification and acid deposition, exhaust from cars, trucks, and buses is a major one.

Motor vehicles release grease, antifreeze, and other liquids, as well as oil, which land on roads, parking lots, and driveways and ultimately tend to wash down into surface water or groundwater. The sheer number of motor vehicles around the world makes these uncontrolled and unquantified excretions serious sources of water pollution.

What kinds of pollutants go down the drain?

Prior to about 1950 the chemical composition of soap was relatively straightforward. The petrochemical industry, which was flourishing by the mid-twentieth century, reconfigured soap chemistry (as it similarly influenced many other domestic products), introducing attractive features such as fragrances as well as environmentally damaging ones such as phosphates. Household cleaning agents (not an entirely accurate term) now deliver significant amounts of chemical pollution in wastewater drained from kitchen sinks and washing machines into sewage systems ill equipped to handle them, and into groundwater. Many other products most consumers rely on without understanding the pernicious relationship between cleaning and contaminating, such as drain cleaners, degreasers, and the like, also end up in surface and groundwater.

In fact, we dispose of a large number of new and largely synthetic domestic products in ways that inevitably lead them to our waters. We excrete pharmaceuticals in our urine and fecal waste, because our bodies only partially metabolize the drugs we use. Antidepressants have been found in fish, and acetaminophen in river water. Many expired medications are simply poured down the drain. Topical medicinal creams, cosmetics, and sunscreens go down the shower drain when we wash them off and into lakes and oceans when we swim. The quantity of household pollutants—pills, cosmetics, cleaning products, and lawn products—that end up in waters is very large but we have too little data at present to understand their long-term environmental and human health impacts. They fit into the disturbing group of contaminants of emerging concern. One of the most difficult current water-pollution-control problems is the insidious introduction of small amounts of harmful chemicals flowing from our own houses and apartments. Many of them are composed of new chemicals being registered, but not necessarily regulated, by the thousands every day.

How is water pollution controlled in the United States?

The Clean Water Act is the main reason US waters are now in relatively good condition compared to their condition prior to the act and compared to current conditions of waters in many other places around the world. The law, originally passed by Congress in 1972, set a strong national framework for water pollution control at a time when garbage, sewage, and oil slicks were common sights on the surface of lakes, rivers, ponds, and bays. We no longer see much of this in the United States thanks to this law. Although it only addresses surface waters (not groundwater), does not address every water pollution problem, and needs updating, the Clean Water Act is still the key to clean water throughout the country.

The heart of the act is the limits it imposes on discharges of major industrial pollutants and municipal sewage into the country's surface water bodies. It requires any company, city, town, or individual who pollutes with what is called a "point source discharge" to get a permit under the National Pollutant Discharge Elimination System (NPDES). The permit typically has effluent limits preset by regulation for specific pollutants based on industry-wide technology standards, as well as additional provisions, normally based on state water quality standards, designed to protect the uses of the particular water body. For example, an electroplater discharging wastewater containing copper into a stream may have a technology-based effluent limit for the copper, but it may need to meet more stringent limits for the copper in order to comply with state water quality standards to protect the health of the particular aquatic life in the stream.

Like many other federal environmental laws, the Clean Water Act directs the Environmental Protection Agency to write regulations, issue permits, and enforce them—in short, to implement the NPDES permit program. Importantly, like these other laws, it envisions that the states, one by one, will take over most implementation responsibilities applying the same or stricter standards, leaving the EPA only with an oversight role, including enforcement if necessary. At present, almost every state has primary authority to implement and enforce the NPDES program, and the EPA is in the back seat.

Although the Clean Water Act does not address nonpoint source pollution forcefully, which is a defect in the statute, one historically underused requirement of the act has been invoked more often in the last several years, thanks to litigation by environmental groups filed in over thirty states. This is the requirement that states establish total maximum daily loads (TMDLs) of pollutants for water bodies the state has identified as impaired to the point that they cannot meet the state's water quality standards. TMDLs determine the amount of pollution such a water body can tolerate and still meet these standards. They can be followed by implementation plans to improve the impaired waters and they can address nonpoint sources as well as point source pollution (although the agricultural sector, among others, has pushed back, suing the EPA on its inclusion of nonpoint source pollution in TMDL allocations). Because TMDLs are not directly enforceable, but must be implemented through other actions, they remain less effective than the act's permit program.

Nevertheless, TMDL implementation has engaged regulators and others in important questions. For instance, what are the main contributors to water pollution, if not only big point source dischargers? In answer to this question, some TMDLs focus specifically on nonpoint sources. For example, The TMDL for the Los Angeles River addresses trash directly disposed of by people and carried into the river by stormwater runoff because it causes such significant water quality problems. Even more novel are TMDLs that focus largely on air deposition of pollutants such as mercury into waters, indirectly addressing needed controls on air emissions that have serious impacts on water quality. Should water pollution control strategies be based on larger hydrological contexts than individual rivers, lakes, and streams—such as watersheds? In answer to this question, watershed approaches have been tried, for example, in the multistate Chesapeake Bay TMDL, where nonpoint source agricultural discharges of nitrogen, phosphorus, and sediments are the main causes of serious water quality issues. Delaware, Maryland, New York, Pennsylvania, Virginia, West Virginia, and the District of Columbia participate in this TMDL.

In the TMDL program, Congress recognized, but did not fully embrace, the notion that a holistic approach, dealing with cumulative impacts from multiple sources from multiple environmental media, is what is needed to satisfy clean water goals. TMDLs provide laboratories to test this notion.

How is water pollution controlled in other countries?

Many countries have laws addressing water pollution similar to those in the United States. Some are as, if not more effective than US laws. Others are less so. As is the case with other environmental laws, much depends on the ability of individual countries to implement and enforce them. This is a particular challenge in developing countries where funds may be lacking and the governmental infrastructure for environmental protection may be weak. India, for example, has had a water act since 1974 but still struggles with serious water pollution.

What are wetlands?

Wetlands are places inundated or saturated with water often enough and long enough so that the water influences the quality of the soil and the kinds of plant and animal communities that live there. Wetlands cover about 6 percent of the earth's surface and can be found on every continent, including subglacially in Antarctica based on recent discoveries made there.[12] Often called swamps, marshes, bogs, or fens depending on the kinds of plant life they support, they can be any size, from large tracts of land to small depressions. Oceans, lakes, rivers, and streams themselves are not wetlands.

Wetlands are divided into two categories: tidal and nontidal. Tidal wetlands are found in coastal areas where fresh and salt water tend to mix, such as Atlantic salt marshes and tropical mangrove swamps. Nontidal, or inland, wetlands occur along rivers and streams, in low-lying areas where ground and surface water meet, and in isolated spots on dry land. Examples are wet meadows, wooded swamps, tundra wetlands, and prairie potholes.

Defining wetlands is difficult. The presence or absence of water is not necessarily a good indicator of whether an area is in fact a wetland. The water saturation may be visible or not; so some wetlands, including parts of the Florida Everglades often appear dry. Conversely, some areas that get very wet after rain and stay that way for some time may not be wetlands if they lack the specific characteristics of a wetland, such as soil type, hydrology, and vegetation. A puddle in an unpaved driveway is likely not a wetland.

This definitional difficulty explains why in 2004 a bitter and disbelieving John Rapanos took a *New York Times* reporter for a bumpy ride in a jeep over the cornfield he once had hopes of developing into a mall. These hopes were frustrated in 1989 when the Michigan Department of Environmental Quality determined part of it to be a wetland that he had filled with sand. The legal battles that ensued were ferocious, almost landing Rapanos in jail, and entangling state and federal judges and finally the US Supreme Court, which is why the *Times* was interested.[13] Wetlands are lightning rods for clashes between naturalists and developers, libertarians and regulators, and government and business. The clashes arise because wetlands, being at the intersection of land and water, can appear to be land. For people like John Rapanos, a wetland is a simple commonsense concept; in fact, it is a complex scientific one. Wetlands are also among the most important features of our planet's surface, providing many protections against such threats as storms and species loss.

What are regulated wetlands?

In the context of environmental protection the regulatory definition of a word may have serious economic, political, and, of course, environmental implications. Because the definition will likely create binding, enforceable consequences, it is of keen interest to affected parties. In the United States, perhaps no other environmental regulatory term has had as stormy and passionate a history as has the term "wetlands" as it is defined in regulations implementing the Clean Water Act.

Section 404 of the act generally forbids filling in wetlands and other waters (streams, lakes, and so forth) unless a permit is obtained from the US Army Corps of Engineers. The EPA and the Corps jointly administer this federal permit program. To determine which areas are wetlands for the purpose of regulation, the EPA and the Corps use the same basic regulatory definition: Wetlands are "areas that are inundated or saturated by surface or groundwater at a frequency and duration sufficient to support, and that under normal circumstances do support, a prevalence of vegetation typically adapted for life in saturated soil conditions."[14]

This definition has proven to be a political and legal punching bag. For several years, the EPA and the Corps used different procedures to identify specific areas as wetlands, finally agreeing on one in a 1989 Wetlands Delineation Manual. It provided greater consistency; it also expanded the scope of what areas met the definition of "wetland." In 1991, the George H. W. Bush administration, under pressure from groups representing such interests as agriculture and oil, made major revisions to the 1989 Delineation Manual. These revisions defined wetlands in a way that greatly reduced the acreage subject to regulation. The scientific and environmental communities quickly attacked the revisions. As a result, the EPA and the Corps reverted to a Corps guidance manual from 1987, which they continue to use, with modest updates, to determine whether an area satisfies the regulatory definition of "wetland."

The US Supreme Court further muddied the waters when in 2006 in John Rapanos's case it failed to reach agreement on the extent of the Clean Water Act's regulatory jurisdiction over "waters of the United States" (an important term in the act, particularly as it relates to wetlands) and sent the case back to the lower courts. The regulated community as well as the regulators were left with no clear legal guidance. Seeking clarity for all concerned, including the environment, in 2015 the EPA published a new regulation called the Clean Water Rule, defining "waters of the United States" again. Not surprisingly, it is being challenged in several courts, and will inevitably return to the Supreme Court, where the answer to the very important question, what wetlands (and other related waterways) are regulated, may very well get even more murky.

One might view this troubled history as a mild curiosity. It is more than that: millions of acres of wetlands that should be protected—and the streams that feed them—have been caught in a confusing and complex legal tangle. Moreover, this sort of legal definitional uncertainty and controversy is frustrating: regulators have difficulty enforcing the law; and business interests lack clear guidance to pursue activities in places that might turn out to be regulated wetlands, or might not.

Why are wetlands important?

Wetlands are critically important to nurture habitat for thousands of species of plants and animals, to absorb floodwater and runoff, to trap pollutants, to provide food, and to offer recreational opportunities. Also, they are often uncommonly beautiful places.

Wetlands are sometimes called "nurseries of life" because they are home to a vast array of biologically diverse species. They provide abundant vegetation and water conditions that are inviting to terrestrial and aquatic creatures in some of the most productive ecosystems in the world. Like tropical rain forests and coral reefs, they can be teeming with life. Wetlands degradation has been identified as a leading cause of species extinction.

Wetlands are also called nature's sponges because of their ability to absorb and slow the movement of surface and groundwater. This capacity is especially valuable in reducing flooding and erosion, especially in coastal areas that are vulnerable to powerful hurricanes and storm surges. For example, wetlands loss in the Mississippi Delta aggravated the impact of Hurricane Katrina on the US Gulf Coast in 2005.

Wetlands are cleansing agents and water filters. When water enters a wetland, its pace is slowed as it maneuvers around plant life. During this process, pollutants in the water, from roads, sewage, agricultural waste, and other sources sink to the wetland floor or are absorbed by plant roots or soil. By the time water leaves the wetland it has in effect been scrubbed of its pollutant load, making it healthier to support animal and plant life and to drink and swim in. Hundreds of artificial wetlands have been constructed to treat contaminated water from sources such as sewage treatment plants as a cost-effective way to rid their wastewater of contaminants.

Wetlands have also been called the earth's supermarket because they are hugely important global food sources. The wetland rice paddies of Asia and West Africa provide rice to billions of people. The wetlands of the Mississippi Delta are essential for the shrimp, oysters, and crabs enjoyed by many Americans.

The importance of wetlands for recreational uses is well established. Long before they were recognized for habitat protection and flood and pollution control, people were ambling and canoeing through them, fishing, hunting, and birding.

Although the very important role wetlands play is now well understood and well documented, this was not always the case. Until the last few decades, in many parts of the world wetlands have been maligned as wastelands; swamps, bogs, and marshes have had negative, if not forbidding, connotations. Indiscriminate destruction of wetlands was virtually unchecked, often for reasons that seemed good at the time. For example, Peter the Great built St. Petersburg on wetlands, and significant sections of Bangkok, Amsterdam, Venice, New York City, Boston, Washington, DC, and San Francisco were built on wetlands.

Do wetlands contribute to disease?

Wetlands are sometimes blamed for being breeding grounds for disease-bearing mosquitoes. Actually, they are home to many mosquito-eating species—fish, birds, insects, and amphibians—all of which help keep the mosquito population down. They have, however, been linked to West Nile virus (WNV), a recent global health concern. The EPA has reported that the principal mosquito species that carry WNV in the United States do not prefer healthy wetlands. Rather, they gravitate to human-made habitats like the stagnant water that collects in containers in people's yards, or to wetlands degraded by human activity. The EPA advises that draining or filling wetlands is not appropriate for WNV mosquito control. Rather, it recommends, for example, protecting wetlands from degradation, eliminating standing-water containers, reducing the presence of contaminated water that attracts mosquitoes, and installing and repairing screens.[15]

Are wetlands disappearing?

Yes. The international community is in general agreement that they are disappearing at an alarming rate. Among the major contributors to wetlands loss and degradation are highway, housing, and commercial construction; mining; logging; dredging, damming, and diking; air and water pollution; agricultural activities; and storms. Some estimates show losses globally of 50 percent of the wetlands that existed in 1900. The United States shares this rate of loss: over half of the estimated 220 million acres of wetland present in the forty-eight contiguous states in the 1600s are gone. According to a study by the US National Oceanic and Atmospheric Administration, between 2004 and 2009 coastal areas in the United States lost wetlands at a rate of 80,000 acres a year, a 25 percent increase over the previous six-year study period, or approximately the equivalent of seven US football fields every hour.[16] In addition, degradation of existing wetlands has reduced their benefits.

How can we protect wetlands?

The most powerful tools for protecting wetlands are laws and their vigorous enforcement. The wetlands regulatory program administered by the EPA and the US Army Corps of Engineers helps prevent the indiscriminate filling of wetlands in the United States, although thousands of permits that allow some filling are issued each year. Many states, cities, and towns also have rules for wetlands protection. It takes strong political will to stop development, however, and regulators sometimes do not have it, or favor business opportunity over wetlands protection. Such seemed to be the case when in the 1980s the Pyramid Corporation pushed to site a mall in the 32-acre red maple Sweeden's Swamp in Attleboro, Massachusetts. Initially, the local office of the Corps denied construction rights to Pyramid because there were clearly alternatives less damaging to the swamp, but the Washington, DC office of the Corps overturned the local office. Pyramid had jumped through almost all the regulatory hurdles when the EPA stepped in and blocked construction to protect the wetland. Pyramid went to court and the EPA won. The Attleboro mall is a classic example of the many hard-fought wetlands battles that involve development interests.

Because government resources—and sometimes political backbone—are in short supply to investigate and enforce wetlands violations, nonregulatory solutions are especially important. Examples are land acquisition and tax incentives for donating wetlands. Seventy-five percent of US wetlands are in private hands, so individual and corporate responsibility is key. Choosing uplands (nonwetlands) for construction, farming, and the like, reducing the flow of pollutants into wetlands, and supporting wetlands conservation are examples of responsible personal and corporate behavior.

Like the United States, many other countries have laws and programs to protect wetlands. International concern is reflected in the Convention on Wetlands of International Importance, called the Ramsar Convention for the city in Iran where it convened in 1971. The convention produced a treaty focusing on identifying wetlands and on international cooperation for their conservation and wise use. Over 150 countries, including the United States, participate.

How is drinking water protected?

Drinking water is, of course, special. While it is important to protect rivers, lakes, and streams enough to make them fishable and swimmable (goals of the Clean Water Act), it is critical to make water, including groundwater, safe enough to drink. While it is unsustainable to kill fish by polluting water, it is devastating to deliver disease, illness, and death to people, mostly children, from unsafe drinking water. In 2012, according to United Nations data, 783 million people or 11 percent of the world's population were without good drinking water. In sub-Saharan Africa it was 40 percent.[17]

In the United States, the 1974 Safe Drinking Water Act is the main reason Americans enjoy peace of mind about their drinking water, as do people in other developed countries with similar protections. The act requires the EPA to establish standards limiting the levels of contaminants in public water systems. Like other US environmental laws, it envisions that states will adopt these, or stricter, standards and enforce them. Today the states are primarily responsible for Safe Drinking Water Act implementation.

There are some chinks in the regulatory armor provided by the Safe Drinking Water Act, however. Individual states and municipalities fill some. But coverage isn't consistent. First, to be regulated a public water system needs to serve at least twenty-five people or have at least fifteen service connections. This covers about 85 percent of the population. The remaining 15 percent rely on their own private wells and are not subject to EPA standards. Even if regulated by states, these wells usually are not inspected regularly. Second, even public water supplies that are regulated by the EPA violate drinking water standards from time to time, so tap water isn't guaranteed to be pristine or even safe to drink. This unfortunate reality was brought home dramatically in the systemic breakdown in 2014 of regulatory control of the Flint, Michigan public water system and the resulting serious lead contamination of the drinking water of thousands of Flint residents. Moreover, the standards themselves sometimes have been caught in heated policy disagreements: What, for example, should the standard at the tap be for water coming from miles of old lead pipes if the replacement cost is enormous, even though lead is known to be very harmful to children in small concentrations? Or, what standard should apply to naturally occurring contaminants like arsenic, a known poison? The regulatory answers to these and other thorny questions have not satisfied everyone and have included public disputes when the actual standards have been proposed or changed. Finally, water served in certain situations, particularly on commercial airplanes, has proved very difficult to regulate. A significant number of airplane samples taken by the EPA in 2004 tested positive for bacteria.[18] Ten years later test results are not promising; and some trip advisors still suggest that passengers not drink from airplane bulk water supplies or use airplane ice cubes.

The European Union's Drinking Water Directive is illustrative of drinking water legal protections in other countries. But protections vary greatly, especially between the developing and developed world.

Is water becoming scarce?

Signs of water scarcity—which can be defined as either not enough water (quantity), or not enough safe water (quality), or both—are very clear in much of the world. The United Nations has identified it as a main global problem for the twenty-first century.

Population increase combined with an increase in demand for food are root causes. The United Nations projects that over the next forty years water use will grow at more than twice the rate of the exploding world population. It also projects a shift in diet from primarily starch-based foods, which are water-efficient, to meat and dairy, which are not. (It takes over six times more water to produce a pound of beef than a pound of rice.) Agriculture accounts for about 70 percent of freshwater withdrawals (often for irrigation), and these are projected to increase substantially as a larger population and water-guzzling food sources also increase. Given how minute the earth's supply of fresh water is, pollution is also a major contributor to water scarcity because it reduces the amount of water that can be used productively.

The demands on water resources are evident in many parts of the world. In the western United States, drought and water usage have created such severe water scarcity that in heavily populated California in 2015 mandatory water rationing was introduced. The Jordan River, shared by Jordan and Israel (and across whose waters—"the river is deep and the river is wide"—Michael rowed his boat ashore in the famous folk song), is now often dry because of water withdrawals for irrigation by both countries; and the Dead Sea, fed by the Jordan, is shrinking dramatically because the river is no longer able to regularly feed it. The conditions of important aquifers are also telling. Many of these are being drained faster than they can recharge. In the United States, both the Edwards Aquifer and the Ogallala Aquifer face these threats. Coastal aquifers face additional threats as salt water intrudes when they are pumped faster than they are replenished. Salt water is useless for drinking and irrigation. The physical realities of major surface water bodies color in the picture. Rivers like the Nile, the Yellow River, the Colorado River, and the Rio Grande are diminishing as water is pulled out of them for irrigation.

How can water quality be further improved?

In the United States, with some of the most comprehensive water pollution laws in the world, data on the quality of the nation's water is still patchy. About 70 percent of its lakes and streams, 45 percent of its rivers, ponds, and reservoirs, and 60 percent of its bays and estuaries remain unassessed. What we do know about these important resources is not comforting: a significant percentage of those that have been assessed do not meet state water quality standards. So despite important improvements in water quality in the last fifty years, whatever is being done now is still inadequate. In the developing world drinking water quality in particular remains an acute problem.

Further necessary steps, in addition to greater access to improved drinking water sources in the developing world, include the following. First, the nitrogen, phosphorus, and sediments humans send into water need to be reduced. This means, among other things, rethinking how agriculture and stormwater management are practiced globally. Second, insidious, bioaccumulative, persistent pollutants need to be controlled. For these especially, this means application of the precautionary principle and aggressive regulation. Third, the industrial world needs to understand the effects of the chemicals it creates and employs before it discharges them into surface and groundwater. Fourth, in the United States, the Clean Water Act needs upgrading to enable appropriate regulation of sources, particularly nonpoint sources, and a holistic approach to water protection. Moreover, the act unfortunately focuses little on pollution prevention, and much on pollution control, a focus that should be shifted. At the same time, research on water pollution needs more congressional funding, especially with respect to toxic and new pollutants. An up-to-date set of amendments could remedy these and other shortcomings of this monumental statutory workhorse. Finally, we all need more information and education, a responsibility, especially, of the industrialized world, about the effects on water of the products we use and the behaviors we are accustomed to so we can maximally protect it and intelligently participate in setting water pollution policy.

6

AIR

Why is clean air important?

Each person takes in more than three thousand gallons of air a day to stay alive. The quality of that air is key to good health. Moreover, polluted air affects everyone and is unavoidable: although it can collect in large air basins (areas often surrounded by geographical formations such as mountains), it is not confined to particular spots, as is, for example, the polluted water of a particular river in which you can choose to swim or not.

Air is our atmosphere, the protective gaseous layer that swaddles the earth and separates it from space. The atmosphere extends roughly 350 miles above us and is composed mostly of nitrogen, oxygen, and water vapor. It is a complex system, regulating the heat that enters it and leaves it, cycling carbon through it, shielding us from harmful ultraviolet rays, and influencing weather. The dynamic, delicate chemical and physical balancing act that occurs in the atmosphere is essential to the health of life on the planet. Atmospheric air pollution disrupts this balance and in recent years has become a problem of immense proportions because it causes climate change.

Even more than water, air is a great vehicle for transporting molecules, including pollutants. It can catch and blow them thousands of miles from their source, often mixing them with others along the way. This transport capacity exacerbates air pollution problems. Acadia National Park in coastal Maine, an ostensibly pristine place, suffers unhealthy concentrations of both visible and invisible air pollution delivered to it from upwind urban locations, especially the New York metropolitan area, home to hundreds of thousands of motor vehicles and to many polluting industries.

What is air pollution?

Air pollution is anything that enters the air and causes harm to humans, other species, or the ecosystems the air supports, or that interferes visibly with our enjoyment of the environment. We often associate air pollution with outdoor (ambient) air. But increasingly indoor air pollution, from such things as microfibers in fabrics, aerosol sprays, and cigarette smoke, is recognized as a major health problem. We also usually think of air pollution as the product of industrialization, emitted from factory smokestacks or from automobile tailpipes. Almost all of it is. But some of the most deadly air pollutants occur naturally and may be inhaled inside or outside. For example, radon, a naturally occurring substance, seeps from the ground into residential basements silently and odorlessly, and is highly poisonous. Volcanic ash, also naturally occurring, can pollute the air with particles producing effects similar to industrial pollutants.

Air pollutants are often divided into two groups: primary and secondary. Primary air pollutants are emitted directly into the air from a polluting source, such as carbon monoxide from an automobile. Secondary pollutants form when the primary ones react with other chemicals (or each other) in the atmosphere creating new ones. A common example is ground-level ozone, a very nasty secondary air pollutant that is inhaled with every breath, and which is harmful to living things.

Why is air pollution a problem?

Air pollution is a problem largely because it is a major contributor to serious health issues such as respiratory, neurological, and cardiovascular diseases. The World Health Organization (WHO) estimates that yearly 7 million premature deaths are linked to air pollution.[1] In the United States, research from the Massachusetts Institute of Technology shows that air pollution accounts for about 200,000 premature deaths a year (the main source of which is motor vehicles).[2] It can be most harmful for children, the elderly, and people who are already sick. Great athletes and the general population are vulnerable as well. China made extensive efforts to clean up its very polluted air in preparation for the 2008 Beijing Olympics to protect participants and spectators. Badly polluted air can be fatal quickly. In December 1952 the world took notice of this for probably the first time after an unusual weather phenomenon (an air inversion) in London. Four thousand people died there over the course of five days, and thousands more in the following weeks in what has come to be known as "the Great Smog." The victims had breathed fog mixed with smoke from factories, buses, and domestic fires; their lungs were clogged and irritated by the very small particles, mostly from coal (some of it burned for fuel in the cold weather), contained in these sources. The Great Smog was shocking: cities had suffered from bad air for centuries; but now that bad air could be lethal. In December 1984 this reality was brought home again, dramatically, at the Union Carbide plant in Bhopal, India. Leaking industrial vapors killed 4,000 people on the spot and injured thousands more, making it among the planet's worst civilian pollution disasters. As horrific as these two events were, however, long-term exposure to moderate levels of air pollution is even more problematic. This is the kind of exposure practically everyone experiences because air pollution is pervasive. Most problematic of all, though, is the impact of air pollution on our atmosphere in the form of greenhouse gases causing climate change.

The problems that air pollution present to humans, the species primarily responsible for them, are suffered by other living species. Also of concern is the problem it presents for our built environment. The Parthenon and the Great Pyramids, for example, have suffered major structural and aesthetic damage as a result of the corrosive effects of relatively recent air pollution, largely from motor vehicles. And air pollution is darkening the Taj Mahal's ineffable white marble.

Why are children especially vulnerable to air pollution?

Children breathe much more air per pound of body weight than adults. Their respiratory systems are still developing: they have fewer alveoli, the tiny sacs in the lungs where oxygen and carbon dioxide are exchanged. They are much more active, often breathing through their mouths (and losing the benefit of nasal filtration of pollutants). They spend lots of time outdoors, often during the day when pollutant levels are high, and they spend it closer to the ground than adults (in strollers or as youngsters only a couple of feet tall), where especially harmful pollutants like car exhaust are denser. These factors also cause susceptibility to polluted indoor air, from tobacco smoke and other sources in poorly ventilated rooms. Moreover, children, unless under adult supervision, might not adopt the protections adults often do, for example, by responding to air quality warnings and staying inside. The exposure of children to polluted air while playing in a park or walking home on a hot city sidewalk can cause a range of problems from minor coughs and days missed at school to exacerbation of existing lung diseases such as asthma and cystic fibrosis. Globally it is recognized as an important public health issue.

This special childhood vulnerability is true as well with respect to other kinds of pollution for similar reasons. For instance, children take in more pollution than adults pound for pound, so their bodies receive higher doses of pollution; they also live in closer proximity to dirt, dust, and toxins on the ground, which are brought inside their bodies not only by breathing, but also by putting things in their mouths. Finally, children have more years ahead of them than adults to take pollutants into their bodies where they can accumulate (for example, as do lead and other heavy metals) and where some of them such as certain carcinogens (radiation, for example) have a greater likelihood to cause disease than they would if exposure occurred in adulthood.

What are the major air pollutants?

There are many, many air pollutants. Some are well known, well understood, and regulated to one degree or another; others are present in the air, but not yet understood well enough to control; still others are being formed all the time as humans continue to introduce new compounds into the air where they may chemically react with others creating still more compounds. Importantly, levels once considered safe for some chemicals and air pollutants, upon further study with new data, may not be. So identifying major air pollutants requires continuous scientific attention and regulatory changes. A good source of information on the universe of air pollutants, at least in the United States, is the EPA.[3] But the EPA is not keeping pace with all the chemicals in circulation, and there is no comprehensive, commonly agreed-upon air pollution catalogue.

It is helpful, however, to divide major air pollutants into three main categories. The first category is what are called the criteria air pollutants, the ones that are widely recognized as both very harmful and ubiquitous. Humans inhale significant quantities of them every day. In the United States, because of their widespread health and environmental impacts, and because they are well known and relatively well understood, they are the main focus of air pollution control across the entire country and the only pollutants subject to National Ambient Air Quality Standards. There are six criteria pollutants: ground-level ozone, particulate matter, carbon monoxide, nitrogen dioxide, sulfur dioxide, and lead. The second category covers the main greenhouse gases. These have profound global impacts associated with climate change. The third category covers additional air pollutants considered highly toxic and known as the toxic or hazardous air pollutants.

These three categories are not entirely separate: the pollutants in the first two may also have toxic characteristics, and the criteria and toxic air pollutants may also contribute to climate change.

What is ozone?

Ozone (O_3) is a gas made up of three oxygen atoms. It is very unstable and reacts readily with other chemicals in the presence of sunlight. It can be either good or bad, depending on its location and the process by which it is made, even though both kinds have the same chemical composition.

"Good" or stratospheric ozone resides naturally in the earth's upper atmosphere, about six to thirty miles above the earth's surface. It is created naturally when atmospheric oxygen (O_2) is heated by sunlight, breaking it up and freeing an oxygen atom. This single, now free and chemically excited atom then bonds with other oxygen atoms to make ozone. It is good because it protects the planet from the sun's harmful cancer-causing ultraviolet rays. Ninety percent of the earth's ozone is stratospheric.

Ground-level ozone is the "bad" ozone. Typically, it is not emitted directly into the air and is not natural. Rather, it is created in the troposphere (the lowest level of the atmosphere where living things take in air) through a very complex process in which nitrogen oxides, carbon monoxide, and volatile organic compounds react with sunlight, again freeing oxygen atoms that unite to form O_3. Not surprisingly, this ground-level phenomenon occurs most often on hot summer days. So temperature can increase bad ozone levels even without an increase in ozone-forming emissions. Sometimes high ozone levels are detected in cold places. This likely happens when it is trapped in a snowy valley with cars, such as a big ski area.

What are volatile organic compounds?

Volatile organic compounds, or VOCs as they are known to the people in the chemical industry and to the people who regulate air pollution, are organic compounds (compounds containing carbon) that evaporate very quickly at room temperature and under normal atmospheric pressure. VOCs are ubiquitous. Most products from the petrochemical industry contain VOCs. They are found, for example, in gasoline, in paint solvents, in inks, in the dry cleaning process, and in consumer products. The smell of bug spray or a new carpet or nail polish or even perfume and air freshener is the smell of VOCs as they vaporize in the air. VOCs can be carcinogenic. Benzene, a VOC and known carcinogen, for instance, is in automobile exhaust and tobacco smoke. Because VOCs react with nitrogen oxides and sunlight to form ground-level ozone, they are of great concern as an air pollutant and regulated as "ozone precursors." In fact, they are a main cause of ground-level ozone. VOCs can also come from natural sources such as vegetation.

Why is ground-level ozone harmful?

Ground-level ozone, even in relatively small amounts, can cause serious health effects, especially to children, older adults, and people with lung disease. It exacerbates conditions such as asthma, chronic bronchitis, and emphysema, and can inhibit breathing. In healthy athletes it can permanently damage lungs, which is why noontime jogs in polluted cities are discouraged on hot days, and why frequent exposure to it is often described as a repeated sunburn on the lungs. Such health effects are why the media commonly report ozone levels year-round and issue ozone advisories of dangerous levels. Ground-level ozone can travel, often influenced by weather patterns and topography, so even rural areas may have unhealthy amounts of it.

Ground-level ozone is also bad for the environment ecologically. It is especially bad for sensitive plants and for plants during the growing season. Cottonwood, ponderosa pine, quaking aspen, and black cherry trees, all common in North America, are known to be sensitive to ozone. Ozone's ability to get into plants through their pores weakens them and makes them susceptible to disease. Finally, ozone can cause visible damage to plant leaves, which may not be fatal to the plant but is ugly to see in a park, a yard, or on a hiking trail.

What is the ozone hole?

The ozone hole is the dramatic thinning of the protective stratospheric ozone layer over Antarctica allowing harmful ultra-violet rays to reach the earth and its human population. British scientists first described it in 1985, causing much alarm. The hole has been closely watched ever since. Shortly after its discovery the international community galvanized into action enacting the Montreal Protocol of 1987, which phases out chlorofluorocarbons (CFCs), the chemicals widely believed to cause stratospheric ozone depletion, not only over Antarctica but also around the globe. This happens because when these CFCs reach the ozone layer they are exposed to ultraviolet rays and break down, releasing chlorine which breaks up the ozone molecules, and thus "depletes" the ozone layer.

The history of CFC reduction is a "good news" story. The message it sends is better yet: very serious human-made global environmental impacts can be reversed if the international community confronts them quickly, scientifically, and deliberately. In the early twentieth century, after leaking toxic chemicals in refrigerators caused several fatal accidents, three American corporations, General Motors, Frigidaire, and DuPont, collaborated to find a nontoxic refrigerant.

They found it in CFC, which is not only nontoxic but also nonflammable. It was patented with the trade name Freon. Soon Freon was widely used in large refrigerators and air conditioners. Because it seemed safe, it was often designated as the only coolant allowed in public buildings. After World War II CFCs began to be used widely, especially as propellants in aerosol containers such as hair and insect sprays. By the 1960s they made it easy to put air conditioning units in automobiles and residences. They became a worldwide blockbuster business producing more than one million tons of CFC yearly.

Although CFCs seemed safe for humans, by the 1980s scientists began to make the connection between alarming signs of ozone depletion in the upper atmosphere, especially the hole over Antarctica, and the presence of CFCs, which by then were considered to be the key destructive agent. Given the urgency of the situation, the Montreal Protocol was quickly signed by 27 nations, and amended in 1990 (other amendments followed), with more forceful terms calling for elimination of production by 2000. The protocol included enforcement provisions (economic and trade penalties), recycling programs, the development of substitutes, and funds to help developing nations comply. A total of 197 countries have signed it, making it the first treaty in the history of the United Nations to have been ratified by all its members. It has caused the phase-out of 98 percent of ozone-depleting substances worldwide, and the ozone hole appears to be shrinking. On the twenty-fifth anniversary of the protocol, the World Bank reported that by 2065, because of it, just in the United States, 6.3 million fewer people will have died of skin cancer and $4.2 trillion in health care costs will have been avoided.[4]

What is particulate matter?

As its name suggests, particulate matter (PM) covers the vast array of small bits of solid and liquid material that appear in our atmosphere, including such things as tiny bits of acids, metals, dust, and soil. The term "aerosols" is also sometimes used for PM, although technically aerosols are not only particles, but also the air in which the particles are suspended.

Throughout the world, two main PM categories are recognized as pollutants; both affect human health. The first, PM_{10}, or large PM, refers to particles above ten micrometers (a fraction of the width of a human hair). These are small enough to enter the lungs and cause health problems, whereas larger particles are generally filtered out and don't get into the lungs. The second, $PM_{2.5}$, or fine PM, refers to yet smaller particles, particles so small that they can be absorbed by the alveoli in the lungs where gas exchange happens, and can even find their way into the bloodstream. $PM_{2.5}$ therefore presents special health concerns.

Why is particulate matter harmful?

In the long list of harmful air pollutants, the World Health Organization ranks fine particulate matter as having the biggest impact on human health. This status derives no doubt from the ability of fine PM to travel deep into the human body and from the fact that it is present everywhere. WHO identifies fine PM worldwide as a major cause of all lung cancer deaths, chronic obstructive pulmonary disease deaths, and heart disease and strokes.[5] It can aggravate asthma, which is a major health problem and getting worse. Children, the elderly, and people with preexisting heart and lung conditions like emphysema are especially vulnerable to particulate matter in their lungs. Its economic costs, in terms of job and school absences, and medical treatments, are enormous.

Particle pollution also affects visibility, making it harder to see behind the wheel as the particles refract light, and harder to enjoy the physical environment through the haze it makes. And particulates travel: diesel exhaust from trucks on Los Angeles freeways can end up over Grand Canyon National Park in Arizona. The EPA identifies particle pollution as the main reason why visibility can drop from 140 miles to as little as 35 in the scenic areas of the western United States and from 90 miles to as low as 15 in eastern scenic areas.[6]

What is asthma, and what does it have to do with air pollution?

Asthma is a chronic, noncommunicable disease that inflames and narrows the lungs and causes such symptoms as wheezing, breathlessness, and chest tightening. The World Health Organization estimates that worldwide 235 million people suffer from it. WHO also identifies it as the most common chronic disease among children.[7] The occurrence of asthma is increasing. In the United States, the EPA reports that about 26 million people, or one in twelve, have asthma and that the number is increasing dramatically.[8] The American Lung Association reports that in 2011 asthma caused over 3,300 deaths.[9] Children and low-income and minority populations are disproportionately affected.

Air pollution, inside and outside, is recognized as a key trigger for asthma attacks, along with allergens such as pollen and mold; genetic predisposition also plays a part. Ozone pollution, in particular, beyond directly triggering an attack, can aggravate an underlying asthma condition and make people more susceptible to other asthma triggers. This ozone link is of great concern to health specialists and has been documented by correlations between days with high ozone concentrations and increased use of asthma medication by children and increased emergency room visits.

What is smog?

The word "smog" first appeared in the early twentieth century to describe the foggy conditions present in industrial cities like London, where the air contained large quantities of smoke from factories and coal-burning furnaces. "Smog" combines the words smoke and fog to describe the visibly gritty air of such places especially on damp, dreary days. This kind of smog is industrial smog usually containing ozone and particulate matter from burning fossil fuels. It has been greatly reduced through regulation in developed countries over the last several decades.

In the later twentieth century with the proliferation of motor vehicles, another form of smog, photochemical smog, also started occurring and is now pervasive in urban settings. In fact, photochemical smog is a persistent, serious health and aesthetic problem practically everywhere, accounting for thousands of premature deaths in the United States and around the globe. It is formed when nitrogen oxides and ozone react with sunlight. Although ozone is invisible, the addition of other chemicals and particulate matter to the mix creates the haze and reduced visibility we associate with photochemical smog. Look out the window of an airplane as it descends into Denver or New Delhi on a hot summer day and you will likely see a yellow hazy ring on the horizon. That is photochemical smog.

What is a temperature inversion?

Normally, air near the earth's surface is warmer than air higher in the atmosphere. It becomes increasingly cold as it goes up; this keeps the air in motion. A temperature inversion occurs when cold air at the surface becomes stuck below the lighter warm air above it, reversing the norm and preventing air circulation. This phenomenon can happen, for example, when cold winds bear down on a city surrounded by mountains or nestled in a valley, and stalls. Here a temperature inversion traps pollutants and increases their intensity as motor vehicles and other combustion sources dump them into the trapped air. They occur regularly in places such as Mexico City, which is very polluted and located in a valley, and in many, many other large and small cities around the world. In the United States, Los Angeles, car-dependent and nestled between the Pacific Ocean and a ring of mountains, is well known for temperature inversions.

Why is carbon monoxide a major air pollutant?

This is mainly because when breathed into the lungs carbon monoxide (CO) gets into the bloodstream and quickly binds to hemoglobin in blood cells. This blocks the ability of these cells to release oxygen into the body, especially to vital organs like the heart and brain. It is odorless, colorless, and tasteless, so it is very hard to detect. Large amounts can overcome someone in minutes, causing suffocation and death. At lower levels CO poisoning can create a range of symptoms, usually reversible but sometimes causing permanent damage. CO is also a player in the production of ground-level ozone, one of the most pernicious air pollutants, as we have seen.

Why are nitrogen oxides major air pollutants?

Nitrogen oxides (NO_x) are major contributors to ground-level ozone production. They also contribute to fine particle pollution when they combine with chemicals like ammonia and water. They are major components of acid rain. Although the whole NO_x family of compounds—including nitric acid and nitrous acid—is of concern, the key family member is nitrogen dioxide (NO_2). This is largely because emissions that form NO_2 usually lead to the formation of other nitrogen oxides. So controlling NO_2 reduces exposure to other pollutants in the NO_x family.

Exposure to nitrogen dioxide is linked to respiratory problems such as airway inflammation in healthy people, and aggravated symptoms in people with asthma. NO_2 concentrations are generally higher near motor vehicles and roadways than they are at other locations. Considering, by way of example, that about 15 percent of all housing units in the United States are within three hundred feet of a major road, railway, or airport (many of them no doubt homes to economically disadvantaged people with multiple health and social stressors), NO_2 is a major contributor to health issues and medical costs.

Why is sulfur dioxide a major air pollutant?

Sulfur dioxide ranks high as a pollutant primarily because in the atmosphere it can form tiny particles that can penetrate the lungs. Short-term exposure can produce adverse health effects, especially for people with asthma, children, and the elderly. Like nitrogen oxides, it is a main contributor to acid rain. And just as nitrogen dioxide best represents the nitrogen oxide family of compounds, sulfur dioxide (SO_2) best represents the sulfur oxide (SO_x) family, and for the same reasons: SO_2 emissions usually lead to other SO_x emissions, so controlling SO_2 brings down pollution levels of other members of the family as well. One family member, sulfates, is particularly good at scattering light, producing haze and diminished visibility.

What is acid rain?

Pure water is neither an acid nor a base. In other words, its pH is 7. But rainwater always contains impurities including natural acids from such events as volcanic eruptions, and natural bases such as the ammonia from decaying organic matter. In normal conditions, taking into consideration these impurities, natural rain has pH values between 5 and 7. Acid rain, or more broadly acid deposition, occurs when sulfur dioxide and nitrogen oxides, primarily from human activities, are emitted into the air where they mix with water and other chemicals to form acidic pollutants. When enough of them get there and the pH value of rainwater drops below 5, acid rain conditions exist. Because SO_2 and NO_x dissolve easily in water and can be carried easily by the wind, they end up in rain, sleet, fog, and snow, often hundreds of miles from their sources. Acid deposition can also be dry. This happens in arid settings when these acidic pollutants mix with dust or smoke and settle on buildings, plants, and the ground.

A nineteenth-century English pharmacist, Robert Angus Smith, first noticed acid rain when he found much higher acidity levels in rain falling over cities in Britain compared to lower levels in less-polluted areas. But it was not until the mid-twentieth century that the problem got much attention. And it is not a problem everywhere. In most of the world acid rain is readily neutralized by naturally occurring bases. The oceans, for example, contain neutralizing compounds (although dangerous ocean acidification is increasing), and many landmasses have alkaline soil and limestone deposits, which are also neutralizing.

In places that do not have this neutralizing capacity, like the eastern United States and Canada where thin soil and granite bedrock are common, and in places where acid deposition has blown and collected with sufficient concentration, it has created serious environmental problems, including damage to trees, fish kills, and ecosystem disruption. The built environment, too, from construction materials to statues, is corroded and undermined by acid deposition.

Is lead too heavy to be an air pollutant?

No. Lead is only one, and perhaps the most pernicious (along with mercury), of several toxic or carcinogenic heavy metals that in very fine dust form pollute the air we breathe. Others include arsenic, cadmium, nickel, copper, and iron oxides. Although all of these occur naturally, pollution from heavy metals is primarily the product of industrialization. Because of focused regulatory action over the last few decades, chiefly the requirement to remove lead from gasoline, lead in our atmosphere has dropped dramatically. But during this time lead dust has travelled and settled in soils, in surface, ground-, and drinking water, and in the human body. It persists in these locations for a very long time. Lead paint flaking from old residential housing stock, for example, remains in the soil of yards, where children playing in them many years later inhale lead as they breathe and ingest lead-contaminated dirt from their hands.

Lead accumulates in the body and lodges in the bones. It is especially bad for children, causing neurological problems as the brain develops, which can produce learning disabilities, behavioral issues, and lowered IQs. In adults, elevated blood lead levels can cause cardiovascular problems, especially high blood pressure.

What are the toxic air pollutants?

There is a whole category of air pollutants that is known or suspected to cause cancer or other very serious health impacts such as reproductive problems and birth defects. These are the toxic air pollutants. In the United States the EPA has identified 187 of them,[10] although the list is not comprehensive. Some common examples are perchloroethylene from dry cleaning operations, benzene in gasoline, and methylene chloride, a paint stripper and solvent. Other familiar examples are asbestos, dioxin, and toluene, not to mention heavy metals such as mercury. The Mad Hatter in Lewis Carroll's *Alice in Wonderland* was "mad" with symptoms of craziness because he inhaled mercury fumes while curing furs for hats, as did many nineteenth-century hatmakers. He was afflicted because the mercury had affected his nervous system.

Although people get harmful exposure to air toxics by simply breathing, toxics in air are also constantly being deposited in water and soil where they get ingested by fish, or taken in by fruits and vegetables, or contaminate drinking water. Children are especially vulnerable. Some air toxics (mercury again is a good example) accumulate in body and plant tissues, so predators at the top of the food chain, like humans, can take in large concentrations from contaminated food.

What is indoor air pollution?

Indoor air pollution is the unhealthy air inside residential and commercial buildings. It can come from outside through ventilation systems and open windows and doors or from a large variety of sources inside. Because we spend so much time inside and because indoor air pollution is less diluted than pollution in the ambient air, it is a significant health problem.

Two common indoor air pollutants are carbon monoxide, discussed above, and radon, which is also colorless, odorless, and tasteless. Indoor carbon monoxide sources include leaky chimneys, space heaters, wood stoves, and car exhaust in enclosed garages. We all have heard of tragic deaths resulting from people being overcome by CO at home. Many homes contain carbon monoxide detectors because of this. Radon is naturally occurring and less familiar. It is produced by the decay of uranium in soil and frequently finds its way into residential basements. Remarkably, it is the second leading cause of lung cancer after smoking. In fact, lung cancer is its only known impact on humans, but it is a very big one. The synergistic effects of radon and smoking put smokers at great risk. Radon is so pervasive and harmful that in the United States the Surgeon General has urged Americans to test their homes for it and reduce the levels if necessary. WHO sees it as a worldwide health risk and has started an international radon project to address it.[11] Secondhand smoke, which is the third leading cause of lung cancer, is also well known. It is particularly harmful to children; for instance, it can exacerbate childhood asthma and bronchitis.

Indoor air is polluted by many other very dangerous materials and compounds and we inhale them unwittingly all the time: microfibers in fabrics, the off-gases of new rugs and new cars, particulates in hairsprays, and the cleaning agents we use to polish furniture are just a few common examples. The smells we detect from some of these things are often VOCs.

In developing countries a large percentage of people rely on coal and biomass (plants and animal waste such as wood, grasses, and dung) for fuel burned in simple stoves inside simple dwellings. Women and children especially are exposed to high concentrations of soot and other pollutants from these fuels. They are thought to be responsible for significant numbers of deaths and chronic ailments in these locations.

What are the main sources of air pollution?

There are many, but a single ubiquitous, overwhelmingly important one exists: fossil fuels. Having gotten directly to the point, let us back up for a moment and provide some context. Air pollution sources produced by human activity fall into two main categories: mobile sources and stationary sources. Fossil fuels play a dominant role in both, but each category contains other important sources of air pollution. Some are natural, like sea salt sprays, volcanic eruptions, dust storms, forest fires, and the processes of bacterial growth and decay. Humans are responsible for most sources, however, and these are the ones that have the greatest long and short-term impacts.

What are fossil fuels, and why are they so harmful?

Fossil fuels chemically are hydrocarbons. They are nonrenewable resources that formed from the compression, under layers of rock over very long periods of time, of the remains of prehistoric carbon-based plants and animals. When burned they release energy. The most common are coal, oil, and natural gas. They are nonrenewable because it took millions of years to produce them and takes only minutes to consume them.

Unless you believe that human development over the last few centuries has been completely misguided, then you cannot conclude that fossil fuels are simply bad. They are largely responsible for remarkable quality of-life improvements and technological achievements since the Industrial Revolution. They are the world's primary energy source and have been for hundreds of years. They fuel our factories and transportation systems; they give us electricity. Without them we could not have put a man on the moon. But the negative consequences of our heavy dependence on fossil fuels are overtaking the benefits they have conferred. They have become especially harmful because under combustion they deliver much more air pollution than any other source, emitting all six of the criteria air pollutants: nitrogen dioxide, sulfur dioxide, carbon monoxide, particulates, ozone, and lead (and other heavy metals) as well as creating lots of carbon dioxide, a leading greenhouse gas. Indeed, we can trace many of the worst air pollution problems and health outcomes to fossil fuels, from acid rain and asthma, to oil spills and climate change.

What are mobile sources of air pollution?

Mobile sources include cars, and all the other machines similarly powered by fossil fuels: trucks, buses, trains, and boats; farm and construction equipment; and planes. We breathe air pollution from these sources at the dock when a boat's outboard motor is idling, and walking on the sidewalk a few feet from the cars on the street beside us. Mobile sources also include such machines as gas-powered lawn mowers, all-terrain vehicles, and snowmobiles, and hand-held equipment like gas-powered saws and leaf blowers. These emit the same chemicals as motor vehicles but are often not required to have air pollution controls on them, as are cars, so whoever is sitting on a power lawn mower to clip the grass is likely inhaling some very unhealthy stuff.

Another example is school buses. The diesel exhaust from them has been recognized by the American Academy of Pediatrics as a major source of serious air pollution for children (who breathe the exhaust both inside and outside the buses), largely because of the significant particle pollution it contains.[12] Most school buses in the United States run on diesel, which is one of the dirtiest fossil fuels.

What are stationary sources of air pollution?

As the term suggests, stationary sources are sources that do not move. Before the dominance of motor vehicles in the mid-twentieth century, they were the main sources of air pollution. Familiar examples today are power plants, metal smelters, pulp and paper mills, petroleum refineries, chemical plants, municipal waste incinerators, and cement plants. Examples on a smaller scale are wood-burning stoves, and residential oil and gas furnaces.

Coal-fired power plants are particularly problematic: they are the biggest source of carbon dioxide and sulfur dioxide emissions in the United States; and they produce more toxic air emissions than any other US industrial source. They are major emitters of heavy metals such as mercury and particulate matter in the form of soot. Many do not have up-to-date pollution control devices; and even when regulated they pour major pollutants into the air. Worldwide there are about 2,300 coal-fired plants, over half of them in China and the United States. Several US plants are shutting down with many more closures expected by 2020. In China, India, and several other developing countries, however, they are increasing in number, so they present a major global challenge.

Ironically, some air pollution controls on stationary sources themselves contribute to complex air pollution issues. For instance, in the United States increased smoke stack height (five hundred feet or higher) is a technique used mostly at coal-fired power plants. In 2010 the US General Accounting Office reported that 284 tall stacks operated at 172 coal power plants, a third of them in the Ohio River Valley.[13] The idea behind tall stacks is that they can disperse pollutants and dilute them to acceptable local air quality levels in compliance with the state's regulations. But tall stacks have contributed to broader air pollution problems. It turns out that they do not necessarily dilute pollutants to acceptable levels. They generally just blow them farther away, and higher, where emissions like sulfur dioxide get more time to form ozone and particle pollution, some of it acid rain. Certainly tall stacks can reduce soot near the plant, but this same soot settles in distant lakes and parks, or lingers in the air of downwind states.

What are fugitive emissions?

They are unintended releases of pollutants into the air, often as fumes or leaks escaping from large or small containers. Industrial operations with holding tanks, chemical vats, and waste lagoons offer many opportunities for unintended vaporization and leaks of hazardous chemicals, which are hard to detect and control.

Fugitive emissions are consequential because we breathe them in all the time as gaseous pollutants and as large and fine particulate matter.

The fumes we smell at the gas pump are fugitive emissions of gas vapors; the familiar smells from printing operations and paint cans are fugitive emissions of volatile organic compounds. These contribute to smog at ground level and to climate change in our atmosphere. If you live near a petrochemical plant or oil refinery you also smell these as VOCs when leaks and accidents occur. In 2015 a methane leak of epic proportions from a broken underground pipe occurred at the Aliso Canyon gas storage facility in the southern California Porter Ranch community. It sickened residents and spewed about 97,000 metric tons of methane, a major greenhouse gas, into the air over several months before it was contained. The climate impacts of this event were significant, and it highlights the dangers of subterranean gas operations as well as of aging infrastructures. Fugitive emissions of methane from oil wells and hydrofracking operations are also of increasing concern in the context of climate change.

Fugitive dust is another kind of fugitive emission. It is the particulate matter stirred up from soil and other friable material. It comes, for example, from roadways where pavement, tires, and debris are constantly pulverized, from construction and demolition activities, from unpaved roads and parking lots, from farming operations, from leaf blowers, and from sand blasting.

How is air pollution controlled in the United States?

It is controlled primarily by implementation and enforcement of the nation's air pollution legislation, the Clean Air Act of 1970 and its major 1977 and 1990 amendments; some other federal environmental laws address certain aspects of the problem, such as the workplace air pollution regulated by the Occupational Safety and Health Act. But it is this statute, and the state and local air pollution control programs in force under Clean Air Act authority, that has dramatically reduced air pollution in the United States. We have a long road ahead to bring air quality up to acceptable levels. For example, millions of people in the United States still live in areas that exceed ozone levels considered safe. But the Clean Air Act has improved the quality of the lives of Americans greatly.

For stationary air pollution sources, like the other major environmental laws in the United States, the Clean Air Act sets broad national standards, most importantly the health-based National Ambient Air Quality Standards (NAAQS). These govern emissions of the six criteria pollutants by setting the legally permissible upper limit for each one. States are expected to develop state implementation plans (SIPs) to meet the NAAQS, which they implement and enforce after EPA approval, although the EPA retains authority to take enforcement actions for a state and to step back in and impose federal regulations if a SIP falls short. States have a variety of ways to meet NAAQS standards in their SIPs. The most common are regulations limiting end-of-stack emissions from industrial air pollution sources by requiring devices such as scrubbers and baghouses to capture pollutants in air emissions. But other effective mechanisms have been included in SIPs, such as local ordinances limiting the burning of leaves or gas-powered leaf blowers. Some SIP provisions can be controversial. For example, Massachusetts imposed a parking freeze on the City of Cambridge (a booming urban area and home of the Massachusetts Institute of Technology and Harvard University) in its original SIP as a way of reducing ozone and carbon monoxide pollution from cars. The freeze strictly limited commercial parking and was very controversial. Developers complained that it stifled growth; neighborhood activists who hoped it would stifle growth, supported it. Revisions to the original SIP have been proposed to provide the City with more parking flexibility.

The Clean Air Act also includes "technology-forcing" requirements (as do some other environmental laws). These requirements come into play, for example, for new (or significantly modified) stationary sources of air pollution, which must have a Clean Air Act permit (normally issued by a state) in order to be built. They are linked to how well the state or local air district in which the source will be located complies with the applicable NAAQS through its SIP. This, in essence, is how they work: For each criteria pollutant (that is, pollutants for which there is a NAAQS), each state is divided into those areas meeting the standard (called attainment areas), and those that are not meeting the standard (called nonattainment areas). In attainment areas, new sources must install best available control technology (BACT) in order to prevent significant deterioration of air quality. Importantly, BACT can be existing, accessible technology taking cost into consideration. In contrast, in nonattainment areas, the source must install technology that meets the lowest achievable emissions rate, looking to technology that has been demonstrated to work anywhere in the world and without regard to cost, thus appropriately exacting more pollution reductions from the source because it is already in an overpolluted location. The effect is technology-forcing by encouraging the most advanced pollution-control technologies in the world.

Another example of Clean Air Act requirements that push technology forward are the New Source Performance Standards or NSPS. NSPS are applicable to new (and modified or reconstructed) stationary sources of pollution. Unlike SIP-based standards for criteria pollutants, which are dependent on particular locations (attainment areas and nonattainment areas), the NSPS are national standards that the EPA promulgates by source category. They provide a technology floor for new sources and are included in the permit for these sources. The EPA is also authorized to set national emissions standards for many existing industrial sources. Implementation of these standards then falls to the states. Recently, the EPA has used this authority to promulgate its Clean Power Plan to regulate carbon dioxide emissions from both coal- and gas-fired power plants in an effort to address climate change.

Air pollution's great ability to travel has created implementation challenges. First among these challenges is what is known as the "ozone transport problem." This is the puzzle that confounds states in the eastern United States receiving dirty air from the Ohio Valley, but having no authority to regulate its sources. For years, eastern states have had tougher and more costly air pollution requirements than rust belt states that enjoy cheaper and dirtier energy; and the eastern states have complained bitterly about it. The EPA responded in 2011 with the "cross-state air pollution rule," which requires midwestern states with coal-fired power plants to cut back emissions of ozone and particulate matter (which are subject to NAAQS) that head east to the Atlantic coast. In 2014, the US Supreme Court upheld the bitterly contested rule. According to the EPA, implementation of the rule will avoid annually 13,000 to 34,000 premature deaths, 400,000 aggravated asthma conditions, and 1.8 million days missed at work or school.[14]

Separate from the NAAQS and NSPS, the Clean Air Act has also enabled the EPA to establish emission standards for hazardous air pollutants, to administer an acid-rain program, and to control ozone-depleting pollutants, especially chlorofluorocarbons.

When it comes to mobile sources the EPA takes the regulatory lead on the theory that cars and trucks are built, bought, and sold in a truly national market and should thus be governed by a single national set of rules that are applied to car manufacturers and cannot be implemented through a SIP. The only exception to this federal preemption is California, which the Clean Air Act allows to have its own mobile source regulations as long as they are as protective as the federal standards. This nod to California is based on the State's pioneering efforts to control air pollution starting in the 1950s. The Clean Air Act enables other states to adopt California's standards in lieu of the federal ones; in practice there is collaboration between California and the EPA in developing national standards.

The Clean Air Act has since its inception been a contentious area between the EPA and industry. The main flashpoint is the regulations the EPA is required to produce to implement the broad mandate of the statute. The pattern is as follows: the EPA proposes a regulation; industry objects usually on the basis that it will destroy the industry or be too costly or kill jobs; the EPA tinkers with the regulation and issues a final rule; industry sues the EPA; and a court, often the US Supreme Court, decides whether the regulation is really what Congress had in mind when it passed the statute. The same pattern occurs in regulatory challenges brought under the other environmental statutes, but it has been particularly pronounced in Clean Air Act legal battles.

This regulatory pull and tug between regulators and industry can sometimes result in better regulations and sometimes not. Nor is it only a US phenomenon. The huge Volkswagen software scandal of 2015 can be traced in part to vigorous regulatory push-back by European automakers against strict emissions tests proposed in European legislative bodies.

How much has the Clean Air Act helped reduce air pollution?

The following EPA statistics show the percent improvement in air quality in the United States based on concentrations of the criteria pollutants in 2015 (except as noted) versus 1980:[15]

Carbon monoxide	84 percent improvement
Lead	99 percent
Nitrogen dioxide	58 percent
Ozone	32 percent
PM_{10}	39 percent (1990 vs. 2015)
$PM_{2.5}$	37 percent (2000 vs. 2015)
Sulfur dioxide	84 percent

In 2010, the fortieth anniversary year of the EPA, the agency reported that fine-particle and ozone programs had prevented more than 160,000 premature deaths. New cars and trucks were up to 95 percent cleaner than older models thanks to such technology as catalytic converters. New construction and agriculture equipment emitted 90 percent less particle pollution and nitrogen oxides than previous models. Because of rules issued in 1990, toxic emissions from industry were estimated to be reduced by 1.7 million tons per year, and acid deposition in the Midwest and Northeast decreased by more than 30 percent. Reductions in particle pollution saved 20,000 to 50,000 lives yearly. The phase-out of ozone-depleting chemicals, notably CFCs, will reduce the occurrence of nonmelanoma skin cancer by an estimated 295 million between 1990 and 2165.[16]

There is, of course, one overwhelmingly important problem with this optimistic picture. It is our collective failure, so far, to reduce greenhouse gas emissions enough to effectively address climate change. Moreover, despite important air quality improvements as a result of the Clean Air Act, according to the American Lung Association's "State of the Air" report for 2015, more than 40 percent of Americans (about 138 million people) live in counties where air is unhealthy to breathe because of ozone and particle pollution.[17]

The quality of the air is not always obvious, either. One reason is the constant circulation of the air in our atmosphere; another is the fact that some air pollution is odorless and colorless. Despite this, simple observation in some places will show that the air is polluted. For example, most industrial smokestacks emit visible pollution. The exhaust from jet planes, from diesel trucks and buses, and from the chimney of a wood stove or fireplace carries visible pollutants and emits odors. Many densely populated cities across the globe, including New Delhi, Beijing, Los Angeles, Houston, and Paris, have noticeable smog in the air.

What are other countries doing to control air pollution?

Many countries have air-pollution control legislation. For example, the European Union has developed extensive legislation that includes health-based standards similar to the Clean Air Act's NAAQS. Member countries in turn have national laws reflecting these standards and other features of EU air legislation.

In Asia, with its many developing nations and its steep recent increase in overall emissions, air pollution control is a particularly pressing issue. India has had an air act since 1981. China in 2014 passed major amendments to its environmental protection law, in large part to address suffocating air pollution. The success of any environmental legislation, however, depends on actual implementation and enforcement, which is particularly challenging in the developing world.

Increasingly, governments and nongovernmental organizations are providing readily available air-pollution databases. In the United States the national Air Quality Index maintained by the EPA is a good online place to look for information on particular US locations.[18] A similar resource for several European locations is Air Quality Now.[19] The *World Air Quality Index* provides global information.[20]

How can air quality be further improved?

There are many ways, but here are some particularly important ones. First, the world needs to wean itself from reliance on the car and other things powered by fossil fuels such as coal-fired power plants. Second, currently unregulated—or underregulated—air pollution sources need to be regulated. These include planes, trains, and ships; large agricultural operations, which are significant sources of methane from livestock and carbon from open burning of agricultural fields; and consumer products.

In addition, more research needs to be done on the pollution soup that is our air. We are breathing in chemicals that we often do not understand and are probably harmful. This means that we need to invest more time and money in research and we need to be more cautious about giving chemicals and chemical companies a pass when a potentially harmful substance is about to enter the market and atmosphere. In the United States, the NAAQS are the critically important centerpiece for health-based air pollution control. Because they necessarily are derived from the scientific information currently available when they are written, the Clean Air Act wisely is set up to enable revisions of them periodically, as well as parallel revisions to state SIPs. The NAAQS, however, are not routinely upgraded. They are also buffeted by the political process, which includes influences that are not science based. In the US Senate, for example, the 2015 incoming majority leader vowed to block the entire suite of pending air regulations designed to bring ozone and sulfur standards down to levels considered safe by the scientific community. Air quality can be improved if Congress and the public enable the EPA, relying primarily on good science, to revise and upgrade these standards regularly to reflect new data. The same is true for the toxic air pollutants, which need more regulatory attention.

Finally, we all need to be better educated about air pollution so we can maximally protect ourselves from it, and intelligently participate in setting air pollution policy on a national and global scale.

7

ECOSYSTEMS

What is an ecosystem?

The environment is often seen as made up of distinct parts operating more or less independently of each other. Viewed this way, protecting the environment means protecting distinctly different categories of things: the oceans, endangered species, the air we breathe, and environmental problem-solving is approached in terms of disconnected challenges. We regulate air pollution and water pollution, but we don't often tackle them together, connecting the dots between, for example, mercury emitted from power plants, mercury in water, and mercury in tuna.

The term "ecosystem" captures an important alternative principle: the interconnectedness of all natural things and phenomena. In 1962 in *Silent Spring* Rachel Carson described it as "ecology."[1] A decade later another environmental trailblazer, Barry Commoner, anchored a bestselling book, *The Closing Circle*, in this concept. The first of the book's four laws of ecology is "everything is connected to everything else."[2] It wasn't until the 1990s, however, that ecosystem protection gained prominence.

An ecosystem (short for "ecological system") is a network of living and nonliving things all of which are, either directly or indirectly, interdependent, and operating, whether large or small, as a system. An ecosystem can be huge like the Gulf of Mexico, or tiny like a little tidal pool. Each contains elements interacting with each other in ways that create an ecological unit. In such a unit, every component depends in some way on every other. So for example, the Gulf of Mexico provides a warm, swampy environment for the bald cypress, which in turn supports wildlife and provides storm protection there. In the tidal pool, seaweed, happy in the aquatic environment, feeds the resident abalone. Sea otters from the larger coastal ecosystem in turn feed on the abalone. The earth is a series of ecosystems loosely laced together, and the earth itself is in a sense one huge ecosystem.

Where ecosystems begin and end is subjective, and they can overlap. Although they were once viewed as stable, closed, reliable systems, they are actually dynamic places subject to and changeable by natural factors such as climate. Humans are almost always part of ecosystems, and we have a major, often destructive, influence on them.

What do ecosystems do for us?

People need ecosystems, but they are poorly understood and we tend to take them for granted. It is not obvious, for example, that wetlands, extremely important and fast-disappearing ecosystems worldwide, are also important flood-control mechanisms, habitats for birds and animals, and water purifiers. The benefits of parking lots, however, are obvious, and sometimes they destroy wetlands. Human activity has changed ecosystems by encroaching on them, often for very good reasons, but the significance to ecologists of the resulting negative impacts has only started to emerge. It is very difficult for us to grasp these impacts, just as it makes sense that someone pulling into a supermarket parking lot would concentrate on their grocery list and not think—or even know about—the ecosystem disruption this convenient acre of blacktop causes.

Perhaps that is why the United Nations, recognizing that over the last fifty years ecosystem change has been dramatic, sponsored the Millennium Ecosystem Assessment (MA), a major undertaking involving many experts worldwide. Among other things, the MA identified the key benefits ecosystems provide. "Ecosystem services," as these benefits are known, are immensely valuable, including for the human species, and, according to the findings of the MA, are seriously at risk.[3]

The MA identified four main, sometimes overlapping, categories of ecosystem services: "provisioning services," such as food, timber, and medicines; "regulating services," such as pollination, flood and erosion control, and water purification; "cultural services," such as religious values and recreation; and "basic supporting services," such as photosynthesis, that make the other services possible.

Let us return to the Gulf of Mexico for a moment, where cypress swamps play an important flood control role and provide birdlife habitat. This is an example of a regulating service. Cypress is also logged and sold for various purposes. The ecosystem is thus furnishing a provisioning service with the logging. But by depleting the cypress, the logging has undermined protections from hurricanes like Katrina, and support for birdlife the trees could have provided. This is a classic example of the challenges and risks presented as our increasing human population takes the services of ecosystems and at the same time diminishes them. Other famous examples are the destruction of the Amazon rain forest and the collapse of the Atlantic cod fisheries in the 1990s from overfishing.

There is another scenario, however, in which ecosystem services offer sustainable and economically attractive alternatives. The Catskill Mountains north of New York City provide an example. Dependent on a natural water supply from the Catskills for millions of users, which had been degraded by development, and facing the need to comply with federal drinking water standards, New York City had a choice: install a filtration plant to purify the degraded water at an estimated $4 to 8 billion in capital costs plus $300 million per year of operating costs or, alternatively, develop and implement a Catskill watershed protection program for less than $2 billion. In the early 1990s the city chose the latter. It includes such elements as land purchases, stormwater retrofits, septic system upgrades, agricultural controls, and stream management. The program remains a success and there continues to be no need for an expensive filtration system.

What is biodiversity?

Biodiversity (short for "biological diversity") is the variety of life in all its forms, and how these life forms relate to each other. Like the concept of ecosystems, despite its profound importance, biodiversity came relatively late to the environmental lexicon, first appearing in the late 1960s. Since the 1980s, through work by scientists such as the prominent biologist and champion of biodiversity E. O. Wilson, it has become an extremely important component of environmental policymaking and problem-solving, encompassing three major categories.

Species biodiversity concerns the range of species of plants, animals, and microorganisms in a particular area. It is, for example, the collection of rabbits, chipmunks, voles, robins, irises, dandelions, milkweed, bees, wasps, earthworms, mushrooms, fungi, bacteria, and people in my springtime New England backyard—only a fraction of the many forms of life teeming in such a space. A backyard in central Florida might look something like mine, but it probably supports different species, and possibly more of them. Higher species diversity occurs in warmer climates, especially in the tropics.

Genetic biodiversity has to do with genetic differences within species. Siamese cats are not genetically the same as Maine coon cats, although they belong to the same species. We are genetically different from our siblings although we come from the same gene pool. Farmed salmon in pens off the Maine coast are genetically different from wild Atlantic salmon of the same species.

Ecological biodiversity has to do with variety in ecosystems. Rainforests, deserts, forests, and ponds are examples of different kinds of ecosystems, and each has various subtypes. Forests are ecosystems but maple and oak forests in the Green Mountains are not like the aspen and pine forests in the Rockies; vernal pools are ecosystems, but the vernal pools people might spot near a trail in the Vermont Green Mountains are not the same as the ones they would find hiking in the Idaho Rockies.

What is a species?

Scientists have not settled on a single definition, and there is considerable scientific, and philosophical, debate on what this term actually means. Even Darwin did not attempt to resolve the question when pondering the origin of species. Discoveries in the field of microbiology concerning, for example, our knowledge of DNA confound the problem. There is no doubt, however, that the notion of species is very important: species are the most basic elements of biological classification; they are central to the study of ecosystems and biodiversity; laws have been written to protect them. Most important, a living species represents an evolutionary process extending over millions of years. As a result, it is by definition a remarkably resilient and adaptive organism no doubt containing the best possible biochemical mix to survive.

In light of the importance of species in all sorts of contexts, good working definitions are essential, and they do exist. Here is one from the EPA: a species is "a group of organisms made up of similar individuals that are capable of breeding with one another."[4] Species are usually named in two parts, first the larger genus, then the species, which is a part of the genus. So humans are the species, *Homo sapiens*. We are part of the genus, *Homo*, its only remaining member. All others, such as *Homo erectus*, are extinct, although many of us also have genes inherited from *Homo neanderthalensis*.

How many species live on Earth?

This is one of the most fundamental questions of science. There is no firm answer, partly because "species" is hard to define; partly because, even with good working definitions, we have not collected enough relevant data; partly because new species keep being discovered all the time; and partly because we simply do not invest the financial resources needed to refine our knowledge. Reliable estimates do exist, however. In 2011 the Census on Marine Life announced that there are 8.7 million species on Earth, of which 2.2 million reside in the oceans. The authors of the study that produced these numbers also point out that, remarkably, 86 percent of Earth's estimated existing species, and 91 percent of those in our oceans have not yet been described.[5] A leading ecologist has observed that we would be embarrassed as we stumbled to answer a question alien visitors to our planet might ask: how many species live here?[6] But we would have no problem finding out all the batting averages, earned-run averages, or other statistics from 1900 to the present of all major league baseball teams, if an extraterrestrial were to ask us for those data.

How fast is the planet losing species?

Species loss is natural. The planet used to lose them at a natural rate (the rate of extinctions before humans became the main cause) of about one to five per year. But the rate of species loss is in no way natural today. The United Nations reports that because of human

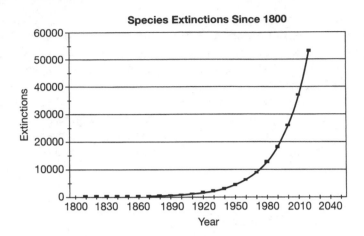

Figure 7.1 Species extinctions over time.

Source: Center for Biological Diversity. http://biologicaldiversity.org/programs/population_and_sustainability/extinction/.

activity, species are disappearing at 50 to 100 times the natural rate, as depicted in Figure 7.1. Thirty-four thousand plants and 5,200 animal species are projected soon to be among those lost, along with steep declines in favorite animals such as lions, tigers, elephants, and whales. One in eight birds faces extinction.[7]

This is why we are in what is being called the sixth extinction, the worst period of species destruction since the dinosaurs were wiped out 65 million years ago—and the only one not caused by natural events such as asteroids, volcanoes, or the gradual warming of the earth. It is directly the result of human activities, including, among others, urbanization, deforestation, pollution, and climate change.

Another term describing the same general phenomenon is "Anthropocene" (from *anthropos*, Greek for "humankind" and *kaines*, Greek for "new"). This is an informally recognized epoch, often considered to begin with the Industrial Revolution, popularized by chemist and Nobel Laureate Paul Crutzen and Eugene Stoermer in 2000.[8] The International Union of Geological Sciences, the organization charged with defining the earth's time scale, has established an Anthropocene working group to decide whether the Anthropocene should be considered a geological epoch at the same level as the current Holocene and other geological epochs, such as the preceding Pleistocene. In any case, the term "Anthropocene" captures a very important fact: we are living in an unprecedented period when humans are causing extremely negative and consequential changes in our environment, and we are aware of our responsibility for it.

Why should we be concerned about species loss?

For many reasons, especially these three: species ensure balanced, healthy ecosystems; they provide us with templates for innovations; and they are beautiful. All of these benefits, not to mention the economic advantages that often accompany them, are diminished with species loss.

Nature out of balance is terrifying, as it should be. Throughout history people have feared it, from the locust swarms dreaded in the Bible to the terror one feels watching Alfred Hitchcock's movie *The Birds*, where the bird population overwhelms the human one. Maintaining balance in nature is very complicated. The presence of different species relating to each other in various ways is essential to achieving it. Consider, for example, the grey wolf in the Yellowstone National Park ecosystem. The grey wolf was decimated throughout the western United States in the early twentieth century by hunters and farmers concerned that their herds were food for the wolves. In the 1990s the wolf was reintroduced to Yellowstone in part to control the burgeoning elk population (no longer kept in check by the wolves) and to revive the aspen, willows, and other flora the elk herds had overconsumed and trampled. Their return thereby created better habitat for birds, beavers, and other wildlife, and even helped the threatened grizzly bear recover. Grey wolves are problematic for some farmers. But they play an important role in a healthy, balanced ecosystem. They are especially important as a "keystone species," that is, one whose loss can fundamentally change an entire ecosystem. Similar observations could be made about the contributions of sea turtles, sharks, elephants, bees, and practically every species, except *Homo sapiens*, to balanced and healthy ecosystems.

Some of the best innovations attributed to the human species come directly from, or are inspired by, our examination of other ones. The contributions of living species are most dramatic in the drugs people rely on. This makes sense when one remembers that species evolve over millennia developing ingenious chemical means to survive all along the way. Taxol, a leading cancer drug, comes from the Pacific yew tree, long considered a junk tree and frequently destroyed in logging operations. It was discovered in the 1980s by researchers under contract with the National Cancer Institute (NCI) to find natural products that might fight cancer. In 1992 the Food and Drug Administration approved Taxol for the treatment of ovarian cancer. According to the NCI it is the bestselling cancer drug, with sales of over $1.5 billion.[9] There are many, many examples of plant-derived prescription drugs. One of the most well-known over-the-counter painkillers, aspirin, was originally derived from the bark and leaves of the willow tree. Bayer marketed it producing great relief to millions of people and staggering revenue for the company. Penicillin, a very important antibiotic, is a naturally occurring fungus that was accidently discovered. Animal species contribute as well. Recently, researchers appear to have uncovered the genetic reason why elephants have low cancer rates, perhaps pointing the way to better cancer treatments for humans.[10] Species contribute not just to medicines, although that contribution is immense. Amateur mountaineer and inventor George de Mestral became fascinated with the burrs he could not pull off his dog's fur and his own pants after a hike. He examined them under a microscope, saw tiny tenacious hooks, and developed the prototype for Velcro.

The beauty of the earth's vast array of species is stunning; it also is not replicable. Imagine the world without peacocks, flamingos, lions, sea coral, or the grey wolf. Think of the artistic creativity these and other beings like them inspire: the idea of the Garden of Eden, lion statues guarding Hindu temples or framing the steps of the main branch of the New York Public Library, horses on the Parthenon friezes or in Picasso's Guernica, lilies in Monet's pond. How could such beautiful living things ever be extinct? In the 1930s about 7 to 10 million elephants roamed in Africa. Today there are 300,000 with the numbers dropping fast. The Asiatic lion until the late nineteenth century was widespread throughout Asia. It is the species Daniel encountered in the lion's den and the one that parades at the Ishtar Gate. Now only a few hundred survive and in only one place: India's Gir Forest. Ironically, this magnificent lion risks extinction because its beauty made it a prize trophy for sport hunters. One British officer reportedly killed fifty of them in less than two years in the late 1850s.[11]

If there are millions of species, can the planet spare some of them?

This question has been the source of conflict between, for example, developers and conservationists and commercial ventures and regulators for years, especially since passage in the United States of the landmark Endangered Species Act in 1973. As is so often the case when it comes to big questions on the environment, imbedded in it are practical issues about competing societal needs and values, and moral issues about the stewardship responsibilities of the human species for future generations and for other species. Surely humans have implicitly answered "yes" to the question over and over again since we have knowingly caused the extinction of many species in the last fifty or so years. Whether that is the right answer—and whether species loss from human activity is ever warranted—is vigorously debated, as it was, for example, during the famous spotted owl controversy. A better answer would be that humans should allow species loss only for the very best reasons, having considered all the available data and every possible alternative. We rarely try to do that. More important, we probably are not even able to. This is because we know too little about how our planet really works, about the secrets its species hold, and about the long-term impacts such loss may bring, to eliminate without serious risk flora and fauna that have lived successfully here for eons.

Ultimately, then, the responsible answer must be that setting aside natural extinctions, we cannot spare any species. One simply cannot conclude that a particular species has no practical value mainly because we have no idea what we are missing from most species losses. As the Amazon rain forest diminishes, for example, along with many untold species, bioprospecting for ideas by pharmaceutical companies increases, because they know what they might be missing (perhaps another blockbuster cancer drug). We have no reliable sense of what the world's ecosystems would be like without bees, which have given us since the time of the Pyramids not only honey but pollination of many food crops. We do know with certainty, however, that their populations are dramatically diminishing.

Why is the spotted owl so controversial?

The northern spotted owl is a medium-sized chocolate brown bird with white spots that lives in the old growth forests of the Pacific northwestern United States and nearby Canada. It likes old growth forests because they contain a mix of species, standing and dead trees, and lots of open space for flight under a multilayered canopy—features that take 150 to 200 years to establish. It stays in the same geographic area with the same mate for its entire life. And it is impatient with disturbances, which is awkward because this owl shares its habitat with the multibillion dollar logging industry: old growth forests are home to commercially valuable trees like cedars, firs, and spruces. In the American Pacific Northwest old growth timber harvests were 5 billion board feet per year in 1989, 10 times the number of board feet in 1940.

In 1990 the spotted owl was listed as a threatened species under the Endangered Species Act, the primary threat being the destruction of the old growth forests by loggers. (Canada also declared it endangered under similar authority.) Logging was restricted as a result. A monumental clash ensued between loggers and environmentalists: between, ostensibly at least, jobs and a bird. The logging industry claimed that tens of thousands of jobs would be lost. The environmentalists claimed that not only the spotted owl, but the entire old growth ecosystem was at risk because spotted owls are an "indicator species," like the proverbial canary in the coal mine, that gauges the health of the ecosystem in which it resides, and portends the loss of other species there. Everyone agreed that saving the spotted owl would cost jobs, but the environmentalists argued that those jobs would soon be gone anyway once the rest of these forests were cut down.

The spotted owl controversy raises not only the jobs versus environment issue, but also many others: Should we care that a lovely bird will be lost at our hands? What is our responsibility to protect not only this bird, but other species this bird warns us about? What might this species offer us that we do not yet know about, and that will be lost forever with its extinction? How important is this timber, after all? Are there viable substitutes? How long need we hold up logging while pursuing them?

Different people will answer these questions differently. Consider violin bows. A good violinist might be tempted to choose a bow made of wood from the endangered Brazilian perambuco tree. It is very flexible and sturdy and has been the preferred choice of bow-makers for 250 years. A beginner with concerns about the environment might feel better choosing a carbon fiber bow, which is sold everywhere, and, although it may not be as good, does not deplete the perambuco forests. What should a responsible violinist do? One could suggest that this person either find a marvelous old peram-buco bow and reuse it, or go for carbon fiber, or possibly get a new perambuco but generously support the International Perambuco Conservation Initiative.

What is the Endangered Species Act?

The Endangered Species Act (ESA) is the only US environmental law that focuses directly on biodiversity. President Richard Nixon signed it into law in 1973, two years after he signed the Clean Air Act.

The ESA starts with these thoughtful admissions and serious global environmental commitment:

(1) Various species of fish, wildlife, and plants in the United States have been rendered extinct as a consequence of economic growth and development untempered by adequate concern and conservation;

(2) other species of fish, wildlife, and plants have been so depleted in numbers that they are in danger of or threatened with extinction;

(3) these species of fish, wildlife, and plants are of esthetic, eco-logical, educational, historical, recreational, and scientific value to the Nation and its people;

(4) the United States has pledged itself as a sovereign state in the international community to conserve to the extent practi-cable the various species of fish or wildlife and plants facing extinction.[12]

The ESA empowers the Department of the Interior and the Fish and Wildlife Service along with the Marine Fisheries Service to list species that are either endangered (in danger of extinction) or threat-ened (likely to become endangered in the foreseeable future) as these concepts are defined in government regulations. Concurrent with the listing process, these agencies are supposed to designate "critical habitats" for them. Moreover, government actions must not, under the ESA, jeopardize listed species or negatively affect their habitat. The act extends to restrictions on private rights: the ESA may be violated when, for example, a homeowner disturbs the critical habitat of an endangered species while clearing a wooded parcel to make a lawn, or a farmer destroys animals listed as endangered to protect crops. It has also been used to protect species at risk from climate change. An example is the polar bear, which has been listed as threatened because the sea ice on which it depends for survival is melting.

The ESA has been the subject of some of the most hard-fought court cases. The spotted owl controversy described above arose from the action of the Fish and Wildlife Service to list it and protect its critical habitat, old growth forests. Not surprisingly, ESA-generated conflicts have often involved clashes between efforts to protect private property rights and efforts to protect endangered species.

How many species are endangered?

Too many to list here. As of October 2016, the US Fish and Wildlife Service has listed 2,277 species worldwide as endangered or threatened, with 1,604 occurring in the United States.[13] This list, as might be expected, is dynamic. Species are added and removed as facts change. It is by definition incomplete because, as stated earlier, we have identified only a small portion of the species, extant or extinct, on the planet. A good resource for finding out the current status of extinct and endangered species worldwide is the International Union for Conservation of Nature (IUCN) Red List. It is easily accessible online.[14] For a very sobering experience, one might go to the extinct species list there (which covers only species extinct after the 1500s), and contemplate for a moment the fact that every one of these over eight hundred plants and animals flourished at one time and was likely taken to extinction by human activity. These include the beautiful passenger pigeon, which could fly at 60 miles per hour and numbered in the billions until it was brought abruptly to extinction on American dinner tables. Its last member, Martha, died in the Cincinnati Zoo in 1914.

What are invasive species?

These are species that are brought from their home ecosystem to a new one and are flourishing there. They can be large or small, plant or animal. Invasive species are often successful and multiply because their adopted environment does not contain the natural predators or competing species that keep them in check back at home. They are transported mostly by human activity, on ships, in crates, and in ornamental plants that end up outside. Their numbers are increasing with the increased movement of people. Purple loosestrife came to the northeastern United States as an ornamental plant in the 1800s. It looks beautiful covering marshes and wet meadows in summer. But it is clogging out every other plant in the way of its thick matted roots and destroying bird and animal habitat in the process.

In the United States almost half of the listed endangered or threatened species are at risk because of invasive ones. This happens when invasive species take over and may, for example, disrupt food sources, decrease biodiversity, and carry disease. Climate change encourages invasive species, as warming conditions invite them to foreign ecosystems, and as infestations overcome drought-weakened plants.

The Asian carp is an ancient fish that has been prominent in Chinese art, culture, and cuisine for thousands of years. It is no stranger in the United States either. Introduced in the 1800s, it has been fished for food and dumped in particular places to clean up bothersome vegetation. In the 1970s fish farmers in the southern United States brought some from China to clean out their commercial ponds. The carp escaped and have been working their way up the Mississippi River and now threaten the Great Lakes basin. They are very big, jump very high, and are ravenous. If they reach the Great Lakes, they may decimate the commercial and recreational fishing industry and greatly disrupt the ecosystem. They can have a chilling effect on recreational boating, too: they have been known to capsize kayaks. The US Congress has passed several laws to control the marauding Asian carp, as it has been called, and has even tried to cut off passage of these fish from Mississippi waters into the Great Lakes by funding installation of electrical barriers.

Invasive species are not peculiar to the United States—they present a global problem. For example, the European Commission, the executive of the European Union, has described them as "a major threat to native plants and animals in Europe, causing damage worth billions of Euros to the European Economy every year."[15]

Why is genetic diversity important?

The Irish Potato Famine of 1845–1849 resulted in almost two million deaths and forced the emigration of about two million Irish people, many of them to the United States. Its main cause was a potato blight from a fungus that infested, in unusually warm climate conditions, the one or two high-yield varieties of potatoes on which most of the population depended. The fungus was an invasive species, *Phytophthora infestans*, which had probably arrived from the Americas. Entire crops were decimated largely because Irish potatoes lacked genetic diversity: reliance on one or two varieties meant there were none to replace those that could not resist the blight.

The farming practice that caused the Irish Potato Famine is called monoculture: planting the same crop in the same place over and over again. Monoculture is a dominant method of growing crops in the United States. America's Great Plains with their amber waves of grain, California's produce-rich Imperial Valley, and Florida's citrus groves all depend on monoculture farming. It has many benefits: it can be high yield (as the Irish potato was), uniform, and easy to harvest. But monoculture has serious disadvantages as it focuses on relatively few crop varieties. Its lack of genetic diversity is a major one, making crops vulnerable to diseases (and increasing reliance on chemical fertilizers and pesticides to combat them) and making monoculture farmers vulnerable to economically devastating crop losses. Fundamentally, genetic diversity ensures that species can adapt to changing conditions like climate, resist disease, and have enough variety to withstand the elimination of a single one.

Is agriculture a clean, even "green" activity?

As presently performed, agriculture, particularly on a large-scale, is one of the most significant sources of pollution. The quaint oil paintings of nineteenth- and early twentieth-century American single-family farms depict a scene with a few chickens, a small herd of cattle grazing in a nearby pasture, some apple trees, a vegetable garden, and fields of hay and corn bounded by stone fences. "Bucolic" and "pastoral" are words with pleasant connotations often used to describe this tableau. They capture agriculture not only as lovely but also, implicitly, as having a low environmental impact. This is how many people still think of agriculture. Today, however, agriculture rarely looks like the oil paintings. Small farms with mixed uses and recycled byproducts (like the cow manure used on-site as a fertilizer for the fields and gardens, whose crops in turn feed the livestock) have often given way to large agribusinesses where the focus may be on single crops, where huge feedlots replace the small herd, and where synthetic fertilizers replace natural manure. In the United States now most of the meat put on the table is produced on huge industrial farms (often called concentrated animal feeding operations or CAFOs) and the family farm is disappearing, giving way to second-home estates or housing developments or being converted to inns or B&Bs.

Like the mid-twentieth century Green Revolution, which greatly increased outputs with high-yield crops, chemical fertilizers, and pesticides, today's industrial-scale farms greatly increase the efficiency of livestock production using similar techniques. Since 1960 milk, meat, and egg production have increased dramatically. In 1950, it took eighty-four days to grow a five-pound chicken. Fifty years later this bird could be produced in half the time. Farm policy encourages industrial-scale livestock (and produce) farms with subsidies and weak regulation. And the consumer is paying less for industrial farm food. But this efficiency is not without serious environmental consequences. Here are some of them, in addition to surface and groundwater pollution. A CAFO produces huge, concentrated amounts of manure. Because feed is not grown on the farm, the manure is stored—often in open lagoons—rather than being returned to the soil for fertilizer. Odor and seepage into groundwater are major problems. CAFOs keep animals healthy for their short cramped lives by feeding them antibiotics and growth hormones; these, too, end up in problematic places, such as the manure described above and in the bodies of the humans who eat CAFO-produced food. CAFOs emit into the air, among other pollutants, particulates, a main cause of asthma, and methane, a contributor to climate change.

CAFOs now dominate global animal food production. It is estimated that they produce 72 percent of the world's poultry, 43 percent of the world's eggs, and 55 percent of the world's pork.[16] Although they were first developed in the United States and Europe, CAFOs are increasingly being used for animal food production in the developing world.

How is pollution from large-scale animal farms controlled?

In the United States, not very well. The huge volume of manure generated on CAFOs is often not considered a waste subject to regulation under federal waste law because, it is argued, it is often applied as a useful product (fertilizer) on fields, even though such application can result in groundwater contamination and can resemble waste disposal more than fertilizing. The Clean Water Act imposes some controls on CAFOs, but they are weak. States often have "right-to-farm" laws that limit the likelihood that state lawsuits against CAFOs can succeed. At the local level, Boards of Health have some authority to address the public health issues CAFOs raise. In the end, however, the air, surface, groundwater, and nuisance impacts of these operations are not being addressed adequately to protect the public and the environment, despite some eloquent advocates for significant changes in agricultural practices and in the programs of the US Department of Agriculture. The European Union, on the other hand, is a leader in CAFO reforms.

Is soil an ecosystem?

Yes. The familiar expression "cheap as dirt" reflects the low value we place on soil, which some who do value it highly have called Earth's skin. Soil, especially topsoil, the dark carbon- and biota-rich organic material that covers the first few inches of some of the earth's surface and enables plants to grow, is an invaluable resource and an ecosystem. It is home to an enormous number of diverse, especially small, organisms, and it is a major participant in the most basic biological cycles in the global ecological system including the nitrogen and carbon cycles. Topsoil covers only about 10 percent of the earth's surface, and it is rapidly being depleted by such activities as industrial-scale farming and road and building construction, much faster than it can regenerate. By some calculations, at the current rate of depletion, the earth has about sixty years of topsoil left. This is a global problem being felt not just in industrialized countries such as the United States and Russia, but especially in poorer parts of the world.

The Dust Bowl tragedy of the 1930s in the United States occurred because unwise farming practices, aided by strong winds and drought, stripped the fertile Great Plains of the rich soil and sturdy vegetation that had sustained life there for millennia, and that had drawn settlers to it in droves starting in the 1860s, prodded by the Homestead Act. These settlers unwittingly set themselves up for tragedy by plowing away the sturdy prairie grasses (using John Deere's newly invented, fast, and even more sturdy steel plow) to produce wheat eagerly purchased by a growing US population; overgrazing cattle herds further diminished the grasses. The result was bare, desiccated, depleted soil, which blew away in fierce winds. Four hundred thousand people fled or died. John Steinbeck wrote about the tragedy in *The Grapes of Wrath*; and Woody Guthrie sang about it in *Dust Bowl Ballads*. The dust bowl so shocked the United States that the Soil Conservation Service was created, numerous emergency measures were taken by President Franklin Roosevelt, and new soil management techniques were introduced such as crop rotation and cover crops. But problematic agricultural practices, combined with the demands of an expanding population, continue to strain agriculturally productive places.

The Central Valley in California is a current example. It is about 450 miles long and about 50 miles wide. In the early twentieth century the naturalist John Muir described it as "level and flowery, like a lake of pure sunshine."[17] It is among the most fertile valleys in the world and provides one-quarter of the food for the United States. Seventeen percent of the nation's irrigated land is there to support this productivity. The water comes largely from aquifers that are being depleted. Indeed, in the Central Valley significant land subsidence is occurring as groundwater is withdrawn. Much of the productivity, often from industrial-scale farms, depends on chemical fertilizers, pesticides, and antibiotics to sustain profits. The valley has some of the largest CAFOs in the United States and some of the biggest producers of such ubiquitous staples as carrots and tomatoes. The environmental sustainability of the valley is at risk as it struggles with weakened soil, drought, and encroaching suburbia, not to mention pressing social issues arising from the often less than acceptable conditions of the agricultural workers in the valley. But the valley is also the home of many farms practicing sustainable agriculture, which many local organizations and academic institutions support. A sustainable Central Valley would integrate the three pillars of sustainability: environmental protection, economic profitability, and social equity.

Why is ecosystem diversity important?

Ecosystems are interconnected and interdependent, providing mutual support of different kinds and so they need to be diverse. Coral reefs are valuable ecosystems, and currently at great risk, but the oceans would not be healthy places if 50 percent of them were populated by coral reefs, pushing out other marine ecosystems. Moreover, the ecosystem services humans rely on come from diverse sources. Wetlands provide services that are unavailable from forested uplands, which provide services unavailable from wetlands, and so on. If ecosystems get out of balance, as is happening in many places around the globe (for example, with the degradation of tropical rainforests), impacts ripple through others, and their services are lost to humans and other species.

How are ecosystems protected?

In the United States, despite the critical importance of ecosystems and the services they provide, relatively few federal laws directly address protecting ecosystems. This concept was not on the agenda of congressional environmental action during the years that saw the Clean Air and Clean Water Acts enacted. There is no Ecosystems

Protection Act comparable to these laws. This is a foundational weakness in US environmental law.

Some laws, in addition to the Endangered Species Act, provide protections, if not comprehensively. The National Environmental Policy Act requires a close look at the overall environmental impacts of major federal actions. The 1972 Marine Mammal Protection Act, although limited in scope, was the first legislation globally to require an ecosystem approach to marine living resources. Other laws, such as the 1968 Wild and Scenic Rivers Act, the 1972 Coastal Zone Management Act, and the 1976 Fisheries Conservation and Management Act deal with particular ecosystems, although with little attention to their interrelationships. And these laws are relatively ineffective. For instance, the national system established under the Wild and Scenic Rivers Act protects less that one-quarter of one percent of US rivers, whereas 17 percent of US rivers have been modified by large dams with inevitable negative ecosystem impacts.

As is the case in the United States, other countries have a variety of laws to protect ecosystems in a variety of ways. For example, almost all countries have laws requiring environmental impact assessments for major actions affecting the environment. The European Union has a number of laws and directives devoted to biodiversity and species protection including a 1992 Habitats Directive to protect not only animal and plant species but also about two hundred types of habitat. Governments also target specific species. For example, India's Ministry of Environment and Forests in 2009 launched Project Snow Leopard, consistent with India's wildlife legislation, to address the complex challenges presented in conserving the snow leopard and the large and ecologically significant Himalayan range it occupies. The kaleidoscope of laws, and associated policies and initiatives, concerning ecosystem protection currently in play around the world is promising, although not comprehensive. Also important is the work of nongovernmental organizations and the United Nations on this vast and important subject.

What is the relationship between sustainability and ecosystems?

Concerns about sustainability frequently apply to ecosystems and biodiversity. No human activity can be sustainable if it poses significant threats to wetlands, forests, species, or the ecosystem services that make human life not just enjoyable, but possible. However, humans focus much better on short-term rather than long-term goals, while sustainability concerns the future. And when humans contemplate vast stores of resources such as ocean fisheries, forested mountainsides, and fertile plains it is easy to slip into what some have called the "ideology of abundance," which has enabled unsustainable practices for many years. How could people ever deplete a resource so limitless as the fish in the sea?

It is not surprising, then, that the Atlantic cod fishing industry would focus on the short- term goal of a good season's catch and not the long-term prospect that the entire cod fishery could collapse with overfishing, as it did in 1992 off Newfoundland, Canada. Economic losses were estimated to be at least $2 billion. Thousands of people lost their jobs.[18] After over a hundred years of steady yields, the introduction of powerful trawlers equipped with sonar and other technologies helped cause a big spike in the capture of cod stock, followed by the collapse. It was unsustainable. It might have been sustainable had the industry taken only surplus, rather than depleting the critical mass required to keep the cod population intact and degrading its ecosystem, for example, by catching many other noncommercial fish in the process, some of which actually protect cod.

Today, halfway around the world in Cambodia, Tonle Sap Lake, known locally as the Great Lake, serves 1.5 million people, and yields about 300 tons of fish per year. Boat-villages, with stores, houses, and schools, float on it. Cambodia's population is growing fast, about 2 percent a year. Scientists and the local population fear that the lake is at risk largely from overfishing and other stressors as a growing population bears down on it. The Tonle Sap is not an isolated scenario. The United Nations estimates that a large portion of the world's fish stock is at risk and unsustainable if expected growth and consumption patterns continue.[19]

Nor is it surprising that the short-term benefits of industrial-scale farming, like the seasonal cod catch before collapse, make it hard to see the long-term dangers of this prevalent farming approach. Many ecologists believe the current agricultural practices are not sustainable into future generations.

Is biodiversity loss as important as other environmental problems?

There are many understandable reasons for biodiversity loss. Among them are the pressures of explosive population growth, particularly in developing countries, requiring, for example, more deforested land for crops, more fishing for sustenance, and more reaping of commercially valuable things, such as ivory tusks, to make money for food. In developed countries the consumers' desire for a variety of attractive foods, as well as general dependence in these places on perfect produce with a long shelf life, have pushed agricultural practices into chemistry labs. Here the development of artificial fertilizers, pesticides, herbicides, and genetically altered seeds positively influence the bottom line of farm revenues, the satisfaction of consumers, and marketability. Development interests all over the world, encouraged by more people and an eager market, seek more land for roads, houses, shopping malls, resorts, and industrial parks, some of the most enticing of which are in ecologically sensitive areas. All of these threaten species, ecosystem, and genetic biodiversity.

It is not surprising, then, that biodiversity protection raises important moral and practical questions or that it frustrates the commercial agricultural sector, which relies on monoculture farming, genetic engineering, and chemicals to produce and sell the food expected in highly competitive world markets to demanding consumers. The questions become more complicated when one considers that some of these same practices help rice farmers in densely populated southeast Asia increase their yield, which not only provides food, but also can reduce the pressure for agricultural expansion and its resulting threat to certain ecosystems. It has been a frustration for real estate developers, too, who for years have been blocked (or at least slowed down) by people concerned about rain forests, wetlands, or particular species, which are ultimately concerns about biodiversity.

But biodiversity is not a trivial requirement for a healthy planet. It is a central one, whose loss threatens ecosystems, species, and their genetic underpinnings. Nor is it an issue separate from, or lower priority than, other environmental problems. Biodiversity, largely by keeping ecosystems stable, plays a role in mitigating pollution and climate change, just as these problems play a role in biodiversity loss: everything is connected to everything else. And it is not a red herring: no one disputes that the earth is losing biodiversity at a very fast pace.

So a serious tension exists between human activity and biodiversity. The need to address this tension is reflected in the United Nation's Convention on Biological Diversity (CBD) to which almost two hundred nations are parties (but not the United States). It was under the authority of the CBD that in 2010 many countries agreed to establish a strategic plan for biodiversity as "the basis for halting and eventually reversing the loss of biodiversity of the planet."[20] 2011 through 2020 was designated as the United Nations Decade on Biodiversity to support this goal.

8

CLIMATE CHANGE

What is climate change?

Climate change means long-term changes in atmospheric conditions—including temperature, wind patterns, and precipitation. Although climate fluctuations such as the great ice age cycles have happened in varying degrees many times throughout history, there is broad agreement that over the last sixty-five or so years the planet has been warming at an unnatural and unprecedented rate. This clearly correlates with increased consumption of fossil fuels, with the cluster of chemicals called greenhouse gases, and with the associated phenomenon known as the greenhouse effect. Climate change, as the term is presently used, is anthropogenic: that is, caused by humans.

Climate change is complex. Among the many complexities we encounter when we study it is that the climate is influenced by unpredictable events, such as shifts in the world economy that change industrial production and hence greenhouse gas emissions. Moreover, it is a planetary, not local, problem, and it requires a global, interdisciplinary, and intergovernmental commitment to find solutions, solutions that may upend traditional geopolitical relationships and customary day-to-day activities. One thing is certain, however: it is happening. No responsible expert denies its existence, its fundamental causes, and the great danger it poses if we act too casually to address it.

Are weather and climate the same?

No, although it may not always be easy to determine when one turns into the other. Weather describes short-term, fluctuating atmospheric conditions in a relatively small area. Climate, on the other hand, refers to average weather conditions over many years. For example, the climate in southern California is warm and sunny, but tomorrow's weather in Los Angeles may be cool and cloudy. It is tempting to suffer through an unusually cold spell and interpret it as an indication that the planet is not really warming. The cold spell, however, is weather, not climate.

People sometimes wonder how scientists can predict climate change fifty years out, and not weather a month away. When we choose a raincoat rather than a windbreaker as we head out the door in the morning, we are relying on fairly precise information about dynamic weather conditions described in the daily forecast. Sometimes this information is presented as a probability—"a 90 percent chance of rain" means choose the raincoat. Predictions about climate do not involve this kind of precision, because they look for long-term trends over decades. No one knows whether it will rain one month from now in Denver—weather is too variable for that, but it is possible to predict climate conditions in the western United States over the next many years. Similarly, it is wise for us to know how much money we need to get through the next week, but it gets harder to maintain that level of precision in long-term planning. It is possible, however, to predict our monetary needs years from now, relying on records of money spent in the past and expected future expenses over decades, in a process somewhat like predicting climate.

Are climate change and global warming the same?

Not exactly, although the two are often used interchangeably. Global warming refers to the recent rise in the earth's surface temperature associated with the increase in greenhouse gases. Climate change encompasses a larger spectrum of atmospheric conditions including changes in precipitation and wind patterns. Most scientists prefer "climate change." For example, the Intergovernmental Panel on Climate Change (IPCC) uses it, as does the US National Aeronautics and Space Administration. But the public may relate better to the term "global warming" and the public has tended to use it more, at least until recently. In this book, we normally use the term "climate change."

What is the Intergovernmental Panel on Climate Change?

The Intergovernmental Panel on Climate Change (IPCC) is the most authoritative source of scientific information about climate change, its environmental and socioeconomic impacts, and ways to address it. Headquartered in Bern, Switzerland, it was established by the United Nations Environment Programme and the World Meteorological Organization in 1988 with endorsement by the United Nations General Assembly. It enlists thousands of experts throughout the world reflecting a range of views and specializations who voluntarily review and assess current information. Governments and observer organizations nominate them. The IPCC produces extensive periodic reports as well as many supporting documents. It greatly influences climate policy and intergovernmental negotiations on climate while itself remaining policy-neutral. In 2007 the IPCC and former US Vice President Al Gore shared the Nobel Peace Prize for their efforts to educate the world on climate change and on how to counteract it.

How do we know that the earth is getting warmer?

Taking the earth's temperature is not easy, and many factors that are hard to predict influence it. Volcanic eruptions, for instance, can change global temperatures, although their overall impact on climate is small and generally short-lived compared to the human impact. The huge eruption in 1991 of the Philippines' Mount Pinatubo spewed gases that reflected sunlight and cooled the earth's surface for three years (by about 1° F worldwide at most).

But reliable sources of data exist to measure climate, as do reliable mechanisms to predict climate trends into the future. In particular, thousands of temperature stations throughout the world record land and ocean temperatures regularly, and scientists combine these data to produce an average global temperature every month. Accuracy has increased over time, with the help of satellite measurements introduced in 1979. Scientists also observe physical evidence of warming: rising sea levels, receding glaciers, increased snowmelt, and moister and more turbulent air. To discover likely trends over decades they employ sophisticated computer models that use historical data and future projections, such as the predicted presence of greenhouse gases or El Niño cycles. A particularly detailed analysis using all available temperature data was based on measurements from 36,866 stations going back to 1753.[1]

The results of running models based on these data with the most accurate assumptions available have led climate scientists to conclude that the earth is getting warmer, at a very fast pace. The IPCC in 2013 stated: "Warming of the climate system is unequivocal, and since the 1950s, many of the observed changes are unprecedented over decades to millennia. The atmosphere and ocean have warmed, the amounts of snow and ice have diminished, sea level has risen, and the concentrations of greenhouse gases have increased."[2]

Average global temperatures are predicted to increase by .5 to 8.6 degrees Fahrenheit by 2100, with a likely increase of 2.7 degrees, depending on the extent of greenhouse gas emissions. In the United States, the average temperature is projected to go up by about 3 to 12 degrees Fahrenheit.[3]

Are humans really the main cause of climate change?

The scientific community agrees that the dramatic increase in greenhouse gases, especially carbon dioxide, is primarily caused by three hundred years of industrialization.[4] This increase spiked in the late twentieth century as dependence on carbon-emitting fossil fuels grew (see Figure 8.1). Industrialized countries, with the United States for years first among them, bear almost all of the responsibility. This climate culpability, however, may shift as more countries (China and India, for example) continue to industrialize. Since 2006 China has outpaced the United States as the top CO_2 emitter, although per capita China's emissions still fall far behind those of the United States.

Human-caused CO_2 emissions in the atmosphere would be even higher if the oceans were not absorbing about one-quarter of the released CO_2. The result is ocean acidification: CO_2 becomes a weak acid in water. Ocean acidification is a serious environmental issue with, for example, likely impacts on many calcifying marine species, such as corals and shellfish that dissolve more easily in acidic water and have greater difficulty building strong shells there.

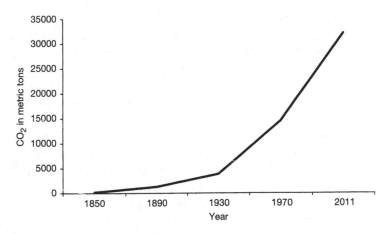

Figure 8.1 Increase in carbon emissions over time.

Source: Based on www.wri.org./blog/2014/05/history-carbon-dioxide-emissions.

Although fossil fuels account for most CO_2 emissions, deforestation and other problematic land-use practices account for a smaller but significant portion as well.

Why is climate change such a big problem?

First, because it is global. No other environmental problem even begins to attain the global scope of climate change. The presence of a very polluted river in, say, Germany does not mean necessarily that rivers elsewhere in Germany or other countries will be polluted, and Germany can reverse that pollution by imposing local controls on discharges into the river. But a coal-fired power plant emitting CO_2 into the air in Germany or the United States does affect climate not just in these places, but everywhere. Controlling the CO_2 in Germany will help, but unless other big polluters like the United States, China, and India also control their own emissions, the climate problem will not be solved. And the inhabitants of distant locations can experience its impacts, such as a farmer in low-lying Bangladesh facing rising seas or a polar bear whose habitat is melting.

The problem also has enormous momentum: even if we slow down climate change, it will continue to have a major impact on fundamentally important things—food supplies, water resources, ecosystems, and the built environment—long into the future. One reason for this momentum is that greenhouse gases persist in the atmosphere for many years, so even if we radically reduce emissions, the effects of those already present will continue. Another reason concerns the oceans, which hold vast amounts of heat and circulate slowly; the IPCC predicts that even if the surface of the ocean stopped warming, deep ocean water will continue to warm for centuries, causing, among other things, continued sea-level rise.[5] This is true in part because the heat of warming water increases the distance among molecules, leading to expansion.

Finally, unlike any other environmental problem, climate change is truly existential. A polluted river and a toxic waste dump have discreet, knowable impacts, which are unpleasant and unhealthy, but without lethal planetary consequences. There is strong evidence that uncorrected climate change threatens the future well-being, or even existence, of many of the earth's living species, including our own.

What is the greenhouse effect?

Among the gases that make up the earth's atmosphere, a few, the greenhouse gases, determine how much heat will be retained from the sun's radiation. Without them, heat in the sun's visible light, which easily slips through the atmosphere and warms the planet, would be lost by sending back into space longer wavelength infrared radiation. Greenhouse gases block some of this infrared radiation and return it back to the earth. Without greenhouse gases the tropics would be a frigid 14°F, well below the temperature needed to sustain most life as we know it.

The amazing fact is that normally the earth maintains an energy balance between the incoming and outgoing solar energy that produces a livable average temperature. This balance is accomplished through the greenhouse effect: much of the heat emitted back to space from the land and water is absorbed by heat-trapping greenhouse gases capable of catching infrared radiation; the gases in turn redirect the heat down to the ground, rather than letting it escape. The greenhouse effect, then, is an important natural regulator of the earth's temperature. Scientists have known this for more than a century.

The analogy to greenhouses is apt. Normal glass lets in visible light but blocks thermal radiation as greenhouse gases do. So when used in a greenhouse roof, glass lets in the warming visible light but traps the thermal radiation inside the greenhouse. Similarly, as greenhouse gases in the atmosphere increase, more energy is trapped and our greenhouse, the earth, heats up. That is what is happening now.

What are greenhouse gases?

These are gases that trap heat near the earth's surface that otherwise would escape into space. Five are very important: carbon dioxide (CO_2), methane, nitrous oxide, water vapor, and fluorinated gases (the only greenhouse gases that are entirely synthetic). In addition to trapping heat, they share two other physical properties common to the climate change problem: they are long-lived (methane lasts about a decade, CO_2 about a century, nitrous oxide a little over a century, and some of the fluorinated gases thousands of years), and they mix well globally regardless of where they originate.

Carbon dioxide has the greatest impact on climate change, which is why we hear about carbon taxes and carbon footprints and not about methane taxes and methane footprints. In the United States, for example, in 2013, about 82 percent of greenhouse gas emissions produced by humans were CO_2, mostly from fossil fuel combustion in motor vehicles and electricity generating plants, and from industrial processes such as cement, iron, and steel production. Methane was second at 9 percent, mostly from natural gas production, including methane leaks in hydrofracking, from waste landfills, and from agriculture, especially livestock digestive processes and manure. Nitrous oxide accounted for about 6 percent, coming mostly from synthetic fertilizers, but also from fossil fuel combustion in motor vehicles, and from industrial processes such as the production of synthetic fibers. Fluorinated gases were last at 3 percent, but these are very potent with a high global warming potential (the amount of heat a gas traps). One type, the hydrofluorocarbons (HFCs), is used increasingly as a refrigerant in air conditioning, replacing the chlorofluorocarbons banned under the Montreal Protocol to protect the stratospheric ozone layer. Recently, 197 countries adopted ambitious amendments to the Protocol to phase down HFCs.

The most abundant greenhouse gas is water vapor, occurring naturally everywhere, especially in tropical climates where hot temperatures are given a boost by the greenhouse effect caused by water vapor. In the absence of the other greenhouse gases (especially CO_2), however, water vapor would not on its own produce the climate change we are experiencing, in part because it normally has a short life (typically about ten days), often quickly changing to rain or snow, especially in colder places. In fact, greenhouse gases in natural concentrations keep water vapor in the air. But an insidious relationship exists: as excessive greenhouse gases from human activity warm the planet, water vapor increases; because water vapor is a greenhouse gas, this "feedback" adds to the warming process, causing even more water vapor. The IPCC suggests that this water vapor feedback due to CO_2 alone is greatly increasing the greenhouse effect.[6]

What is climate change feedback?

Climate change feedback is something that either speeds up or slows down the climate warming process. It is an important and complicated variable in assessing climate change. The water vapor feedback described above is a classic example. Another is melting Arctic ice: ice reflects heat back into space; the more it melts, the more land and darker water replace it, absorbing and not reflecting back more heat, which leads to more warming. Yet another is permafrost, carbon-rich soil that remains frozen and accounts for about one-quarter of the exposed land area in the northern hemisphere. Permafrost traps carbon compounds from the decay of organic material in the ground, but when it melts, as it is now, these compounds are released. The more its carbon is released, the more permafrost melts because of the greenhouse effect. This is the vicious cycle of positive (heat-increasing) climate change feedback. How fast such melting will occur, and with what other influences, is one of the many questions climate scientists are dealing with. Understanding climate change feedback is key to understanding climate change itself. It also helps explain why aggressive action to reduce greenhouse gases is so important given the nonlinear and unpredictable future possible for a planet warmed by the greenhouse effect.

What do trees have to do with climate change?

There are negative (heat-reducing) climate change feedback mechanisms, too. All vegetation, including trees, takes in carbon from the atmosphere in the process of photosynthesis, storing it as the vegetation grows. Vegetation thus is an example of a carbon "sink." In this way it helps keep atmospheric carbon concentrations down. But when vegetation is removed (for road building, harvesting tropical forests, agricultural development, and other human activities) the carbon reduction mechanism is lost. Forestry experts and climate scientists generally agree that reforestation is an important element of climate change mitigation.

What is a carbon footprint?

A carbon footprint is the amount of CO_2 emitted by a particular place or thing, living or nonliving. (An alternative standard measure for carbon footprints is the "carbon dioxide equivalent" or CO_2e, which measures the bundle of greenhouse gases and converts them into the same amount that CO_2 by itself would create.) This is a useful number, for example, to consumers interested in the climate impact of a product they are buying, or corporations considering different manufacturing options. It can be measured in different ways. The carbon footprint of a plastic bag could be measured simply as its share of the carbon emissions from the stack at the factory where the bag is made. But this would be incomplete because it would not account for the carbon costs of transporting the bag to stores, extracting the petroleum from which it is made, disposing of the bag by burning or recycling, and related indirect carbon-emitting processes; so these variables might (and should) be added into the calculus. Apple, for instance, reports that an iPhone 6s over its lifetime, including production, transport, and use, will be responsible for the emission of 54 kg (119 pounds) of CO_2e.[7]

Another approach is to estimate the carbon footprint of the consumer, not the producer: the factory in Bangladesh that makes high-end clothing has a carbon footprint, but so does the person wearing it while carrying an iPhone in San Francisco. If you assign the person or place for whom these items were made responsibility for the carbon used to make them, San Francisco's ostensibly light carbon footprint looks much heavier and Bangladesh's much lighter.

Indeed, how one measures the carbon footprint of an entire country is very important, especially when trying to determine the fair contributions of countries required to bring down the amount of carbon in the air, and to pay for climate adaptation, both major topics of international climate negotiations. For example, if the metric is total CO_2 emissions, China outpaces the United States; if it is per capita emissions, the United States outpaces China; if it is historical emissions (especially considering that CO_2 stays in the air for many years), the United States pops to the top again, although this metric may be changing as China's total emissions keep rising; if consumption, rather than emissions, is the metric, wealthier countries, the United States and others, again pop to the top greatly outpacing less wealthy countries such as China.

What are climate change deniers thinking?

Senator James Inhofe is a leading voice for those who deny that climate change exists. While Chairman of the Senate Committee on Environment and Public Works, the Committee that oversees the EPA, he authored *The Greatest Hoax: How the Global Warming Conspiracy Threatens Your Future,* published in 2012, five years after thousands of scientists worldwide concluded in the fourth report of the IPCC that "warming of the climate system is unequivocal."[8]

If congressional climate change deniers need proof of climate change closer to home they have a good resource in a 2014 study by the US Global Change Research Program known as the National Climate Assessment. It was prepared under the authority of the Global Change Research Act passed by the US Congress in 2010, written by a team of over three hundred experts, subjected to numerous peer reviews including one by the National Academy of Sciences, and commented on extensively by members of the public prior to its release. The assessment received heavy press coverage, and for good reason. Its findings were unambiguous and alarming: climate change is happening now; it is "primarily due to human-induced emissions of heat-trapping gases"; "it will accelerate significantly if global emissions of heat-trapping gases continue to increase"; and the consequences include more diseases, poorer air quality, infrastructure damage from sea-level rise, and competition for water among countries and communities. The assessment also offered the hopeful but measured prediction that "there is still time to act to limit the amount of change and the extent of damaging impacts."[9]

Despite this broad consensus in the scientific community, there exists a persistent, well-funded, and vocal chorus of people who deny climate change. One wonders what the basis for this denial is given not only the scientific evidence but also the terrible risk to our planet's safety denial could cause. Denial is the better word here, not skepticism, which is a core component of rigorous scientific thinking. For Inhofe a main foundation is the Bible, in particular a line he quotes from Genesis 8:22: "As long as the earth remains there will be springtime and harvest, cold and heat, winter and summer, day and night." On national radio, he explained, "My point is, God's still up there. The arrogance of people to think that we, human beings, would be able to change what He's doing in the climate is to me outrageous."[10] Pope Francis, who in 2015 published an especially influential encyclical on the effects of climate change, has a different view: "We need to care for the earth so that it may continue, as God willed, to be a source of life for the entire human family."[11] The president of the conservative Heartland Institute responded to Pope Francis by saying "the Holy Father is being misled by 'experts' at the United Nations who have not proven worthy of his trust."[12]

For Inhofe and others, the uncertainty that is a necessary part of climate science, and indeed of any science, is used to support denial. Fossil fuel industries cultivate doubt because they fear that effectively addressing climate change will disrupt their investments and enormous profits from these fuels. Using approaches applied by the tobacco industry when it was combating charges that smoking causes lung cancer, the oil and coal industries are known for underwriting campaigns to discredit climate science. Their approaches include raising doubts about undisputed evidence, using seemingly independent organizations to promote their positions and scientific confusion, using spokespersons who make it appear that there is still serious debate among scientists on the issue, emphasizing the number of jobs that might be lost, and using their extraordinary influence to shape government policy. In 2007 the Union of Concerned Scientists harshly criticized Exxon Mobil for such tactics.[13] One convenient target used to undermine climate science is the models climate scientists rely on to predict future trends. Because rigorous science requires any projection to state its statistical uncertainty, deniers can focus on the uncertainty to claim that the projections are unreliable. This is not surprising: it is relatively easy and a standard technique of deniers to plant seeds of doubt by attacking complicated methods. But climate change modeling is a highly respected and crucial scientific tool, certainly more scientific than the book of Genesis or facts manipulated by interested parties.

For many conservatives who have long denied climate change, the rationale finds its way back to some of their basic tenets: big government is bad; what is good for business is good for the country; unfettered markets can solve any problems. Thus, conservative leaders often block government and global initiatives to address climate change, and conservative policymakers speak out against them.

Is it too late to reverse climate change?

Climate change is already being felt globally. The scientific community, the United Nations, and climate change policymakers have set under 2°C (3.6°F) over preindustrial levels as the limit that global temperatures can rise without risking dire consequences. This limit is a central assumption in international negotiations about limiting greenhouse gas emissions, including those concluded in Paris in December 2015. The planet is on track to blow through this increase well before the end of the century unless the greenhouse gas emission spigot is shut down totally now, which is virtually impossible. Carbon dioxide concentrations would need to stay at about 450 parts per million (ppm) to keep the planet at the 2°C limit. By 2013 they were already at 400 ppm—up from 280 in the 1750s, and 316 in 1997. Still, whether it really is too late—whether the irreversible tipping point is near—remains to be seen.

The vocabulary of climate change solutions, however, points to a partial answer. Policy leaders speak of either "adapting to" climate change or "mitigating" it. Reversing it is not part of the vocabulary because, practically speaking, climate change cannot be reversed. But if we move fast enough and aggressively enough to adapt to and mitigate the harm we are inflicting, we might be able to keep impacts down and temperatures below dangerous levels.

What is climate change adaptation?

Climate change adaptation is behavior designed to prepare for climate change impacts expected in the future. It is adaptive to protect coastal wetlands, which blunt storm surges. It is not adaptive to allow the constructions of summer homes on ocean beaches knowing that sea levels are rising and storms are becoming more extreme (although remarkably, some local zoning boards still enable it).

The 2014 Report of the IPCC addresses climate adaptation extensively.[14] Forward-looking cities and businesses factor it into their planning strategies, such as evacuation planning for low-lying areas, shade-producing vegetation plantings, and placement of key electrical stations away from areas that might flood. Recently Logan Airport, New England's largest, located on fill in Boston Harbor, announced plans to spend millions to protect runways from the flooding expected as the Atlantic Ocean rises and storms surge.[15] In 2013 New York City announced an extensive plan to fortify its power grid, build floodwalls, levees, and bulkheads along its 520 miles of coast, and renovate buildings threatened by storms and sea rise. The initial cost was estimated at $20 billion, but then-Mayor Bloomberg noted that the cost of a severe storm like Hurricane Sandy a few decades from now would be $90 billion.[16] Climate change is part of Mayor DiBlasio's "One New York: The Plan for a Strong and Just City," which is intended to build on Bloomberg's plan and expand it to address issues related to poverty. Some jurisdictions, however, still resist: for example, in 2012 the North Carolina legislature voted to disregard climate change predictive data when making its state development plan.[17]

What is climate change mitigation?

Climate change mitigation is the effort to slow down human impacts on the climate system, in particular, the amount of greenhouse gasses (especially carbon dioxide) we are emitting. Energy efficiency and conservation, renewables, nuclear power, a carbon tax, carbon capture, and geoengineering are all forms of climate mitigation. So while adaptation helps us live with the reality of climate change, mitigation is about putting the brakes on it. Mitigation includes everything from changing daily habits, like not idling the car in the driveway while we chat with a neighbor, to redesigning how we pay for reducing the effects of pollution, for example, by taxing it. Scientists, economists, and concerned citizens are pursuing mitigation practically everywhere. Not surprisingly, the IPCC addresses it extensively,[18] as do many other scientific organizations.

Why is energy efficiency an important climate change mitigation tool?

Old refrigerators are not energy efficient—far from it. People who replace them will save money on their electric bills, a great incentive. Cutting back on such electricity guzzlers also mitigates climate change as do smart transportation practices: electricity production and transportation are two of the largest sources of greenhouse gas emissions. Energy- efficient opportunities abound. LED lights, for example use roughly 75 percent less energy and last 35 to 50 times longer than incandescent bulbs. Energy conservation is similar, and has a more direct effect on consumption. Here we are choosing to use less energy rather than better technology. Lowering the thermostat on a cold winter night conserves energy, as does riding a bicycle to work or carpooling. Of course, if the energy we consume came from clean sources—renewables or nuclear, for instance—the need for mitigation itself would be diminished.

What are renewables?

Unlike fossil fuels, which are not renewable, renewables are energy sources that are not depleted as they produce energy; rather, they are quickly replenished, and do not emit harmful amounts of carbon, if any. Solar and wind are prime examples, and are appearing practically everywhere on the global land and seascape, even competing with the oil and gas industry as profit-making propositions. Hydroelectric power from dams is another familiar renewable. Others are biofuels (liquid fuel from plants), waves and tides, and geothermal energy (heat from under the earth's surface). Some of these have their own direct negative environmental impacts. For example, dams have had enormous negative effects on river species and water supplies. Biofuels need heavy carbon-emitting machinery and lots of acreage and fertilizers to grow the plants that supply them. Moreover, all of them require materials and equipment that need to be manufactured, transported, and installed, probably powered by fossil fuel.

Solar power is the most promising of the renewables, and it is enjoying an impressive surge of interest throughout the world. The sun is the source of an abundance of energy, providing far more than humans need. Moreover, it is available and accessible everywhere, thanks largely to solar technologies that have succeeded in converting this energy to useable heat, electricity, and many, many other applications. Photovoltaic cells (PVs), also called solar panels, are particularly important now: they convert solar energy directly to electricity often at the very spot the energy is needed. PVs are appearing on residential and commercial rooftops, on highway signs, telephone poles, and over many acres as solar farms in sun-drenched fields as PVs become increasingly easy to buy and install. Solar heat plants are another important solar technology and operate on a bigger scale: they collect solar energy (often from PVs), then convert it to electricity for transmission to users, much as conventional power plants do.

The speed with which solar energy, especially PVs, has taken off around the globe is remarkable. Prices for rooftop PVs dropped 29 percent from 2010 to 2013 and sales are shooting up. This is all very good news because solar panels emit no carbon pollution and require relatively few other resources as they produce energy. Like other renewables, however, they are not without environmental costs, including hazardous chemicals and energy used in their production, waste byproducts that need disposal, and land use if the panels reside in a field rather than on a roof.

Is nuclear power a viable mitigation option?

Before the Fukushima Daiichi nuclear disaster in Japan in March 2011, the answer to this question might have been yes. Policy leaders and the public were increasingly in favor of nuclear. At the time it happened, several countries were ramping up nuclear power plants as clean, dependable alternatives to fossil fuel power plants, which nuclear plants are—unless they malfunction.

Fukushima melted down and released radioactive material as a result of an earthquake-caused tsunami. It was the worst nuclear disaster since Chernobyl, the nuclear meltdown in the Soviet Union in 1986. It reminded the world again of the great risks present at nuclear power plants because they contain deadly and long-lasting radioactive materials. The cause of the tragedy, an unprecedented natural disaster, underscored the difficulty of anticipating every possible risk, not only natural, but also human from error, war, and terrorism.

Many responsible scientists argue, however, that fear of nuclear energy is out of proportion to its danger. One measure of reactor safety is that France has generated 75 percent of its electricity from nuclear fuel for decades with no serious accidents and no deaths from radioactivity. Nuclear energy now generates about 11 percent of the world's electricity and has prevented an estimated 1.84 million air pollution-related deaths. It has also prevented the release of many gigatons of greenhouse gas that would have been emitted from conventional power plants.

Nuclear power is an important option—but only if plants are properly sited, designed, and overseen, and spent nuclear reactive fuel is carefully disposed of. Proponents are correct that to date deaths and injury from the handful of significant nuclear accidents are far fewer than those caused by fossil fuel air pollution, such as deaths and injury from respiratory diseases, and climate change impacts, such as deaths and injury from heat waves and major floods.

Is hydrofracking part of the solution?

Hydraulic fracturing, often referred to as hydrofracking or just fracking, is a relatively new process that taps oil or natural gas from rock very deep below the earth's surface. It involves drilling wells vertically, and then frequently into horizontal directions extending thousands of feet. To get at the oil or natural gas, large amounts of fluid (hence hydraulic) are shot under great pressure into the rock formations that hold it, fracturing it. The fluid carries small particles (called proppants) that hold the fractures open as well as a variety of chemicals that aid the process. Under pressure from the rock formations, the fluids return to the surface, and the propped-open fractures enable the oil or gas to flow and be removed.

Hydrofracking is of great interest today not for the oil it can access, but for natural gas, which is the main focus of current hydrofracking activities. Natural gas is a cleaner fossil fuel than coal, emitting less carbon, and is readily available, including in the United States, so it is an attractive energy alternative to combat climate change. Like the solar industry, hydrofracking also represents commercial opportunities given the demand for alternatives to carbon-heavy fuel sources. These opportunities are realized not only in the natural gas itself, but also in the land on which lucrative rock formations rest. For example, the financially struggling Pittsburgh Airport received a $50 million signing bonus from a hydrofracking operation located on airport land and may get billions in royalties. This airport sits on the huge Marcellus Shale, a 400 million-year-old sedimentary bedrock layer about 7,000 feet below the earth's surface, estimated to hold 1 trillion cubic feet of natural gas (about 4 percent of total natural gas consumption in the United States in 2014). Many thousands of new wells were hydraulically fractured in the United States between 2011 and 2014, often producing income for commercial and residential landowners.

Whether hydrofracking should be part of the solution to climate change or pressing energy needs is not at all clear, however, and is the subject of vigorous, sometimes heated, debate. Setting aside the fact that the natural gas extracted from hydrofracking is still a fossil fuel, although a relatively clean one, the environmental negative impacts of hydrofracking are not well understood and they may be significant. Some are readily apparent as a matter of common sense, such as the inherent danger of violent and extensive disruption of subterranean bedrock. Increased seismic activity from hydrofracking has been reported in places such as Ohio, Texas, and Oklahoma, as well as the United Kingdom and Canada. Other major concerns are the large amounts of water required in the hydrofracking process, potentially contaminating and draining increasingly depleted clean groundwater supplies; the proper disposal of chemical fluids and contaminated water used in the process; and fugitive emissions of methane, a major greenhouse gas, migrating from hydrofracking wells into groundwater and the ambient air.

In the United States, many sources of public drinking water systems serving many people are near hydrofracking wells. Recognizing that we do not yet know enough, the EPA in 2012 launched a study "to understand the potential impacts of hydraulic fracking on drinking water sources."[19] This was laudable, but disturbing. Essentially it suggests that here the EPA is letting serious problems evolve (giving fracking operations the benefit of the doubt) without full scientific understanding in situations where the potential for such problems is clear. This approach has historically been the source of many environmental difficulties. Some countries and states are applying the precautionary principle, however. By 2016 hydrofracking bans were in place in France, the Netherlands, Scotland, and Germany, and in the states of New York and Maryland. In July 2015 the EPA released a draft of its study, but offered no definitive regulatory steps.

What is carbon capture and sequestration?

Controlling runaway climate change comes down to controlling the amount of carbon dioxide in the air. So when carbon is "captured" and "sequestered" where it won't soon be released again, climate change is being mitigated. This sort of mitigation happens naturally and humans can—and sometimes do—encourage it. Wetlands and peat bogs, for example, capture carbon (like other such natural environments, they are called "carbon sinks" or "carbon reservoirs"), so preserving them is an effective mitigation technique.

Carbon capture and sequestration usually refers, however, to new technologies that would capture carbon from polluting industrial sources, such as power plants, and send it (likely by pipeline) to a safe storage location (for example, in a deep underground rock formation). These technologies may be promising and important, especially if one takes the view that fossil fuels, coal especially, will remain major sources of energy for a long time, no matter how hard we try to wean ourselves from them. But they are expensive and themselves require energy, no doubt from fossil fuels, to work. In addition, they create their own regulatory and environmental problems, transport and leakage being two. Finally, they let us maintain a coal-based energy mentality, distracting us from the key objective: cutting reliance on fossil fuels.

What is geoengineering?

In the climate context the term refers to methods designed to manipulate the environment to fight climate change. Some standard approaches, for instance reforestation and carbon capture, can fall under this broad definition. The term usually has a narrower application, however, referring to more exotically manipulative fixes, most of which are in formative stages. One example is solar radiation management using sulfur dioxide droplets disbursed into the atmosphere that act as mirrors. This would artificially create something like the effects of the Mount Pinatubo volcanic eruption. These sorts of technologies, should they be perfected, are appealing to those who believe the obvious solution—reducing carbon emissions dramatically—is out of reach. To others they are considered to be dangerous tinkerings with large natural systems.

How does a tax on carbon mitigate climate change?

Many policymakers and economists believe that taxing carbon is the best way to shift away from fossil fuels. The theory is that CO_2 emitters are not paying their full freight because every ton emitted produces quantifiable damage to the planet. The tax is needed to counteract this damage by paying for medical, environmental remediation, population movement, and other expenses resulting from climate change. If the cost of a product such as gasoline increases, consumers will use less or stop buying it, and investors, producers, and consumers will look for alternatives. This will increase conservation and reliance on renewable energy sources and will encourage people to make lifestyle changes, such as using mass transit. Carbon taxing has been enacted in a few countries as a climate mitigation tool (Sweden and Ireland, for example). But it has met stiff resistance in the United States, largely because of objections to additional taxation and the powerful fossil fuel lobby. Boulder, Colorado has a carbon tax, however, and other regions of the United States are considering it.

Are there laws that address climate change?

Since the late 1980s, international attention to climate change has been consistent and growing with the United Nations playing the leading role. The 1992 United Nations Framework Convention on Climate Change (UNFCCC), created at the Rio Earth Summit, was the first international agreement on climate change and laid the foundation for the twenty or so international climate conferences and agreements that followed it, including the Kyoto Protocol and the 2015 Paris Agreement. These are not entirely "hard" laws: enforcing them is very difficult. Many countries, however, have passed enforceable laws that address climate change and often help implement these international agreements. The number of laws and countries enacting them is growing, although their complexity and changeability make them impossible to cover in this book. The Columbia Law School Sabin Center for Climate Change maintains an excellent database for those who want up-to-date information.[20]

Judges are also contributing to climate change law. In 2015, for example, a Dutch court, in an opinion with potential impacts on courts in other countries, ordered the government to cut greenhouse gas emissions significantly.[21] Until this ruling, no court anywhere in the world had given such an order. The court reasoned that the government has a legal obligation to protect its citizens from the looming dangers of climate change. Other similar lawsuits are under development. The US Supreme Court has rejected one, but other countries may produce more favorable outcomes, following the lead of the Dutch court.

In the United States the Clean Air Act provides solid authority to regulate greenhouse gases and the industries that emit them, but the statute, originally enacted in 1970, well before climate change was identified as a major environmental problem, was not drafted with this in mind. Because climate change is such a political lightning rod for powerful coal and oil interests, Congress has never amended the act to strengthen its authority to address it. The George W. Bush administration, in particular, blocked any attempt at meaningful progress under the law. It took litigation by several states against Bush's EPA to get the US Supreme Court to rule, in *Massachusetts v. EPA*,[22] that the EPA could indeed regulate greenhouse gases which, fortunately, the incoming Obama administration quickly did. These regulations, including the administration's the Clean Power Plan, are aimed primarily at reducing emissions from coal-fired power plants and motor vehicles. They routinely meet strenuous opposition from industry groups and the politicians they support, so although some are final, some remain in litigation.

What is the Kyoto Protocol?

The Kyoto Protocol is an international agreement that binds certain nations to reductions in greenhouse gases as part of the global effort to address climate change. The Protocol grew out of the UNFCCC signed by 150 nations (including the United States) at the 1992 Earth Summit in Rio, following an IPCC assessment that human activities are changing the climate. It was adopted, with support from the entire international community, and with leadership from the United States during the Clinton administration, in Kyoto Japan in 1997. In 2001, however, under President George W. Bush (and to the surprise and embarrassment of his own EPA Administrator, Christine Whitman, a former New Jersey governor), the United States withdrew its support and became the only one out of the 179 participating nations to vote against implementing it. It went into effect in 2005, with 191 nations as parties. In 2012 the Protocol's first "commitment period" expired. It was extended at the UN Climate Conference in Durban in 2012. Although not the defining international climate change agreement, the Kyoto Protocol is a precursor to the potentially much more successful 2015 Paris Climate Change Conference and the Paris Agreement on climate change that the conference produced.

What is the Paris Climate Change Conference?

The Paris Climate Change Conference took place from November 30 to December 11, 2015 in Paris under the authority of the UNFCCC, the same authority underlying the Kyoto Protocol and other international climate agreements. It was preceded by important negotiations and commitments made in 2014 by the United States and China that helped pave the way. At the conclusion of the Conference 195 countries for the first time committed in the Paris Agreement to participate in lowering greenhouse gas emissions in a variety of ways. The UN Secretary General called it a "monumental triumph."[23] Although some have criticized it, the broad consensus is that the Paris Agreement is a historic turning point in global efforts to address climate change. Among its key features is the participation of both developing and developed countries, something that was not accomplished at Kyoto, and agreement to hold "the increase in global temperature rise to well below 2°C above pre-industrial levels and to pursue efforts to limit temperature increase to 1.5° above pre-industrial levels."[24]Two degrees is widely thought to be the level at which devastating consequences will occur. Other promising features of the agreement are binding commitments by countries to make "nationally determined contributions" to cutting carbon emissions, five-year reviews, adaptation and mitigation strategies, and financial support to be delivered from developed nations to developing ones.[25] The agreement was structured to create no new binding legal obligations, thus avoiding required approval by the US Senate, which would have voted against it. US participation was considered a critical component, one missing in the disappointing Kyoto Protocol.

The Paris commitment by countries to participate did not, however, put the agreement immediately into force. Under the terms of the agreement, at least 55 parties to the UNFCC accounting for at least an estimated 55 percent of total greenhouse gas emissions need to formally join.[26] In September 2016 China and the United States, the top two emitters, ratified the agreement bringing the greenhouse gas percentage close to 55 percent. In November 2016 it went into force, thirty days after the thresholds had been met.

What is climate justice?

The industrialized countries, although representing only about 20 percent of the world's population, are responsible for most of the greenhouse gases in the air. This is the result of many years of productivity that enabled these countries to attain high standards of living and world dominance. They continue to enjoy the products of industrialization even though the factories that make them (and their polluting byproducts, including CO_2) are shifting to less wealthy countries as these countries try to achieve higher standards of living through the same development process. Ironically, climate change will hit them hardest because they usually are located in hotter climates, often in low-lying regions, where impacts from water shortages, flooding, desertification, and the like are greatest. They also lack the financial resources to adapt to these changes. Storm barriers and evacuation routes are expensive to build, and not as pressing as tomorrow's food, water, and shelter.

As the world community struggles to bring global temperatures down and adapt to them, questions of climate justice arise. From a fairness point of view, which countries should reduce their carbon emissions, and by how much? If less wealthy countries are asked to cut emissions, should they receive subsidies or compensation not only because they are poor, but also because they are generally not the cause but the victims of climate change? Should industrial development be curtailed to cool the planet, even if further development is the surest path to a higher standard of living? Can countries in Africa and South America be asked to stop cutting down forests (forests being recognized carbon sinks) when industrialized countries did the same thing in prior centuries to make way for growth? How can developed countries that have become rich through activities that created the climate crisis tell India or China, with millions of people lacking electricity, that they cannot emit the greenhouse gases they may need to produce it?

The 1992 United Nations Framework Convention on Climate Change took a position on the questions posed above, stating that countries should protect the climate system "on the basis of equity and in accordance with their common but differentiated responsibilities and respective capabilities," and that "developed countries should take the lead in combating climate change."[27] It stipulated, moreover, that developed countries should assist developing countries "that are particularly vulnerable to the adverse effects of climate change in meeting costs of adaptation," recognizing that "economic and social development and poverty eradication are the first and overriding priorities of the developing country parties."[28] The Kyoto Protocol implemented these principles with the agreement that developed nations would reduce their greenhouse gas emissions but developing nations would not. How to allocate emissions fairly, as Kyoto attempted to do, remains a very thorny problem. Should emissions allocations be based on current total emissions or historic contributions? Per capita, or by some other measure? The 2015 Paris Agreement recognizes "the specific needs and special circumstances of developing countries,"[29] but does not attempt to allocate emissions among nations.

Climate justice also entails our obligations to future generations because climate will greatly impact our descendants. On behalf of those people who are not yet born should we not do whatever is necessary—even annoying, disruptive, expensive things—now to limit the damage our generation and generations before us have done? This obligation is captured in the concept of intergenerational equity also acknowledged in the Paris Agreement.

What does climate change have to do with world peace?

The Intergovernmental Panel on Climate Change won a Nobel Prize in 2007. This was not a science prize, as one might expect, but the Peace Prize. At the time some people thought it was a stretch, but in retrospect it seems utterly appropriate. Climate change is causing water and food scarcity in such places as the drought-burdened and conflict-riddled Middle East and in flood-ravaged, impoverished Bangladesh. Too few basic resources for too many people coupled with their uneven distribution are a classic formula for conflict and war. Climate change induces these conditions.

And the connection is now being made. Only a few years ago the US military addressed climate change merely as a future threat to specific military installations in flood plains. Now it incorporates climate change into its strategic thinking about extremist groups and political unrest. In 2014 Secretary of State John Kerry said that climate would influence American foreign policy.[30] Also that year, US Department of Defense Secretary Chuck Hagel asserted that climate change poses an immediate threat to national security, with increased risks from terrorism, infectious disease, global poverty, and food shortages.[31] The IPCC has flagged climate change as a source of international conflict.[32] If climate change can cause conflict, the reverse should also be true: adapting to it, mitigating it, and making these efforts cooperatively on an international scale should advance the cause of world peace, as the 2007 Nobel Committee recognized.

9

WASTE

What is waste?

Waste may be the most conceptually difficult term in the environmental lexicon. At one level it is unwanted material, usually the byproduct of industrial production, or sewage, or stuff that has been discarded because it is no longer useful. We use words like "garbage," "junk," or "trash" for household and commercial waste. Material that is completely recycled or reused is not waste. An empty Coke can rattling down the street would not be a waste at all if it had gone directly to a recycling facility. The term is hard to define, however, because it is subjective: the leftovers in the dumpster behind a restaurant are garbage to its owners, but they are food for a homeless person searching for her next meal. One person's waste can truly be another person's raw material. Because of this subjectivity, whether or not something is a waste has generated major disputes, particularly when government decides to regulate it, which can be expensive, especially for industry. For example, is copper slag a waste if the smelting company that created it intends to reuse it or sell it someday, even though in the meantime it is sitting in a pile leaching contaminants into the ground?

Waste is arguably a human invention. From this viewpoint it does not exist at all in nature because almost everything there is at some juncture put to good use: the remains of a lion's kill are food for jackals, and they clean them up nicely. Rather, waste is the result of human production and consumption, which uses raw materials very inefficiently, casting off large quantities of useable material. From this viewpoint, waste can be defined as the opposite of efficiency. To the extent that it represents something of value that becomes an expensive liability rather than a revenue-generating resource, it can be thought of as a market failure.

A simple definition is that waste is the stuff we throw away—garbage. This definition highlights the great challenge facing us now: the fact that nothing really does get thrown away—it just goes somewhere else. Take the dry-cell battery, a common power source in such household items as remote controls, hearing aids, and watches, whose likely fate was once traced by Barry Commoner in his 1971 book *The Closing Circle*.[1] After it is thrown away it may go in the trash, then to a municipal incinerator where it is burned, releasing toxic chemicals, which are caught up in the wind and captured in rain or snow, which is then deposited in lakes where some of the toxic chemicals are taken in by fish in whose organs they accumulate, which fish when eaten by humans cause the deposition of these toxins in their organs, harming them and maybe their fetuses—and on and on. This cycle is predictable unless the battery is properly recycled, a big "if."

Waste can be divided into three categories. Solid waste is the material we commonly refer to as trash or garbage generated in residential and commercial buildings, and it is a major problem globally. Hazardous waste is waste that poses particularly significant threats to public health or the environment and gets special regulatory attention as a result. Radioactive waste comes from nuclear reactors, hospitals, and research facilities.

The term "waste stream" is a related idea and refers broadly to the total flow of waste from various sources to its ultimate destination. Waste streams are broken down into their own categories: municipal, medical, electronic, and nuclear, for example. They change over time as needs for energy and goods and their means of production evolve. In the early twentieth century, coal ash from residential furnaces was a major part of the municipal waste stream; not so today, when coal is no longer burned much as a residential heating source. But coal ash remains in the waste stream of such important sources as coal-fired power plants. Electronic waste, which was not a significant problem a generation ago, is a major waste stream now.

Why is solid waste a problem?

There are four big reasons: first, because there is too much of it; second, because much of it is poorly managed, if at all; third, because many of the materials in it, especially new compounds generated by modern industrial innovation (such as cell phones), are either harmful or poorly understood, or both; and fourth because it is very expensive to drag it from place to place, to try to get rid of it, and to pay for its negative aesthetic, health, and ecological consequences.

The United Nations Environment Programme (UNEP) estimates that every year 11.2 billion tons of solid waste are collected worldwide.[2] Moreover, the pace of waste generation is accelerating as affluence and urbanization rise globally. It is expected to double again by 2025. This is not surprising: the volume of solid waste a country produces directly correlates with how much disposable income its citizens enjoy and how resource-intensive and consumer-based its lifestyle is. In the United States, per capita waste generation is higher than practically anywhere else. The United States makes up 4 percent of the world's population but generates 30 percent of its waste, and each American throws away about 1,650 pounds of garbage every year, about 4.5 pounds per person per day. To put it another way, Americans toss out monthly about as many pounds of garbage as they weigh, which is about twice as much as they tossed out fifty years ago. This phenomenon is replicated in other industrialized countries as shown in Figure 9.1 below.

Very little of the waste generated today is managed optimally. In developed countries this is typically done through some form of recycling, for instance, but often not as aggressively as it should be given the volume produced and the environmental impacts. In 2013 the United States enjoyed a 34 percent recycling rate, which somewhat offsets its staggering waste generation statistics. (This rate, however, masks considerable variation in recycling rates among the states, which roughly range from over 40 percent in California to just 2 percent in Wyoming and Mississippi.) Japan, another highly developed country, does somewhat better: its rubbish generation per person is about half that of the United States, although its recycling rate is a little lower. In the urban areas of some developing countries, in contrast, poor waste management is creating critical situations especially as population increases along with industrialization, although per capita waste generation is often much lower than in developed countries. Different governments have different definitions of recycling, and data are incomplete and dynamic so comparisons are necessarily imperfect.

Poor management of food waste contributes to odor and to disease carried by rats and other animals. Food is organic waste so as

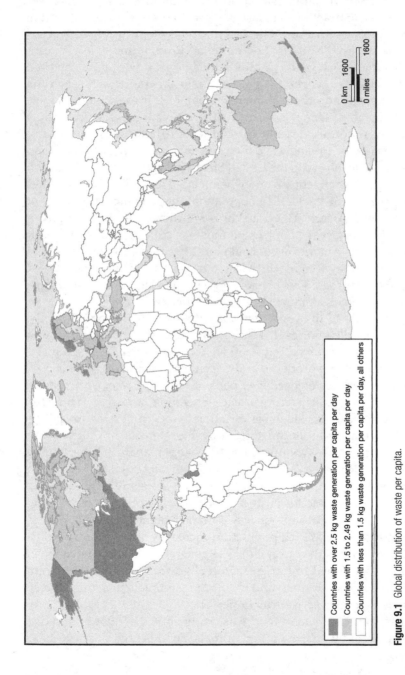

Figure 9.1 Global distribution of waste per capita.

Source: Adapted from http://www.economist.com/blogs/graphicdetail/2012/06/daily-chart-3.

it decomposes it emits methane, a major greenhouse gas contributing to climate change. Packaging is another major waste source. It leaches chemicals into the ground at poorly managed landfills, as does practically everything else that goes into these waste repositories, from worn-out furniture to batteries to paint cans. Incinerated landfill waste does not disappear. Even when solid-waste incinerators are relatively well regulated as they are in the United States, they emit toxic chemicals such as dioxin, lead, and mercury and leave ash piles leaching out these heavy metals into groundwater. The fast-developing electronics industry presents perhaps the most daunting problems, because its rapid growth rate is outstripping humans' ability to properly dispose of its discarded products—such as cell phones, tablets, and their toxic components.

And then there is the cost to society. The World Bank reports that in 2010 globally humans spent over $205 billion dealing with solid waste. In 2025 the cost is expected to escalate to $375 billion.[3] Every year New York City spends about $1.6 billion to handle over 3.5 million tons of garbage using a workforce of over nine thousand people to do it. New York's waste is usually hauled, often by heavily polluting diesel trucks and sometimes by rail, to out-of-state landfills in places as far away as South Carolina.

Finally, one could conclude that the main problem with solid waste is that fundamentally, it is a huge societal lost opportunity— the opportunity lost to conserve or generate energy, the opportunity lost to save materials, the opportunity lost to enhance urban beauty. It is also an opportunity lost to reduce pollution: as a practical matter, every human-generated pollutant is a waste, so conversely, waste is by definition a major source of pollution.

What do Americans discard?

Containers and packaging come in as number one: 27 percent of the total discarded or almost 70 million tons annually. Food, either scraps or spoiled, accounts for 15 percent or about 37 million tons. Plastics are used increasingly, and so plastic wastes account for a significant portion, about 12 percent or 32.5 million tons. This picture is problematic, but it could be worse: some American garbage is not simply thrown out for good; rather, it is increasingly recovered by being reused or recycled. In the United States, as is the case in other developed countries, measurable progress has been made in these important pollution-control areas. The American 2013 recycling rate of 34 percent is up from 9.6 in 1980 and 28.5 in 2000.

The more important point, however, is that Americans have embraced a throwaway culture. Even as the United States promotes recycling and waste minimization, its producers of domestic goods push disposables—water bottles, diapers, mops, coffee filters, containers for the salads we make at salad bars, and the forks we use to eat them. And consumers choose to buy them. The rate of recycling is not keeping pace with generation, especially when it comes to plastics, a particularly pernicious waste stream. Plastics are recycled at a rate of only 9 percent, up from 5 percent in 2000.

Plastics present special environmental problems, especially in the oceans. In particular, they remain in the marine environment for a very long time. One way producers try to address the problem is by making so-called biodegradable plastics. In 2015 a United Nations report concluded, however, that products labeled "biodegradable" will not significantly decrease the amount of plastic in the oceans, or the chemical risk they pose, because to biodegrade, these products require conditions that rarely exist. The report also notes the irony that labeling a product "biodegradable" may actually encourage littering.[4]

Where does garbage go?

Globally, most garbage goes to landfills, although in lower-income countries a larger percentage ends up in open dumps. The largest landfill in the United States—also among the largest in the world—is Apex Regional Landfill just outside Las Vegas. In 2010 it took in 9,000 tons of municipal solid waste a day. Once at a landfill, solid waste is often incinerated. It has been said, however, that the largest dump in the world is the Pacific Garbage Patch, the enormous gyre filled with waste plastics.

What is the difference between an open dump and a landfill?

An open dump is an uncovered area where trash is thrown. Often at some point the trash is burned on site to reduce its volume, but an open dump is usually not carefully designed or maintained; as a result, it releases harmful materials into the air and groundwater, as well as odors. It is a breeding ground for disease-carrying vermin. Open dumps were very common in the United States until the 1980s, when the country became aware of their hazards. In rural places, town dumps held disintegrating oil drums, appliances, and other discards from household and farm operations that resulted in hazardous materials leaching into the ground, and where continuously smoldering refuse released pollutants into the air. Open dumps are still prevalent in developing countries.

Landfills, or sanitary landfills as they are sometimes misleadingly called, are locations on land specifically designed to hold nonhazardous waste indefinitely in an environmentally sound way. They often are lined with synthetic material or dense soils to prevent harmful substances from leaching into groundwater. In addition, they are generally equipped with leachate collection systems, regularly monitored for leaks, covered to prevent wind from dispersing their contents, and organized to keep incompatible material separated. Although these are useful storage techniques, their long-term efficacy is questionable. In the United States landfills are regulated in various ways at the state and local level, but not meaningfully at the federal level. Hazardous waste landfills are very different. They are heavily regulated repositories for discarded materials that have the characteristics of, or are listed as, hazardous wastes as determined by the EPA.

How is waste controlled in the United States?

The most important and comprehensive federal waste control law is the 1976 Resource Conservation and Recovery Act (RCRA). RCRA's focus is hazardous waste management. Other federal laws play important roles, such as the Ocean Dumping Act and the Nuclear Waste Policy Act. The Clean Air and Clean Water Acts also provide controls over some waste-based air emissions and water discharges. For example, the Clean Air Act regulates emissions from solid waste incinerators; the Clean Water Act regulates discharges from sewage treatment plants.

Federal law to control waste was a late arrival in the decade of the 1970s, when Congress enacted the major environmental laws. This congressional foot-dragging was based on the general reluctance to involve the federal government in regulating garbage, a subject that had always been the exclusive domain of state and, especially, local government. Solid waste (conventional commercial and residential garbage) in the United States is still primarily controlled at the local and state level. Plastic bag bans, for example, are appearing in state legislation and local ordinances.

By 1976, however, it was clear (and clearly stated by Congress in RCRA) that the country's economic growth, an improved standard of living, new technologies, and even the success of air and water pollution controls (which generated very large amounts of pollution treatment residues) had caused an enormous increase in waste generation that was exceeding local ability to deal with it.[5] Of greatest concern was hazardous waste.

RCRA's centerpiece is a cradle-to-grave regulatory program designed to manage and, to a lesser extent, minimize the future disposal into the ground and groundwater of hazardous waste generated and handled by ongoing industry. It imposes federally enforceable requirements on three groups of hazardous waste players: those who generate hazardous waste; those who transport it; and facilities that store, treat, or dispose of it. The requirements include responsibilities for all three to maintain a manifest system tracking the waste, as well as specific requirements tailored to each group. For example, hazardous waste facilities are required to get permits with specific waste management provisions, and generators of hazardous waste are required to identify and label their waste as the first step in the manifest system. After revelations in the 1970s about abandoned hazardous waste sites, RCRA was amended in 1984 to require hazardous waste facilities to clean up preexisting contamination at their sites. Mindful of the tradition of local control of garbage, Congress in RCRA leaves nonhazardous waste almost entirely up to state and local governments. Like other major US federal environmental laws, states can run the RCRA hazardous waste program if approved by the EPA, and most do.

One of the challenges for the regulated community is to figure out whether or not a particular waste stream is a regulated hazardous waste at all. In a nutshell, under the EPA's regulations, a hazardous waste is regulated if it is either listed as such by the EPA, or if it exhibits one or more characteristics: toxicity, reactivity, ignitability, or carcinogenicity. Household hazardous waste is exempt from RCRA, which may make sense because of the federal government's reluctance to regulate people's activities in their homes. RCRA's definition of hazardous waste when spelled out in EPA regulations is complex, in part because of the mottled exemption-heavy universe it tries to describe. How did it happen, for example, that coal ash is exempt from regulation even though it exhibits the characteristics of regulated hazardous waste? It is difficult, moreover, to regulate behaviors that appear to take wastes out of circulation, but in fact do not. This is called sham recycling. Is the addition of a hazardous sludge (costly to dispose of as a waste) to cement legitimate or sham recycling?

What are household hazardous wastes?

These are products used around the house or apartment waiting to be disposed of that technically could be federally regulated hazardous waste but are exempt from regulation. Nevertheless, the household hazardous waste stream is significant. The average US household generates about twenty pounds of household hazardous waste per year, a total of about 530,000 tons per year. Here is a partial list of household products that are often hazardous:

- Paints, preservatives, strippers, solvents, and brush cleaners
- Cleaning agents (oven cleaners, floor wax, spot removers, drain cleaners, for example)
- Motor oil, battery acid, gasoline, car wax, antifreeze, degreasers, rust preventatives
- Personal care products (nail polish, for example), medicines
- Pesticides

Cities and towns often have household hazardous waste pick-up days, and some have pharmaceutical take-back programs. Often government agencies and product labels provide information on how properly to handle household hazardous waste. It is left to individuals, then, to decide whether to avail themselves of these environmentally responsible opportunities or just to dispose of household hazardous wastes down a sink, a storm drain, or unmarked in the garbage bin. If they choose the latter approach, these wastes will be improperly disposed of and their hazardous constituents will find their way into ground or surface water, or the air.

What about abandoned hazardous waste sites?

The US Congress believed in 1976 that RCRA had finally "closed the loop" of pollution by wrestling down the last major remaining pollution portal: the industrial hazardous waste stream. But the United States was startled soon after by the tragedy of Love Canal, a residential neighborhood in Niagara Falls, New York built on an abandoned chemical dump. The story of Love Canal was a wake-up call that better laws were needed to deal with hazardous waste, particularly abandoned hazardous waste sites. It is also a parable about corporate responsibility, hidden pollution, and the role of government.

Love Canal is named for William Love, who in the 1890s wanted to connect the Niagara River with Lake Ontario and build a model city. He did not succeed, leaving a trench behind. His land was bought by Hooker Chemical Company (later Occidental Petroleum Corporation), which used the trench to bury 22,000 tons of toxic waste. In 1953, with a warning about the waste to the City of Niagara Falls, Hooker sold the land to it for one dollar. The city built two schools on it, and a residential development followed.

By the mid-1970s basements were filling with chemicals, leaking drums of waste were being uncovered, and Love Canal residents were experiencing notable numbers of miscarriages, birth defects, and illnesses. Hooker denied responsibility, and the city discounted citizen complaints. After significant citizen activism and aggressive press reporting, the EPA investigated, and in 1978 President Jimmy Carter approved emergency financial aid—the first time presidential emergency funds were approved for other than a natural disaster. Over two hundred families were evacuated or agreed to move. The EPA called it at the time "one of the most appalling environmental tragedies in American history."[6] It put a spotlight on the lurking presence of chemical dumpsites and the need for governmental action, beyond RCRA, to address them.

It is not unusual for schools to be built on dumps, as were the Niagara Falls schools, because dump acreage is often cheap. For example, New Bedford, Massachusetts built its high school on a dump, which is now causing problems; and the public high school in the affluent town of Concord, Massachusetts was also built on a dump. Residents of New Bedford and Concord have expressed concern about these siting decisions. The Superfund law is a direct result of Love Canal and a few other notorious waste sites discovered in the 1970s.

What is Superfund?

Superfund is the misnomer commonly used as shorthand for the Comprehensive Environmental Response, Compensation, and Liability Act (CERCLA), which Congress passed in 1980 to deal with hazardous waste sites, including abandoned ones like Love Canal. Other common examples of sites covered by CERCLA are old landfills, military bases, harbors, riverbeds, mines, smelters, and even entire towns, such as Libby, Montana, which is widely contaminated with asbestos. It is a misnomer because the Superfund is simply the fund established by the law for cleanup of these abandoned sites if no responsible parties exist to fund the cleanup. CERCLA, however, contains more important provisions than the fund (which dries up now and then depending on congressional action). The most important are its liability provisions that are designed to force responsible parties who own the site or put the waste there in the first place, such as Love Canal's Hooker Chemical Company, to pay for cleanup costs, reimburse the government for cleanups financed by the fund, and sometimes to perform the cleanup itself. This liability follows them whether they are negligent or not (called strict liability); whether they originally received permission from the government to dispose of the waste there or not; whether they had knowledge of site conditions or not; whether, like Hooker Chemical, they placed notice of danger in the sales document; or whether they dumped hazardous substances at these places decades ago or yesterday. Moreover, at sites where more than one party sent hazardous substances, if it is not possible to determine how much a particular party contributed to the contamination (because there are no site records or waste was not divided on site), all parties are "jointly and severally liable," meaning that a single party could be required to pay for the entire cost of cleanup unless the party can demonstrate that its contribution was "divisible" from the rest of the hazardous substances at the site. Often responsible parties opt to pay cleanup costs to resolve their liability, leaving the actual cleanup to the federal government. Some CERCLA sites have many responsible parties, and it is not uncommon for them to agree collectively to pay for the cleanup, allocating the fair share of costs among each other. This is often a wise choice in light of the liability exposure presented by the strict and joint and several liability standards. If a CERCLA site has no identifiable responsible parties, or if those identified are unable to pay, the site is "orphaned" and the government can pay for the cleanup from the Superfund.

The CERCLA liability approach in which the "polluter pays" has been called grossly unfair, even draconian, but it has been credited with causing a behavioral about-face by the chemical industry (among others) from one with cavalier waste disposal practices to one that pays great attention to the ultimate disposition of its waste stream. CERCLA liability has also raised difficult legal and policy questions. Should a cash-strapped municipality that owns a Superfund site (for example, a former town dump) and clearly sent waste to it, pay millions of dollars to contribute to cleanup costs thereby diverting municipal resources that might be used to buy a fire truck or install a traffic light, two purchases that protect public safety? Should a purchaser of property that subsequently turns out to be a Superfund site contribute to cleanup costs if the purchaser was not fully aware of the contamination at the time of purchase? What if they paid very little for the property knowing it was contaminated? What if contaminated groundwater from an adjacent Superfund site migrated into their abutting land making it part of the site, and making them potentially liable under the law?

Uncontrolled industrial wastes often leach into groundwater. Because of its importance as a source of drinking water, Superfund cleanups often address not just surface pollution, but also groundwater contamination. Groundwater cleanups are difficult, time-consuming, and costly.

How hard is it to clean up groundwater?

Anyone who lives near a big CERCLA site (of which there are over a thousand on the National Priorities List, the list of national priorities among the known hazardous waste sites in the United States and its territories) knows that cleanup, from selecting the right cleanup strategy to declaring the cleanup complete, is a long process. This is in part because the groundwater cleanup portion of the site is most difficult to tackle. It is one thing to cap a landfill containing old hazardous waste drums with vegetation, dense soil, or synthetic covers to cut down on movement of the waste in rain or by wind, or even to dig up the drums and cart them away. It is quite another to reach many feet down to contaminated groundwater and try to return it to drinking water quality, which has often been the CERCLA cleanup objective.

Not only is groundwater deep below the earth's surface, but the aquifers that hold it also are often comprised of craggy, fractured rock where contaminants are hard to locate. The contaminants themselves, moreover, may be difficult to pin down: contaminated oil might float to the top, heavy metals might sink to the bottom, and it may be impossible to get all the contaminated water out and properly clean it at the surface (a common approach called "pump and treat"). Finally, depending on the chemicals and subsurface conditions, the process can take from a few years to decades.

CERCLA sites are only a very small percentage of contaminated groundwater sources. The cleanup challenges they present are one reason why the fast pace of groundwater contamination everywhere—not just from rusting 55-gallon drums of chemical waste, but from fertilizers, pesticides, detergents, and petroleum products—needs to be slowed.

It may come as a surprise, moreover, that petroleum is excluded from CERCLA's definition of "hazardous substance" (a term which helps define the statute's reach), so uncontaminated gasoline and other fuels that may end up in groundwater are not subject to CERCLA cleanups. The EPA and the courts have struggled for years with the scope of this important but vague statutory exclusion.

What are brownfields?

Brownfields are industrial or municipal sites that have been abandoned or lie fallow primarily because potential buyers fear that the possible presence of hazardous substances left there might create complications for redevelopment. This legitimate fear arises because originally (before it was amended) CERCLA imposed liability on any owner of contaminated property—without exception. Brownfields are often contrasted with greenfields, which are undeveloped areas usually outside of cities that are uncontaminated and thus considered good development prospects.

Brownfields are everywhere: they are the empty lot where the local gas station once was, or the fenced-in acre behind the local metal refinishing shop, or the dust-blown remains of the defunct tannery on the other side of town. The EPA estimates that there are more than 450,000 of them in the United States.[7] They represent enormous lost opportunities: for urban revitalization, for the municipal tax base, for commercial investment, and for avoiding the unnecessary use of greenfields for industrial development. Recognizing this, over the last twenty years federal, state, and local governments have made concerted efforts to bring them back to productive use. Some mechanisms employed at the federal level are tax incentives, protections from liability (such as those in the 2002 amendments to CERCLA called the Brownfields Revitalization and Restoration Act), grants to states and other stakeholders, and technical assistance to brownfields communities.

One dramatic example of a potential brownfields revitalization success story is the Fresh Kills Park project on Staten Island in New York City. Fresh Kills was a landfill in a coastal marshland that opened in 1948 and became New York City's main disposal area for household garbage (and by 1991 its only one) until it closed in March 2001. By 1955 it had become the largest in the world. At its peak it received 29,000 tons of garbage a day ferried through New York Harbor by a fleet of barges. It was reopened briefly after 9/11 to receive material from the World Trade Center, where it was carefully screened for remains and effects. The Fresh Kills project would create a 2,200 acre park (three times the size of Central Park in Manhattan) including athletic fields, riding trails, and art installations. If all goes well, it is scheduled to open in 2036.

An increasingly common example of successful brownfields revitalization is golf courses, because they can be built on degraded land and can turn eyesores into profitable and appealing places.

For example, Harborside International Golf Center in Chicago was built on a municipal solid waste landfill; the Old Works course in Anaconda, Montana was designed by Jack Nicklaus and built on a CERCLA site. Golf courses present their own issues, of course, including water use, groundwater contamination from pesticides and fertilizers, and habitat disruption. These are among the reasons why they make sense on previously contaminated land: they are hardly pristine locations, although they appear to be.

How is waste controlled in other countries?

As is the case in the United States, many other countries regulate waste categorizing it as municipal solid waste, hazardous waste, household waste, electronic waste, and so forth. They also have specific laws addressing responsibilities of generators, transporters, and waste facilities such as landfills.

The European Union's Waste Framework Directive, to which members are expected to adhere through their own national legislation, is illustrative. It provides waste definitions and management principles, among other guidance. It applies the "polluter pays" principle as well as extended producer responsibility (EPR). EPR is the idea that producers of products should take back their used goods for eventual recycling. It extends a producer's responsibility to the postconsumer stage and is an increasingly important waste management tool—a common example is spent printer toner that the consumer can send back to the supplier. The directive also includes recycling and recovery targets, and requires member countries to develop waste management plans and waste prevention programs. The directive lays out this hierarchy of waste management practices, from most to least effective: prevention, preparing for re-use, recycling, recovery for other purposes such as energy, and disposal.

Given the high priority everywhere to reduce waste, several legislative tools have been applied around the world to bring the quantity of waste down and manage what is left wisely. For example, plastics are prevalent and particularly environmentally damaging wastes. Some countries have imposed strict controls on plastic bags, and the number is increasing. Bangladesh banned thin plastic bags in 2002 in response to their tendency to clog street drains during floods. Some states in India have imposed similar bans, as have several African countries. Ireland has imposed a tax on plastic bags combined with a public awareness campaign. As is true with other environmental laws and initiatives, waste reduction depends on resources and political will.

What more can be done to reduce waste?

The best way to reduce waste is to stop generating it. Short of that, policymakers and regulators encourage the concept of "integrated waste management." It is frequently applied in efforts by various sectors such as municipalities to bring waste under control. Integrated waste management involves three steps: reducing waste before it enters the waste stream by, for example, eliminating unnecessary packaging; recovering it and separating it for reuse and recycling; and managing what is left through landfilling or incineration in an environmentally sound way.

Much of the solution, however, concerns lifestyle and cultural expectations, especially in affluent segments of the population. Why do affluent people need so many shoes? So many cars? Why are so many newly built suburban houses often oversized McMansions? Lifestyle changes may be occurring, however. According to *Newsweek*, the University of Michigan's Transportation Research Institute reports that in 2011 baby boomers were fifteen times more likely to buy a new car than were millennials.[8] Perhaps this is an early indication that the materialism of the late twentieth century may be giving way to a new simplicity.

Why is recycling important?

The answer to this question seems obvious. Recycling reduces the quantity of waste needing disposal or incineration, and returns material, which would otherwise be lost, into useful circulation. It can also conserve energy. The World Bank reports, for example, that "producing aluminum from recycled aluminum requires 95 percent less energy than producing it from virgin materials."[9] Recycling is promoted, with good reason, as a key component of responsible waste management, which is why it is strongly encouraged by the United Nations and the EPA and why many cities globally have recycling programs.

Some have attempted to debunk recycling, arguing among other things that it is too expensive, that it is stalling after ambitious beginnings, that there is plenty of landfill space, that its costs outweigh its benefits. These people have rightly been rebutted by responsible environmental policymakers who point out the flaws in such analyses, including misunderstandings about landfill capacity and cost, and about the significant benefits of preserving natural resources and the costs of extracting them.

Is it possible to eliminate waste altogether?

Zero waste may appear to be an impossible goal. Actually, it is a reasonable aspiration aiming to significantly reduce—and finally eliminate—the waste humans dispose of. Rather than cradle-to-grave (the usual grave being a landfill, dump, air, or water), from this point of view waste is seen as a potential resource or residual product, recycled in the cradle in effect, and replicating natural cycles more than current industrial ones. Proponents recognize that the ultimate goal is elusive. So they recommend incremental approaches including community recycling, energy conservation, and closed loop industrial processes that incorporate byproducts into manufacturing operations. The idea is gaining currency and shows up in our daily lives. Many grocery stores, for instance, now encourage reusable shopping bags. Carpooling and public transit are encouraged through government incentives. Residential composting of vegetable waste returns it as organic fertilizer to backyard gardens.

Zero waste has been legislated in some places. In Buenos Aires, without significant population growth, the amount of trash sent to landfills grew from 1.4 to 2.2 million tons between 2002 and 2011. In 2005, aware of this trend, the city responded with its so-called zero waste law that required a reduction of 75 percent in waste sent to landfills—an ambitious goal, but one that stimulated new approaches to waste reduction in the city. The city of Seattle, Washington adopted a zero waste guiding principle for its 1998 solid waste management plan. Several other US cities have such goals. In each case, the idea is not to drop immediately to zero waste. Rather, it is to encourage serious thought and action, in order to get to zero waste sometime.

10

THE BUILT ENVIRONMENT

What is the built environment?

The term "built environment" refers to the places that people have designed and constructed for living, working, and recreation. It includes homes, commercial buildings, highways, parks—every place that has been altered by humans for our safety, comfort, convenience, and pleasure. The built environment, which inevitably changes or replaces the natural one, is a defining feature of our planet.

What does the built environment have to do with environmental protection?

Land—forests, wetlands, deserts, meadows, mountains—serves many functions crucial for our sustained well-being and that of every other species. It covers just 30 percent of the earth's surface, and much of that is already in use or being degraded. Land is an immensely important resource, but humans often do not treat it as such.

Decisions on where to build a highway, how to develop a housing subdivision, and whether a town's playing fields should be artificial turf or grass all concern how land will be used, and they all have impacts on the environment. The easiest route for the highway might be through a wetland or an old growth forest, but the route would diminish the many services these ecosystems provide. The housing subdivision might be an escape from the city, but it would put more cars on the road polluting the air and contain bigger lots and structures breaking up existing natural habitats. Artificial turf at a suburban high school might be easier to maintain than grass, but it also might leach pollutants, reduce soil permeability, and increase runoff.

In the United States since the 1950s, the built environment has gobbled up a staggering amount of land. In 1982 there were about 71 million acres of developed land. In 2007 there were more than 111 million, an increase of over 50 percent. In the last 50 years about 4 million miles of highways have been laid down. By 2010 paved parking spaces and roads covered about 24,000 square miles—almost the size of West Virginia. In western states, where population is growing fastest, economically stressed ranchers are selling private ranchland near urban centers to developers serving people who want large tracts for suburban homes. On the other side of the country in New England, a similar phenomenon is occurring. Dairy farmers near growing urban areas are selling their land to developers. Growing urban areas exert intense pressures on all environmental resources. These changes in the landscape have come at the price of natural beauty and ecological balance.

Land must be altered, for better or worse, to accommodate the benefits of industrialization and the realities of an increasing population. The growth of suburbs is understandable: escape from the dirt and congestion of the city to the verdant quiet and order of outlying towns. In the United States, however, this often occurred without adequate planning and control, which would have considered impacts from roads and buildings on ecosystems, water and air quality, wildlife, and so on. Instead, land-use planning, to the extent that there was any, occurred at the local level and inconsistently. Moreover, development was influenced greatly by the automobile, starting with the Model T Ford in the early twentieth century. The automobile contributed significantly to the explosion of suburban living and its environmental consequences. Dense urban centers sprawled out over large tracts of land, which became suburban, car-dependent locations, consuming many more acres and many more vehicle miles travelled than necessary or desirable; at the same time, lifestyle choices imposed further pressures on the land: chemically fertilized lawns and golf courses; two-, three-, and even four-car garages; shopping malls; and the like. If one travels by plane at night from Atlanta to Boston up the East Coast of the United States and looks out the window, one will see hardly a break in the urban light glow emanating from a thousand miles of cities and suburbs that comprise this very dense corridor.

In the United States these land-use decisions have been subsidized by taxpayers who often had less say in them than those who benefitted. The subsidies enabled new roads, utilities, and schools in outlying areas. Recreational sprawl—the roads, condos, and power lines needed to service ski areas and resorts, for example—also is often subsidized by taxpayers. Trying now in the twenty-first century to retrofit wise transportation, housing, and other land-use policies is practically impossible. The fractured and myopic land-use decisions that characterized post-World War II America continue and are being repeated elsewhere around the globe. All of this growth of the built environment has degraded land, and in some instances completely eliminated its natural utility. At the same time, unregulated growth has squandered opportunities to reduce air pollution, protect groundwater and ecosystems, and encourage healthy living. In short, it has not been smart growth.

What is smart growth?

Smart growth, sometimes called sustainable communities or the compact city, is basically the opposite of the sprawl described above. It is a planning approach with several main elements: compact mixed uses with homes, shops, places where people work, and schools existing together in the same area, instead of acres of houses connected to everything else by roads; mixed housing stock available to different social strata and ages instead of separate wealthy and low-income neighborhoods; pedestrian, bicycle, and mass-transit options for getting to work and school, instead of reliance on the single-occupant vehicle; preservation of open space by clustering housing and reusing existing vacant or abandoned lots, sometimes called brownfields, instead of occupying greenfields with office parks and shopping malls; and public involvement in planning decisions, instead of top-down decision-making by officials and developers. Smart growth aims to create economic and social vitality, to benefit the environment by reducing pollution and the conversion of land to impermeable blacktop and chemically fertilized lawns, and even to address the obesity epidemic by encouraging walking and cycling. A common smart-growth slogan is "live, work, and play neighborhoods."

The EPA, the US Department of Housing and Urban Development, and planning and environmental organizations worldwide embrace smart growth. Many communities in the United States and elsewhere do as well. Denver, Colorado and Melbourne, Australia offer just two good examples. Several states have enacted legislation or implemented policies reflecting smart-growth principles. For example, in 2008 California passed smart-growth legislation, followed by Maryland in 2009; moreover, many states have incentive programs to encourage smart growth and discourage sprawl.

Smart growth is not new. Much of the credit for these sensible ideas comes from Jane Jacobs, the urbanist and activist. Her 1961 book *The Death and Life of American Cities*—the *Silent Spring* of urban planning—promoted walkability, short blocks, mixed uses, and community involvement. It eschewed the car-centered approach to urban planning popular in the United States after World War II. Actually, Jacobs was not fighting sprawl. She was fighting the bulldozing of New York City neighborhoods (and beautiful Washington Square Park) for the massive highway system that Robert Moses, the mid-twentieth century New York City Parks Commissioner and master builder, envisioned and largely implemented from Long Island to Connecticut, enabling the sprawl that surrounds the city. (Moses was a complicated figure: he also gave the New York metropolitan area Jones Beach State Park and Lincoln Center for the Performing Arts, among other landmarks.)

Moreover, smart-growth principles highlight the hidden fact that cities such as New York and San Francisco and the density that epitomizes them, although sometimes viewed in contrast to the perceived beauty of Westchester and Marin Counties, are highly efficient and environmentally responsible places notwithstanding their special environmental problems. This is largely because of their tiny per capita footprint, relative walkability, and public transit systems. In a 2004 *New Yorker* article, David Owen made a strong case that "by most significant measures, New York is the greenest community in the United States, and one of the greenest in the world."[1] The measures reported in the article included fossil fuel usage, modes of transportation, energy consumption, and land use.

But smart growth is not easy to implement, nor is it a panacea. For one thing, in the United States traditional zoning laws which favor separating uses (industrial zones, residential zones, agricultural zones) actually inhibit smart growth, as does most US transportation policy, which heavily favors highways over public transit. The Interstate Highway System, created by an act of Congress in 1956, is a prime example. It covers over 46,000 miles and is a profound endorsement of private over public transit and single cars over multipassenger vehicles, both of which are discouraged in smart-growth planning. Imagine if the United States had an Interstate Railway System as comprehensive, well-maintained, and well-funded as its interstate highways, and as reliable and state of the art as those in Europe and Japan.

Some argue that smart growth has not yet resulted in its expected benefits. Others worry that in distressed city locations smart growth so achieves its revitalization goals that gentrification and the displacement of lower-income and aging populations occurs. Still others argue "not in my back yard" when established suburban neighborhoods are threatened with reconfiguration along smart-growth lines. It is clear, however, that this is an important idea in land-use planning that promises significant social, environmental, and even economic returns.

What is wrong with NIMBY?

Not in my back yard (NIMBY) is a reaction against land uses that seem unpleasant to live near: a sewage treatment plant, a power line, a shopping mall, a bus terminal, a nursing home, a high-rise building. It is not flattering to be told you have a NIMBY bias, but it is a common reaction to practically any piece of the built environment that offends one's sense of safety, beauty, or quality of life. Other related acronyms, some more serious than others, are LULU (locally unwanted land use); NIABY (not in anyone's backyard); and BANANA (build absolutely nothing anywhere near anybody).

The problem with NIMBY is that people who employ it usually acknowledge the importance of the land use at issue, but want it located somewhere else and can afford the time and money to mount objections. Cape Wind, the proposed wind farm off Cape Cod in Massachusetts, would have produced renewable carbon-free energy but it was vigorously and successfully opposed by wealthy summer residents of the Cape, Martha's Vineyard, and Nantucket, many of whom objected to the aesthetic impacts the wind farm would have on them. They had no general objection to wind farms, just to those in view from their homes and sailboats. NIMBY reactions are not confined to the United States. For example, opponents to the siting of wind farms in the United Kingdom have raised similar objections.

What special environmental challenges do cities present?

More than half the world's population now lives in urban areas. In 1950, only 30 percent were urban dwellers. Whereas in 1950 the world had two megacities (metropolitan areas with over 10 million inhabitants), New York and Tokyo, in 2015 there are 35 megacities, many of which are in developing countries. This trend will continue as the global population continues to explode and people gravitate to urban places, which offer jobs and other opportunities. The pace of urbanization is fastest in the developing world, but it is happening in the developed world as well. Moreover, as suburban commuter times increase, existing urban centers like New York, Boston, and San Francisco are increasingly attractive places to live, with housing becoming affordable only for wealthy buyers and with less wealthy residents either dying off or being priced out.

Even though cities hold increasingly greater numbers of people, in the United States at least, their environmental problems have historically been given short shrift. Environmental laws in the United States were first promoted by conservationists and the affluent to protect iconic rural and suburban landscapes. Their perspectives were reflected in the laws themselves and in their implementation. In 1970 a senator from Maine, not a member of Congress from the Bronx, championed the Clean Water and Clean Air Acts. The goals of the Clean Water Act were fishable, swimmable water, but not necessarily in urban waterways. Boston Harbor received the City's sewage until 1991 and still receives sewage overflow (although the harbor is much cleaner now than twenty years ago), as does New York Harbor. Similarly, air quality in cities is consistently poorer than in suburban and rural areas, so more city dwellers are exposed to air pollution with its attendant health problems. Effective regulation of diesel buses, truck traffic, and the like—key contributors to air pollution in cities, and often emitted a few feet from pedestrians and bicyclists inhaling it—has not been a primary focus of environmental policymakers and regulators. Old housing stock, covered with lead paint, is primarily an urban problem. Soil adjacent to wooden structures closely packed in cities such as Baltimore and Boston is often highly contaminated with lead where urban gardens grow and toddlers play. Similarly, old lead pipes under city streets send drinking water to urban faucets; this water is sometimes badly contaminated with lead, as in Flint, Michigan.

In addition to fairly obvious environmental challenges, especially concerning air quality, cities are typically hotter than other places. The EPA reports that the annual mean temperature in a city with 1 million people can be up to 5.4 degrees Fahrenheit warmer than its surroundings. At night the difference can be up to 22 degrees.[2] Heat is especially bad for sensitive populations, such as the elderly, and it is uncomfortable, especially if one cannot afford air conditioning. This problem can be mitigated by saving land for parks (even pocket parks), creating green roofs (such as the one over Chicago's eleven-story City Hall, constructed as part of the City's Urban Heat Island Initiative), planting sidewalk trees, and incorporating heat impacts into urban planning processes.

Finally, it is hard to keep cities clean. In New York City, it is reported that about a half a million dogs leave over 20,000 tons of fecal matter and 1 million gallons of urine on the streets every year.[3] New York and other places have "poop scoop" laws. But dog fecal matter and other waste often flush into storm drains and end up in urban waterways.

Can landowners do anything they want on their property?

The notion that one's home is one's castle runs deep. It greatly influences the extent to which government regulates what private landowners can do to their property. Unfortunately, land and soil, especially in private hands—one's castle—enjoy fewer comprehensive legal protections than do air and water. In fact, in the United States, government, both local and federal, is loath to regulate the behavior of people on their own property. Few legislators would support a proposal to limit the size of houses to save energy, or limit the number of garages in a new single family home if other zoning requirements are satisfied, or prohibit paved driveways or chemical fertilizers without a very compelling reason to do so.

The United States has no federal soil or land protection law similar to, for example, its federal air and water laws, although this idea is not outlandish: at the same time in the 1970s when Congress was passing the Clean Air and Water Acts, a companion law, the National Land Use Planning Act, was voted on. Its sponsor, Senator Henry Jackson, introduced it by saying "intelligent land-use planning and management provides the single most important institutional device for preserving and enhancing the environment, for ecologically sound development, and for maintaining conditions capable of supporting a quality life and providing the material means necessary to improve the national standard of living."[4] The legislation failed by a few votes, and has never been attempted again.

This is unfortunate. Consider Hurricane Katrina: if the land comprising the Mississippi delta had been protected through multistate planning and if the natural wetland buffers there had not been manipulated and destroyed to make way for development and industry, Hurricane Katrina almost certainly would not have packed the devastating wallop that killed approximately a thousand people, crippled the economy, and scarred the natural beauty of New Orleans and other Gulf Coast areas.

The United States is not alone. Developing countries may be replicating our mistakes. For example, Ho Chi Minh City is a growing metropolis of over 8 million people practically at sea level. Its streets flood with tidal changes. Some of Vietnam's tallest skyscrapers are under construction there, yet attention to the vulnerable location on which they sit is just beginning.

Is there anything a landowner in the United States cannot do?

Setting aside large-scale emissions into the air and discharges into water, or releases of highly toxic chemicals into the ground, with few exceptions landowners have considerable latitude to build, cut down trees, dig holes, engage in polluting activities, and impose other alterations on the land they own, with significant effects on the surrounding environment. Across the United States restrictions, if any, are imposed in widely varying ways with widely varying effects by local zoning and planning boards. Some of these are not insignificant: environmental standards in local subdivision rules and groundwater and wetland restrictions can protect environmental values in the development context at the local level. A few federal laws address particular values that can constrain building. The Historic Preservation Act, for example, requires a close look at development that will affect historic sites or cultural artifacts, although compliance is sometimes weak. The Coastal Zone Management Act gently prods states to develop plans to preserve coastal areas.

Occasionally, the federal government or a state does impose a significant restriction on what people can do on their land. One scenario is when a landowner wants to develop land in an environmentally sensitive area requiring a federal or state permit (a wetland or coastal beach, for example) and government forbids it on environmental grounds. This is the situation that faced developer John Rapanos, who wanted to build a mall in a wetland. Another frequent and related landowner complaint is that by forbidding a profitable use such as a residential development to protect an environmental resource, the government is in effect "taking" land, in the constitutional sense of the word. Landowners have argued right up to the US Supreme Court that although they still own the land it is worthless, and they should be compensated under the Fifth Amendment, which provides that private property should not "be taken for public use, without just compensation." In most of these cases the landowners have lost where they can point only to diminished land values and where productive, less intensive, uses of the land remain.

Despite strongly held notions that private property rights are sacrosanct and that owners should be compensated when government regulations cause their property values to drop, concerns about the environment have broadened the philosophical and legal discussions of what these rights really are. The foundational National Environmental Policy Act, for example, describes "each generation as trustee of the environment for succeeding generations."[5] If this is the case, then many behaviors on private land with long-term impacts should be reconsidered and checked, starting perhaps by discouraging the excesses practiced by owners of suburban property, including preferences for large lots, the liberal use of water and fertilizer for lawns, and the choice to live in a car-dependent location. Notions of smart growth and sustainable communities concern giving people alternative choices about where and how they want to live. Land-use and tax policies—as well as social values—that favor sprawl undermine these goals.

How do public lands help protect the environment?

About 25 percent of the United States' roughly 2.5 billion acres of land is owned by the federal government for the public. (This does not include land reserved for Indian tribes or the military.) Almost all the rest is privately owned except for tracts owned by states. The built environment, very visible in much of the country, is basically absent on public land. This might not have been the case: in the nineteenth century federal law encouraged settlement of the West by redistributing federally owned public land to homesteaders, in effect a huge giveaway. In the twentieth century, however, the emphasis shifted to retention of public land as conservationists found their voice; the result was curtailment of development on it.

Four agencies manage federal public land now, primarily for preservation, recreation, and extraction of natural resources. The Bureau of Land Management controls about 250 million acres designated for multiple uses, including recreation, energy development, grazing, and conservation; it also controls about 700 million acres of subsurface mineral resources that can be extracted and bought by private parties. The Forest Service controls about 200 million acres, also designated for multiple uses including timber harvesting, grazing, recreation, and habitat preservation. The Fish and Wildlife Service controls about 90 million acres primarily to protect plants and animals; this acreage includes the important National Wildlife Refuge System. The National Park Service controls approximately 80 million acres for purposes of resource conservation and public enjoyment.

Public land plays a major role in protecting species, water, air, and biodiversity. It provides deep, deep natural beauty not just in the United States, but around the world. It also has huge economic value. Timber harvesting; copper, mercury, and nickel mining; oil and gas drilling; grazing; and commercial development all beckon on US federal land. So it is not surprising that this acreage has been the source of great conflict between commercial interests and environmentalists. The conflicts play out in Congress, which over the years has produced a ragged patchwork of poorly coordinated laws, and in the courts. Such conflicts will continue as land and the resources residing in it diminish, and a growing population extends its reach.

Finally, public lands in the United States and elsewhere in the world should not be seen as the only solution to wildlife protection, healthy ecosystems, and the many other values which public lands help protect. One cannot just put a fence around these lands. Inevitably threats will appear: contaminated groundwater, invasive species, climate change, airplane noise and exhaust, long-distance transport of air pollutants, and myriad others from catastrophic to minor incremental ones. The few remaining Asiatic lions are safer in India's Gir Forest than they are in the wild, but a single deadly infestation could wipe them all out. Ideally they should be in more than one park, perhaps in other countries. Like every other environmental challenge, systemic, sustainable approaches need be applied. Public lands are wonderful and crucial, but only part of the solution.

11

ENVIRONMENTAL JUSTICE

How is justice a part of environmental protection?

A safe, healthy environment is considered by many to be a basic human right. Like any goal embraced and implemented in various ways by all levels of government, environmental protection should be administered as justly and fairly as possible. However, actions taken to protect the environment are usually considered in the context of economics, practicality, and the interests of empowered people. Issues of justice and fairness are not at the front end of such actions. These issues include procedural justice (do all affected people have a voice and are these voices heard by decision-makers?); distributive justice (are burdens and benefits being shared in a way that reflects the abilities and responsibilities of all parties?); and corrective justice (do decisions account for past behaviors that have contributed to the environmental problems being addressed?). Environmental justice addresses the complex problem of fundamental fairness in international environmental agreements, and in national, state, and local environmental laws and policies.

Earlier in this book, fairness and justice were considered in the context of the global community where it informs international relationships and responsibilities, especially between developed and developing nations, and in the particular context of global responsibilities for mitigating and adapting to climate change, where justice is an important factor. Over the last thirty years environmental justice has been the subject of serious concern among environmental policymakers and social justice and civil rights activists in many contexts, in part because notions of justice and fairness have so often been marginalized in environmental law and policy. Although it is in the United States where the idea has come into sharpest focus, today environmental justice is the subject of serious study, discussion, and action in many places on every continent. An example is from Latin America: in 2001 Brazil hosted the first international colloquium on environmental justice in that part of the world. Movements in Kenya and Nigeria exemplify the importance of environmental justice in Africa, and they are growing in India. The idea of environmental justice has begun to deepen governmental responses to environmental issues globally, and has greatly expanded the number of groups who have or should have a voice in decisions about environmental protection.

When does an environmental justice concern arise?

An environmental justice concern arises when some level of government is considering taking an action that might disproportionately impact a vulnerable population: for example, when polluting sources such as chemical factories, bus depots, urban freeways, or power generating plants cluster in areas where the residents are already burdened with pollution, health and social problems, or economic disadvantage; or when that population has little political clout, has been discounted by government for some reason, has not had an opportunity to participate in the decision-making process, or has been discriminated against. This is a phenomenon that falls largely on low-income and nonwhite communities.

Convent, Louisiana is a low-income African American community located in what has come to be known as "cancer alley" (also known as "petrochemical corridor"). Cancer alley stretches over one hundred miles along the Mississippi River between Baton Rouge and New Orleans, Louisiana. About one million people live there. It got its name because of the high rate of cancer among its residents and the more than 150 oil refineries, toxic-waste dumps, and other noxious industrial facilities located there. The toxins released reach close to one hundred thirty million pounds per year, or about one-sixteenth of the total amount released nationwide. In 1996 Shintech Corporation announced plans to site a polyvinyl chloride plant in Convent, which would pump significant amounts of additional toxins into the polluted air. In 1999 it pulled these plans after an intense reaction from the community, pressure from the Congressional Black Caucus, and a civil rights complaint filed by environmental justice activists. Although some residents of Convent supported locating the plant in their community because it would bring jobs, as did the local chapter of the NAACP, in 2005 Shintech settled on the city of Plaquemine, a more affluent area thirty-six miles away, to site the plant. The result enjoyed praise from the EPA, which had been asked to investigate, and is viewed as a victory for environmental justice advocates. The Shintech controversy classically demonstrates the significance environmental justice concerns can, and should, have in the context of environmental protection.

What is an environmental justice population?

There is no general definition. In the United States the EPA recognizes three groups—minority, low-income, and indigenous populations—but does not offer a definition of the term. States sometimes have their own definitions, usually in formal state environmental justice policies. Whether a particular community falls within a particular definition often depends on such factors as what level of poverty constitutes low income. For example, the Massachusetts Environmental Justice Policy for its Executive Office of Environmental Affairs states: "Environmental justice population means a neighborhood whose annual median household income is equal to or less than 65 percent of the statewide median or whose population is made up 25 percent minority, foreign born, or lacking English language proficiency." The policy then goes on to further define "foreign born," "low income," and "lacking English proficiency."[1] Government agencies sometimes try to map areas as potential environmental justice communities to help determine whether a particular government action may raise environmental justice concerns. This has proven to be a difficult endeavor.

How is environmental justice defined?

The EPA offers, perhaps, the best working definition. Environmental justice is "the fair treatment and meaningful involvement of all people regardless of race, color, national origin, or income, with respect to the development, implementation, and enforcement of environmental laws, regulations, and policies."[2] The definition tracks the 1964 Civil Rights Act with its specification of race, color, and national origin—and, importantly, adds income to it.

The definition has two very different parts. Fair treatment focuses on the disproportionate burdens that minority and low-income populations can suffer. For example, polluting facilities have been sited with greater frequency in minority and low-income communities, while affluent white communities are generally more successful in keeping them out of their backyards. Meaningful involvement focuses on giving community members a reasonable opportunity to express their views and influence decisions, when, for example, a chemical plant like Shintech is proposed to be sited in their midst. Creating meaningful involvement can be as straightforward as holding public hearings in accessible locations with translation services. Given the enormous disparity in resources and political influence between community groups and corporate interests and between the disenfranchised and the politically empowered, environmental justice is a difficult goal to attain, although a very important one.

Unlike most other environmental protection goals, such as clean air, swimmable water, and pollution prevention, which focus on sources of pollution and how to protect important resources from them, environmental justice focuses on particular groups of people affected by pollution and how to ensure they are not shouldering a disproportionate burden of society's unhealthy byproducts.

Other terms, particularly "environmental equity" and "environmental racism," have also been used to capture the idea, and have somewhat different connotations. "Environmental equity" was the term initially used by the EPA (and rejected by environmental justice advocates). It has a soft tone and implies the redistribution of risk rather than risk reduction. The term "environmental justice" was adopted by the Clinton administration and continues to be used by the US government. "Environmental racism" is a more pointed term focusing on racial animus, a recognized cause of environmental injustices.

What is the environmental justice movement?

The environmental justice movement, although increasingly global, started in the United States where it remains an important component of the national dialogue on environmental protection and social justice. Its roots are in the civil rights movement of the 1960s, but it took shape in the 1980s when strong correlations started to be drawn between environmentally harmful governmental decisions, such as the siting of hazardous waste facilities, and communities of color. These correlations came into sharp focus in 1982 when nonviolent demonstrations occurred in Warren County, North Carolina, whose population was predominantly African American. Citizens objected to the siting of a hazardous waste landfill there, asserting that the siting decision was based on racial demographics. Over five hundred protesters were arrested. Research by the US government[3] and scholars confirmed that nonwhite communities bore a disproportionate share of environmental risks and yet had little or no voice in environmental decisions. This was further elaborated in a highly significant study published by the United Church of Christ in 1987, "A National Report on Racial and Socio-economic Characteristics of Communities with Hazardous Waste Sites."[4] This early activism and scholarship laid the foundation for the environmental justice movement.

Environmental justice activists have continued to use tools such as street protests and hard data to raise awareness. They also have used the courts and government agency administrative proceedings to challenge unfair practices. The Shintech controversy described above shows how some of these tools can come into play. In the second decade of the twenty-first century the environmental justice movement in the United States and elsewhere includes a wide spectrum of voices such as Latino farm workers, African Americans, low-income neighborhood activists, Native Americans, and other indigenous populations. Sometimes the interests of different environmental justice groups are not the same, but they share the same basic premise: people who are disadvantaged or subject to discrimination should not bear disproportionate environmental burdens and they need to be informed and part of the decision-making process on matters that affect their well-being.

How is environmental justice promoted in the United States?

The term "environmental justice" appears nowhere in the many environmental laws passed by the US Congress in the 1970s and 1980s. There is no language on environmental justice in the Civil Rights Act of 1964. Although in recent years some members of the US

Congress have submitted environmental justice bills, thus far none have been enacted. Thus there is relatively little incentive for governments or courts to promote this notion of fundamental fairness, although several court cases have been filed, relying on the Equal Protection clause of the US Constitution or helpful language in the Civil Rights Act. Very few plaintiffs have prevailed in such lawsuits.

However, in light of pressure from leaders of the environmental justice movement and the importance of this constituency to him, in 1995, aware that Congress would not act, President Clinton issued an Environmental Justice Executive Order that directed the federal government to address environmental justice issues in various ways.[5] The executive order is not enforceable in court and it applies directly only to federal government operations, but it provided great momentum and established practices that advanced environmental justice goals. It has been reaffirmed by all subsequent presidents. The George W. Bush administration slowed governmental momentum, but in the Obama administration environmental justice responsibilities again became a presence in governmental actions. For example, because of the order an environmental justice analysis is now expected to be done before issuing a federal permit to a polluting facility planned to be built in a low-income or minority community, and information about the permit may be translated into a language other than English if that is the language spoken in the community. Moreover, federal regulations now often address the impacts of the regulation on environmental justice populations. In addition, several states now have environmental justice policies, and a few have environmental justice statutes. But it is important to know that claims of environmental injustice in court have difficulty succeeding, and, in the absence of firm law, it is hard to drive this goal into the workings and decisions of government.

What are the main barriers to achieving environmental justice in the United States?

The main barrier is the unequal political and economic power that exists between enfranchised, monied people and corporations, and disenfranchised low-income and nonwhite people. This imbalance is experienced in many areas of American life. And it manifests itself in many subtler ways throughout the social fabric. The sometimes unjust governmental implementation of environmental protection is part of this entrenched fabric.

Another important barrier is the lack of congressional action in creating laws (or amending current ones) to achieve environmental justice. Clearly such action would be difficult in the current congressional climate.

What more can be done to achieve environmental justice?

Perhaps the most potent forward action is to educate the public that environmental law and policy are not immune to issues of fairness and justice; and that all people should share the polluting byproducts of industrialization, including upper socioeconomic classes who are often better equipped than others to fight environmental degradation in their communities, and who often contribute more to environmental problems than poor and vulnerable people. In addition, it is important to give those experiencing environmental injustice the tools necessary to participate fully in environmental decisions and financing to provide them legal and technical support. Actions like these will advance environmental justice principles everywhere.

12

ENVIRONMENTAL PROTECTION AND THE ECONOMY

Are environmental protection and economic growth compatible?

Without doubt, economic growth has put an enormous strain on the environmental resources that power it. In fact, the environment would not need so much protecting but for the Industrial Revolution and what followed: dependence on fossil fuels, synthetic chemicals, and all the byproducts of industry that have entered Earth's air and water. The Industrial Revolution radically changed much of the world in immensely positive ways, and very few would argue that we should return to the world that preceded it. We are learning, however, that the strain it imposed is becoming so severe that current economic growth and unsustainable environmental degradation are often companions.

The extent of the strain depends on how wisely we use our natural resources, and how we manage and conserve them. The economy relies on natural resources: without them our industries cannot produce the goods we need. But energy derived from coal, for example, pollutes the air and changes the climate. Dirty air can create health crises, and sea-level rise from climate change can flood agricultural lands with salt water, bringing higher human and economic costs. Energy processes derived from the sun, on the other hand, do not harm the environment to the same degree, and may carry lower correlated costs. In the long run, then, choosing solar power or other renewable energy sources for a factory reflects good public policy and makes good economic sense.

Economic growth, moreover, is an incomplete measure of a healthy economy, in part because it does not account for environmental impacts. Why is an increase in the sale of domestic automobiles seen as a positive economic marker? Yes, it shows growth, but is this growth sustainable if it relies on fossil fuels, which are depletable resources and which warm the planet? Why are housing starts reported as a positive economic indicator? They indicate growth of an important economic sector, but not necessarily sustainable growth if they create new sprawling housing subdivisions that require extensive roads and break ecosystems apart. Growth is a standard measure of economic success, but without careful management, in the present century it is a likely path to a fundamental and potentially catastrophic depletion of land, species, water, and air. The answer to the question, therefore, is a qualified yes: economic growth is compatible with environmental protection if it is undertaken wisely, consistent with sustainable development goals.

Even so, whenever environmental regulations impose compliance costs on industry—for catalytic converters in cars or scrubbers on air emissions stacks—a common response from affected companies and industry groups is that these will be the death knell for the industry; that in some respects economic success and environmental protection operate at cross purposes. For example, regulation of CFCs (the chemicals that were depleting the ozone layer) in the 1990s was met with resistance by industry, whose lobbyists said such regulation would create deep economic and social disruption. In the United States this has been a concern since environmental regulations first appeared in the 1970s, and it continues today when new ones are proposed. While it is true that new regulations normally impose costs on affected industries, the dire warnings have proven false. CFCs were phased out but without the consequences industry feared. The requirements for catalytic converters and smokestack scrubbers decried by industry created a global market dominated by US manufacturers. In the forty-plus years of air pollution regulation, which have seen significant improvement in air quality in the United States and related health benefits, the national gross domestic product (GDP), the most relied upon—although flawed—quantitative measure of economic progress, has risen over 140 percent.

Notwithstanding resistance from industry, as the public shows a growing desire to buy products from environmentally responsible companies, and companies see the savings to be enjoyed by environmentally sustainable production methods, environmental concerns are increasingly being reflected in how businesses operate. Many companies are now seeing the connection between a positive bottom line and an environmental ethos, between environmental protection and economic success.

How accurate is the gross domestic product as an economic measurement tool?

The GDP is a measure of economic activity based on a set of calculations concerning goods and services bought and sold. Since the mid-twentieth century a country's GDP has been viewed as an excellent indicator of its economic well-being. It is, however, a crude measure in many respects and is increasingly under scrutiny by mainstream economists, governments, and international organizations. The European Union has a Beyond GDP Initiative. In the United States, some states are reconsidering it. The GDP nevertheless has a tremendous influence on economic policy.

Among its defects is its failure to account for the environmental costs of economic activity, because these often are incurred outside of the market and so are not measured. As explained in the 2005 United Nations Millennium Assessment, the loss of a natural resource represents the loss of a capital asset. Yet a country could cut down its forests and deplete its fisheries and this would show as a positive gain in GDP (a measure of current economic well-being), without showing a corresponding decline in assets (a measure of wealth which is highly relevant to future well-being).[1] Similarly, the cost and depreciation of a factory is calculated as part of the GDP, but not the cost of the depreciation of the degraded air that receives the factory's smoky waste, or the health costs imposed on individuals and society breathing the polluted air, costs known in economic terms as externalities.

Not surprisingly, as countries and economists become better educated on the consequences of industrial pollution, discomfort with the GDP has increased. Growth and consumption, key development values in the twentieth century that are central to the calculation of the GDP, are not sustainable in the twenty-first without attending to their costly byproducts and measuring them.

What is an externality?

An externality is a cost or benefit arising from the production or consumption of goods that affects parties who are not involved in these activities. For example, the full costs of pollution are normally not borne by the individual or factory producing it. These costs are negative externalities. A vaccination is an example of a positive externality. Here, the person receiving and paying for the vaccination is getting protection from disease, but is also conferring a benefit on other people by not spreading the disease to them.

Internal costs are reflected in the price we pay for things. External costs are not. This is an extremely important feature of our market system, which has great relevance for the environment. For instance, costs internal to the production of a car include steel, labor, and energy. External costs include air and water pollution caused by the emission and discharge of waste byproducts. The pollution costs are negative externalities: they are not reflected fully in the price of the car and they are borne by people who are not directly involved in the production or consumption of it; but the steel and labor, of course, are. In essence, these external costs are subsidies from society received by the producer.

It is difficult to put a value on a wetland or forest destroyed by road construction, or a human life lost to asthma; they are outside of—that is, external to—the market. It is because of these externalities that market forces alone cannot be relied on to protect the environment, and one reason why governments need to intervene with regulation—to correct these market failures. If external environmental costs were monetized and incorporated in the cost of the things we buy (internalized), it is very likely their prices would rise and thus that we would find incentives to reduce the costly pollution, or at least understand its consequences. The market would be a more reliable check on pollution because consumers would choose less-polluting alternatives. They would, for example, more likely demand products made from renewable energy sources and recycled material. Cost-benefit analysis, popular with some economists, attempts to price these externalities but is difficult to apply in the environmental context.

What is cost-benefit analysis and why is it difficult to apply?

Cost-benefit analysis (CBA) is a widely used tool that evaluates the net economic effects of environmental regulations and related government policies by quantifying their costs and benefits in monetary terms. In the words of Lisa Heinserling and Frank Ackerman, two leading environmental scholars, "it seeks to perform, for public policy, a calculation that markets perform for the private sector."[2] Private business relies on market responses to make basic decisions on what goods to produce. The behavior of consumers and the costs of production provide the information necessary for a business to know whether a particular product will be profitable. Environmental regulators, however, lack some of these market data when making choices on how to protect the environment. One can speculate, but not know, how much society will benefit or "profit" from cleaner air or water resulting from costly regulations. The benefit to the lumber company of timber from deforested acreage is easy to quantify on the market. It is much harder to quantify the benefit that forested acreage provides—biodiversity, climate change mitigation, natural beauty—when a regulator steps in to limit the timber harvest. It is also difficult to know, in a world of finite financial resources, what the priorities for environmental protection should be. If one had to choose, is it more important to allocate funds to clean up hazardous waste sites, or to retrofit diesel buses? Which one will yield the greater return on the societal investment? What would the consumer prefer? CBA tries to get at the answers to such questions.

Its proponents see CBA as a way to ensure that society is allocating its resources wisely, that is by clarifying, in economic terms, which specific actions are worth taking. They also see it as a more objective means of making decisions because it is based on economic assumptions that are transparent, and ostensibly it imposes discipline into the policymaking process. CBA's critics see it as a probusiness approach that monetizes values that cannot be monetized and that should not carry a price tag in any case, such as a human life or a scenic vista, and which contains conceptual and practical flaws and challenges. Moreover, detractors are wary of what they see as its veneer of objectivity and legitimacy, which actually are shored up with subjective methodologies and questionable data.

In 2015 the US Supreme Court ruled that cost must be considered at the beginning of Clean Air Act rulemaking (the dispute concerned the Environmental Protection Agency's regulation of coal-fired power plants). Industry challengers priced benefits from the regulation at 6 million dollars; the EPA priced it at tens of billions.[3] CBA offers no standard formula for analysis, and is driven by policy perspectives, not just economics, as these widely different figures demonstrate.

Notwithstanding the mixed reviews CBA has received and the political and philosophical controversy it has generated, the US government has applied it ever since President Reagan first required CBA to be used for federal regulation development by Executive Order in 1981. President Obama reaffirmed the use of CBA by Executive Order in 2011. The US Office of Management and Budget (OMB) is responsible for enforcing CBA during regulation development. Some believe that OMB at times abuses this role by closely reviewing regulations (and sometimes blocking them) in ways that extend beyond strictly budgetary considerations. CBA is also applied by other bodies, including the European Union.

Does environmental regulation kill jobs?

Regulators do not want to eliminate jobs, and legislative bodies will not let them. In the United States, regulators often perform an economic impact analysis prior to issuing a regulation, which contains an evaluation of its cost and its effects on the economy. Similarly, when a company is penalized for environmental non-compliance, penalty policies (the guidance documents relied on by government enforcement staff to set the penalty and negotiate a settlement) normally require consideration of the company's ability to pay. The idea is to ensure that businesses are not shut down unless their illegal actions have egregious environmental consequences.

Nevertheless, the death knell argument has continued because it speaks to a strong ideological base, that is, those in favor of limited regulation and opposed to big government; and it raises the specter of job loss for struggling families, such as workers at paper mills in Maine and in the coal mines of Kentucky. For example, the "war on coal," which the US Chamber of Commerce, the National Mining Association, and the Senate Majority Leader from Kentucky accused President Obama of waging, is simply rhetoric designed to derail his air pollution regulations for coal-fired power plants. In fact, in

2012 barely 90,000 people were employed in coal, half of them in two states (Kentucky and West Virginia); a century ago the number was 700,000. By comparison, in 2013 the solar industry employed 143,000 people, up 20 percent from the year before and continuing to grow quickly. Meanwhile, low-cost and readily available natural gas has emerged as a serious coal competitor. At the same time, air pollution regulations have reduced deaths and illness significantly. This is not a war on coal. Rather, the economy is changing to reflect economic opportunity consistent with market forces, improvement in solar and other renewable energy generation technologies, and environmental priorities.

Can environmental regulation be good for business?

Few American business leaders would promote aggressive regulation of their industries. Industry groups such as the American Manufacturing Association, the American Petroleum Institute, and the Chemical Manufacturers Association spend significant parts of their budgets challenging federal environmental regulations and influencing environmental policy. These groups often wage important legal battles in federal courts.

Some features of these regulations, however, help businesses beyond the overarching benefits they receive from a clean environment. One is the level playing field provided by regulations at the federal level, where most of them are based. National, standard, consistent regulation of waste, water, and air provides industry with certainty about its regulatory obligations that is absent when regulation is left entirely up to smaller governmental units, especially states. While it is true that states often regulate environmental matters in partnership with the federal government, the federal government provides a regulatory foundation on which the states base their own requirements and upon which industry relies. Prime examples are federal emission control requirements for cars and federal rules about interstate transport of hazardous waste. Imagine fifty significantly different sets of rules for these important environmental regulations. Indeed, the idea of a level playing field was an important impetus for the congressional drafters of the original environmental statutes.

The enforcement of environmental regulations has also some-times been credited with spurring innovation and efficiency. For example, in 2004 Walmart was subject to an EPA enforcement action for violating anti-idling regulations at loading docks in Massachusetts and Connecticut. As a result of the action, Walmart changed its own rules to limit its seven thousand delivery trucks from idling at loading docks at four thousand facilities across the United States. Idling every truck in such a fleet for one hour a day would burn 2.1 million gallons of fuel per year. The fuel sav-ings for Walmart are considerable, and each year the air receives significantly fewer tons of smog-forming pollutants and carbon dioxide.

Finally, although not a benefit in the conventional sense, the major US environmental statutes all contain significant opportu-nities for affected industries, as well as public interest groups and individuals, to suggest changes to proposed regulations. Every time a regulation is proposed, the statutes require the EPA or other pro-posing government agency to provide a meaningful opportunity for comment. The agency then considers the comments and revises the proposed regulation if the comments improve the regulation. The agency also explains in its response to these comments why it is accepting the comments, or why not. This statutory structure allows industry, within the framework of regulation development, rather than through lobbying or litigation, other common ways to exert influence, to help shape the new requirements affecting them in a constructive way, and to help the agency avoid imposing require-ments that may be inappropriate.

What economic tools can be used to protect the environment?

Governments can and often do introduce economic tools to manip-ulate market behavior, particularly production and consumption practices, in ways that are designed to improve environmental qual-ity. In the United States and elsewhere in the world these supplement the traditional command-and-control approach to environmen-tal regulation described earlier in this book. Whereas regulatory requirements typically drive pollution down to the regulated limit, economic or market-based tools tend to drive pollution to the level that makes economic sense to the polluter. Devices that have been successful or are promising in driving pollution down include subsidies, taxes, marketable permit mechanisms such as the system known as "cap and trade," and disclosure requirements.

What are subsidies and how do they work in the environmental context?

Subsidies are forms of financial support, usually from governments, for activities thought to be socially beneficial. They include tax incentives, grants, and low-interest loans, and they are often used in the environmental context. For example, in the United States the redevelopment of brownfields in cities is promoted by government grants. Municipal recycling programs enjoy subsidies. Federally insured low-interest loans promote energy-efficient home improvements.

However, subsidies are not always good for the environment. For years, government energy subsidies have generously supported the fossil fuel industry. Although recently subsidies are giving solar and other renewables a boost as well, it is a much smaller one: globally in 2011 fossil fuel subsidies reached $500 billion, while renewables received only $88 billion. In the United States, the imbalance is about the same. This is odd not only in light of the climate crisis, but because fossil fuel industries are among the world's most profitable and do not need subsidies. Moreover, sometimes indirect subsidies occur with perverse effects. Roads built to support access to old growth timber in effect subsidize the timber industry with detrimental environmental consequences. To the extent that air or water pollution is not controlled, polluters are in effect being subsidized by the public, which must pay for the health consequences.

The converse of subsidies is taxes and user fees to discourage activities or behaviors perceived as harmful to the environment. For example, Ireland's tax on plastic bags has caused many consumers there to shop with reusable ones. And many economists think that taxing carbon will influence carbon emissions. Solid waste disposal fees create incentives to reduce waste. Where water is scarce, user fees can influence decisions on how long to let water from the tap or the shower run.

Returning to externalities: taxing an activity associated with a negative externality is a good way to correct the externality. Conversely, a subsidy is good way to encourage increased consumption of a good or service with a positive externality. Carbon taxes, then, are a good way to discourage fossil fuel consumption; and brownfields subsidies are a good way to encourage urban redevelopment.

What is cap and trade?

In a cap and trade system the government sets a limit on the total emissions of a particular pollutant, then either allocates or lets industries bid for permits to emit specific amounts up to the set limit; industries that do not use up their permitted allotment can sell the remainder. Once the cap is set, the market controls the price for the right to pollute. In the United States, cap and trade was used with some success during the George H. W. Bush administration to bring down acid rain levels. The approach benefitted from bipartisan support largely because it was not a tax, and because it relied on market principles. It is often mentioned as yet another way to reduce carbon emissions to control climate change and was promoted in the Kyoto Protocol on climate change. Consistent with Kyoto, the European Union has had a greenhouse gas cap and trade program in place since 2005, also with some success.

What does market disclosure have to do with environmental protection?

The Toxics Release Inventory (TRI) is a part of the Emergency Response and Community Right to Know Act, a US law passed in 1986. It was a congressional reaction to the devastating chemical release in 1984 at a Union Carbide plant in Bhopal, India followed in 1985 by a serious release at a similar plant in West Virginia. The TRI requires industries that emit large amounts of chemicals to report them. The data are publically available and readily accessible through a government website. One objective of the TRI is to give communities information about toxic substances nearby so they can plan for emergencies. Another is to provide incentives for companies to improve their environmental performance. The TRI is very successful: chemical releases listed in it have come down dramatically. It is an example of the power of public awareness, and the sensitivity of industry to public pressure. Information such as TRI data is increasingly available. And the public wants it, just as the public wants information about the calorie count and sugar content in foods served in restaurants. The public does have a right to know, as the title of the TRI law states.

Disclosures required of publicly traded businesses, such as in initial public offerings of stock and other relevant descriptions of corporate operations, offer similar opportunities for the public to become aware not only of current environmental legal liabilities, but also of a company's carbon footprint and other information concerning the negative impacts its operations might impose on the environment. Although many policymakers believe such disclosures could influence corporate attention to environmental issues, they are not yet legally required, as is TRI information.

What economic steps to protect the environment are most promising?

Among the tools and concepts currently available, here are some steps that are particularly promising.

- Stop subsidies that promote environmentally unsound practices, and use subsidies as appropriate to promote sound environmental practices.
- Make polluters pay for the costs of pollution by imposing taxes, user fees, and other mechanisms to internalize environmental costs.
- Give consumers and shareholders information about corporate operations and environmental impacts on product labels, in Securities and Exchange Commission filings, and other places, thus enabling them to express their preference for environmentally sound business practices and environmentally friendly goods.
- Modify measurements of national economies such as the GDP to include the benefits of environmental sustainability and the costs of environmental degradation.
- Downplay growth and include sustainable development as a measure of economic success.

Given the appropriately urgent global attention being afforded the environmental problems the world faces, it is not surprising that at the United Nations, in legislative bodies, and within nongovernmental environmental organizations and corporations numerous approaches such as these are being vigorously pursued.

13

THE FUTURE

What are the greatest threats to the environment today?

We all should be deeply concerned about our planet as we move further into the twenty-first century. Even though the science is not completely certain and the facts are evolving, it is clear that we are rapidly depleting our resources in a thoroughly unsustainable way, and that inaction, or inadequate action, is not an option.

There are many threats to the environment right now. The planet—its atmosphere, its oceans, its fresh water, and its land—are under extraordinary stress caused by the human species, the species acclaimed as so adaptable that it controls practically all the others. Yet in this century our species is facing the profoundly ironic question: can we find a way to adapt to, and maybe reverse, the threat that is ourselves? Any list of greatest environmental threats is subjective. Here is one:

- climate change
- biodiversity loss
- dying oceans
- new pollutants
- population
- poverty

Why is climate change one of the greatest environmental threats?

It is actually by far the greatest, in part because it significantly influences practically all the rest. Here is a sample of what may occur as a result of climate change deeper into the twenty-first century.

In the midwestern United States where about 60 million people live in cities such as Chicago, Minneapolis, and Kansas City, temperatures are predicted to increase by 3 degrees Fahrenheit in the next few decades and possibly by over 10 degrees by century's end. In this scenario, Michigan summers would feel like summers in Texas. In the American Southwest, where about 55 million people live in places such as Los Angeles, Denver, and Salt Lake City, and whose population is growing faster than anywhere else in the country, temperature patterns look much the same. They are rising and could get 9 degrees or so warmer by century's end, bringing more severe droughts and more competition for increasingly scarce water resources. In the Northeast, which includes the New York metropolitan area, temperatures could go up 4.5 to 10 degrees, causing flooding in coastal areas and threatening the urban infrastructure.[1]

In the fall of 2014 the *New York Times* published an article titled "Portland Will Still Be Cool, but Anchorage May Be the Place to Be: On a Warmer Planet, Which Cities Will Be Safest?" Looking ahead into the next few decades, the article stated: "Forget most of California and the Southwest (drought, wildfires). Ditto for much of the East Coast and Southeast (heat waves, hurricanes, rising sea levels). Washington, DC, for example, may well be a flood zone by 2100." The article then went on to recommend the Pacific Northwest as a "potential climate refuge." Florida, on the other hand, was described as "ground zero" for climate difficulties.[2] The disarmingly casual tone of the article cannot diminish the shocking future it portrays.

Bangladesh is a low-lying country in southeast Asia, almost one-quarter of which is less than seven feet above sea level; it is the country at greatest risk from sea-level rise. Scientists agree that by 2050, 17 percent of the land could be inundated and 18 million people displaced. By 2100 seas in Bangladesh could rise 13 feet, much faster than the global average, with dire consequences, including mass migration and urban overcrowding.[3]

Snow is an absolute must for the Winter Olympic Games. It is predicted that in 2100, only six of the countries that have hosted these games to date will have enough snow (or cold enough temperatures for artificial snow making) to host them again. By this time, two-thirds of Europe's ski resorts may be out of business for lack of snow. In eastern Canada, by midcentury the ski season could be two or more months shorter. This scenario is hardly as terrifying as the prospects for Bangladesh, but it also indicates much larger problems than recreational, entertainment, and economic losses.[4]

How serious is the future climate change threat?

It is very difficult to answer this question, largely because the answer depends on choices humans will make to address the threat. If the world chooses to institute strong CO_2 emissions controls, the temperature rise by the end of the century is predicted to be about 1°C (1.8°F), with a range from about 0.3° to 1.7°C (0.6° to 3°F). If we choose the status quo—failed international agreements and inadequate regulatory and lifestyle controls by major CO_2 emitting countries—the predicted range of temperature rise by 2100 is 3° to 5.5°C (5.4° to 9.9°F). But, importantly, this does not mean that 10°F is the highest possible temperature rise by 2100, although it is plenty high. Some climate experts analyzing IPCC data suggest that there is a 10 percent probability of temperature rise exceeding 6°C or 11° F.[5] This would be catastrophic. In other circumstances, we take the same level of risk very seriously: how many homeowners would move into a house with a known 10 percent chance of fire and raise a family there without first taking steps to reduce those chances greatly?

Why is biodiversity loss such a great threat?

Species come and go, but rarely do living creatures face mass extinctions. Humans are intrigued by the fifth great extinction that abruptly annihilated the dinosaurs and many other species about 65 million years ago. Our generation is witnessing the sixth great extinction. We have caused it. The threat is enormous because the interconnected web of life—its biodiversity, much of which remains a mystery to humans,—is the essential foundation upon which we thrive. Take away bees, coral reefs, and many of the thousands of species we have yet even to identify, and the entire natural edifice upon which we depend is shaken, its balance undone. The eminent ecologist E. O. Wilson describes our circumstances this way:

When we alter the biosphere in any direction, we move the environment away from the delicate dance of biology. When we destroy ecosystems and extinguish species, we degrade the greatest heritage this planet has to offer and thereby threaten our own existence.

Humanity did not descend as angelic beings into this world. Nor are we aliens who colonized Earth. We evolved here, one among many species, across millions of years, and exist as one organic miracle linked to others. The natural environment we treat with such unnecessary ignorance and recklessness was our cradle and nursery, our school, and remains our one and only home.[6]

Are the oceans really dying?

Until recently, the oceans were thought to be too big to seriously damage, let alone to put into a death spiral. This is no longer the view. Overfishing, pollutants (some of which accumulate in marine organisms), trash, oil spills, acidification, sonar noise, and climate change are all piling on, changing the chemistry of the oceans and disrupting the creatures that live there. These developments affect coastal habitats as well. The human species cannot thrive without healthy oceans.

Why are new pollutants such a great threat?

Many, many pollutants present grave dangers to the environment. New pollutants, that is, those insufficiently understood to safely enter our water and air (in this book sometimes called contaminants of emerging concern or CECs), are particularly unsettling. As described earlier, pharmaceuticals and personal care products are common examples. Some CECs have been contaminating us for years, but have been detected only recently. Others are new creations of our chemistry labs. They are widely used, slip through treatment systems and other controls, and often are associated with pernicious health effects such as endocrine disruption. Nanopollutants fall into this category. CECs are a great threat because we know so little about them while we enjoy their benefits. Like many other twenty-first century environmental pollutants, they eerily call to mind the warnings of *Silent Spring*.

What does population growth have to do with environmental protection?

Like the unprecedented rise in carbon dioxide, the world's population grew in the twentieth century from 1.6 billion to over 6 billion. In other words, in one hundred years it became nearly four times larger. (See Figure 13.1.) In contrast, it took many millennia for the human population to reach 1 billion. This astonishing growth was projected to level off at about 9 billion in 2050—staggering, but mildly reassuring. Recent projections, however, see the explosion extending to the end of the century with an increase to between 9.6 and 12.3 billion by 2100.

Already, the pressures from sharp population increase in the twentieth century are being felt in the environment, and by extension, by humans. In the United States, at the beginning of the twentieth century, the Colorado River delta covered almost 3,000 square miles; it now covers about two hundred and fifty. It once emptied into the Pacific Ocean. Now it dies out fifty miles north. A main reason is diversion of its water to meet the demands of a rapidly growing (and sometimes wasteful) population. The same holds true for other great world rivers, such as the Indus in Pakistan, the Yellow in China, and the Murray in Australia, all under great stress as they

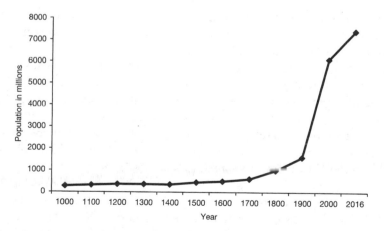

Figure 13.1 Population increase over time.

Source: Based on www.worldometers.info/world-population/world-population-by-year/.

support the people living near them. The fate of these rivers, and of water supplies, is easy to predict if current growth and consumption patterns continue.

As populations increase, especially in developing countries, the demands for food also go up. Deforestation to make room for agriculture is occurring in areas rich in biodiversity, notably in the Amazon tropical rain forests. In Nigeria, where population has quadrupled in the last sixty years, demands for livestock are causing desertification. As its urban population grows, Egypt is losing 3.5 acres an hour of its rich Nile Delta soils. Again, the future is not hard to predict if expected growth and current consumption patterns continue.

By 2100 most of the world's population will reside in dense urban centers. In fact, almost all of the population explosion we are seeing is occurring in these places; according to the World Bank, "by 2050 as many people will live in cities as the population of the whole world in 2000."[7] Many of them are in low-lying coastal areas. Some of the cities with the highest populations at highest risk from the sea-level rise expected over the next several decades are Calcutta, Mumbai, Dhaka, Ho Chi Minh City, and Miami.[8]

How is poverty connected to environmental protection?

The harmful effects of environmental degradation are borne disproportionately by the poor who generally are least responsible for it. Water scarcity and desertification are two examples on a global scale. In the United States the location of polluting facilities correlates with income and race. Poor countries also are on the receiving end of the detritus of industrial success: industrial cast-offs, such as computer parts and discarded smart phones, from richer countries go there; polluting industries relocate there for cheap labor and available land. The poor lack the resources to combat the environmental problems they experience: money is lacking, but so is information and political power, and extreme environmental problems are connected to political disenfranchisement. In 2000, Nelson Mandela asserted that "freedom alone is not enough . . . without time or access to water to irrigate your farm, without the ability to catch fish to feed your family. For this reason the struggle for sustainable development nearly equals the struggle for political freedom."[9]

With development, historically at least, comes pollution: this has been the great irony of the success of the industrialized world. Poverty itself can invite pollution when industrial development is seen as the best way to escape it. The problem going forward is how to achieve development in poorer countries without exacerbating the environmental crisis the world community is now experiencing.

The connection between poverty and pollution in the international context is often characterized as a North–South divide, with generally speaking the North being the developed, richer, countries and the South being the developing, poorer countries. The divide is real, representing two camps with different problems and different approaches to environmental issues on a global scale. It is particularly relevant in the present context of climate change negotiations. The connection between poverty and the environment was brought home pointedly by Pope Francis in his 2015 encyclical. And it was an important subject at the 2015 Paris Climate Change Conference.

Assigning responsibility is not a comfortable exercise. But here it is helpful because it encourages national accountability, both moral and economic. Responsibility for the global environmental challenges we face lies primarily with the industrialized, wealthy countries of the world.

What solutions are most promising?

Although much has been done to protect the environment, much more is needed in light of where we are today—a time fundamentally different from the first Earth Day in 1970 and first UN summit on the environment in 1972. The following are solutions that speak to the future.

Replace fossil fuels with renewables. The increased global attention to this hugely important goal is impressive. Solar energy is a hot market, with China leading the way. Governments are exploring financial means to discourage fossil fuel use. Some countries are taxing carbon. But the effort needs to be ramped up: renewables, especially solar, should be rewarded with subsidies, tax breaks, and political will. Carbon should be aggressively taxed at every governmental level by whatever means that is fair and effective.

Encourage mass transit. About one-third of greenhouse gases globally and significant amounts of other pollutants come from cars. It is estimated that by 2035—twenty or so years from now—globally there will be 1.7 billion cars on the road, double the current number, with much of the increase occurring in China and India (echoing the increases seen in the United States in the twentieth century).[10] Even if alternative fuels replace some fossil fuels powering cars the environmental impacts, including impacts from road construction and maintenance, will be huge. A mass transit infrastructure powered by clean fuel would reduce greenhouse gases and encourage smart growth, with positive impacts on climate, air quality, and ecosystem protection (as vast acreage consumed for highways and sprawl are spared).

Reduce consumption. The United States should not be perceived as a model for the developing world. No family in the United States needs a three-car garage. Disposable plastic bags are not the only way to get food from the supermarket to the kitchen. A weed-free lawn is not beautiful if it requires pesticides, herbicides, and chemical fertilizers that end up, as they inevitably do, in groundwater. We, especially suburban Americans, need to stop and think about practically every purchase we make, every product we consume, every piece of land we alter, and at least wonder whether it is justifiable environmentally, economically, and morally.

Be smart about the introduction of chemicals into the market. For producers this means being transparent and cautious, and looking for less damaging alternatives. For regulators, it means applying the precautionary principle appropriately. For the consumer it means being educated about products we use, and adjusting lifestyles and purchases to minimize environmental harms.

Foster global cooperation. Global environmental problems require global solutions, which require international cooperation. John Lennon urged us to "imagine there are no countries.

It isn't hard to do." Of course one can imagine; but it is probably impossible, and perhaps not even desirable, to transform the governments of the world into one overarching governmental structure. The inviolable notion of national sovereignty, however, needs to be turned on its head: national sovereignty yes, but subservient to intergovernmental cooperation, starting with a more muscular and better funded United Nations. Without question the United Nations has created opportunities for dialogue, for global commitments to reduce pollution, for technology sharing from North to South, and the like. It is an immensely important institution. But with the exception of the Montreal Protocol, not enough has been accomplished concretely in the international community to actually solve environmental problems. The Kyoto Protocol is largely a failure because national self-interest got in the way. A stronger international framework is needed, international cooperation must be fostered, and national interest must be put aside to deal effectively with environmental issues which require global solutions. Implementation of the Paris Agreement is a vital step.

Provide information. Publicly available information and education about the environment are critical components of environmental protection. Research, funding, policy, and law must steer toward more information, greater public awareness, and support for environmental education in schools and at home everywhere. Information also needs to be accurate. Politicians and others who enjoy the bully pulpit must deliver scientifically based, carefully considered facts and hypotheses. If they serve in legislative bodies, they should support laws and policies that fund good environmental science and promote dissemination of information.

Finally, people need to experience the natural environment, which is perhaps the most potent form of environmental information. We need to make sure our children have the ability and time to watch birds fly; to turn over a log and closely observe the life under it and to smell the rich soil supporting that life; and to peer inside a forest thicket, and maybe venture into it. These experiences are attainable, of course, in the wild, but they also exist in urban parks and in pastures, wetlands, and hillsides often only a bus ride away.

Does individual action matter?

Absolutely. At the ballot box; in stores where we choose the products we buy, and at home where we choose how to discard them; in decisions we make on where to live and how to get to work; and in what we teach our children through our actions and in our schools. One can legitimately ask whether the size of the environmental challenges means that individual action is useless. The answer must be that all actions that first do no harm, and second, model sustainable environmental values and behavior, are critically important. These actions include our own and those of educators and their students, of business and political leaders, of parents, and of coworkers, and of neighbors next door.

What is the prognosis for future generations?

The fair answer is that the prognosis is unclear. It depends on how we deal with climate change, population, poverty, and the other pressing environmental issues addressed in this book. From the perspective of this writer, however, the prognosis is good because humans have in the past and can again set aside self-interest and parochialism. We are an adaptive species. We can mitigate the problems we have created—and even reverse some of them—by throttling back consumption, creating clean energy, and directing our considerable intelligence to studying what we are doing and understanding its implications for our children and for the planet we need and love.

NOTES

CHAPTER 1

1. Al Gore, introduction to *Silent Spring* by Rachel Carson (New York: Houghton Mifflin, 1962, with a new introduction by Al Gore, 1994).
2. John Keats, "La Belle Dame Sans Merci," in *The Complete Works of John Keats* (Boston: Houghton Mifflin, 1900).
3. Richard Nixon, "Annual Message to Congress on the State of the Union," January 22, 1970; see Gerhard Peters and John T. Woolley, *The American Presidency Project*, www.presidency.ucsb.edu/ws/?pid=2921.
4. Aristotle, *Politics* 1.8.
5. *Sierra Club v. Morton*, 405 US 727 (1972), 741–42 (Douglas, J., dissenting).
6. *Report of the World Commission on Environment and Development: Our Common Future*, June 1987, Geneva, Switzerland, A/42/427, www.un-documents.net/OCF-02.htm.
7. Plan of Implementation of the World Summit on Sustainable Development, World Summit on Sustainable Development, September 2002, Johannesburg, South Africa, A/CONF.199, www.un.org/esa/sustdev/documents/WSSD_POI_PD/English/WSSD_PlanImpl.pdf.
8. Garrett Hardin, "The Tragedy of the Commons," *Science*, December 13, 1968: 1244, www.sciencemag.org/content/162/3859/1243.full.
9. 42 USC § 6901(b)(3) (1976).

CHAPTER 2

1. Arctic Monitoring and Assessment Programme, "Arctic Pollution Issues: A State of the Arctic Environment Report," cited in "Persistent Organic Pollutants: A Global Issue, A Global Response," last updated September 2, 2016, www.epa.gov/international-cooperation/persistent-organic-pollutants-global-issue-global-response.
2. Michael Pollan, "Precautionary Principle," in "The Year in Ideas: A TO Z," *New York Times Magazine*, December 9, 2001, www.nytimes.com/2001/12/09/magazine/09PRINCIPLE.html.

3. Rio Declaration on Environment and Development, United Nations Conference on Environment and Development, Rio de Janeiro, Brazil, June 1992, A/CONF.151/26 (Vol. I), Principle XV, www.unep.org/Documents. Multilingual/Default.asp?documentid=78&articleid=1163.
4. As reported in National Institute of Environmental Health Sciences, *Your Environment. Your Health*, last reviewed July 15, 2016, www.niehs.nih.gov/health/topics/agents/sya-bpa/.

CHAPTER 3

1. US Const. art. 1, § 8, cl. 3.
2. PA Const. art. 1, § 27.
3. Richard Nixon, "Annual Message to Congress on the State of the Union," January 22, 1970; see Gerhard Peters and John T. Woolley, *The American Presidency Project*, www.presidency.ucsb.edu/ws/?pid=2921.
4. Frederic H. Wagner, "Half Century of American Range Ecology and Management: A Retrospective," in *Foundations of Environmental Sustainability: The Coevolution of Science and Policy*, ed. Larry L. Lockwood, Ronald E. Stewart, and Thomas Dietz (New York: Oxford University Press, 2008), 142.
5. 42 USC § 4321.
6. 42 USC § 4331 (a).
7. *Cherokee Nation v. Georgia*, 30 US (5 Pet.) 1, 17 (1831).
8. US Environmental Protection Agency, Tribal Assumption of Federal Laws— Treatment as a State (TAS), last modified October 28, 2015, www.epa.gov/tribal/tribal-assumption-federal-laws-treatment-state-tas.
9. 42 USC § 6973 (a).
10. Michael Martina, Li Hui, David Stanway, and Stian Reklev, "China to 'Declare War' on Pollution, Premier Says," Reuters, March 14, 2014, www.reuters.com/article/us-china-parliament-pollution-idUSBREA2405W20140305.

CHAPTER 4

1. U.N. Charter art. 1, para. 3.
2. United Nations Environment Programme, "About UNEP," last accessed September 30, 2016, www.unep.org/About/.
3. Rio Declaration on Environment and Development, United Nations Conference on Environment and Development, Rio De Janeiro, Brazil, June 1992, A/CONF.151/26 (Vol. I), www.unep.org/Documents.Multilingual/Default.asp?documentid=78&articleid=1163.
4. Indira Gandhi, "Man and Environment," Plenary Session of the United Nations Conference on Human Environment, Stockholm, June 14, 1972, LASU-LAWS Environmental Blog, http://lasulawsenvironmental.blogspot.com/2012/07/indira-gandhis-speech-at-stockholm.html.
5. Maurice F. Strong, *ECO '92: Critical Challenges and Global Solutions*, Journal of International Affairs 44 (1991), 288–89, www.jstor.org/stable/24357310.

6. Clyde Haberman, "The Snake That's Eating Florida," *New York Times*, April 5, 2015, www.nytimes.com/2015/04/06/us/the-burmese-python-snake-thats-eating-florida.html.
7. A. Hsu, Environmental Performance Index (New Haven, CT: Yale University, 2016), www.epi.yale.edu.

CHAPTER 5

1. "Brunswick Area Saltwater Intrusion Monitoring," US Department of the Interior, US Geological Survey, last modified May 29, 2015, http://ga.water. usgs.gov/projects/intrusion/brunswick.html. See also "Saltwater Intrusion Puts Drinking Water at Risk," *NOAA's State of the Coast*, http://stateofthe-coast.noaa.gov/water_use/groundwater.html (site discontinued).
2. "Groundwater Study Assesses Potential for Contamination of Drinking-Water Aquifers in Los Angeles," US Department of the Interior, US Geological Survey, last modified May 19, 2014, https://www.usgs.gov/news/groundwater-study-assesses-potential-contamination-drinking-water-aquifers-los-angeles.
3. Simon Romero and Christopher Clarey, "Note to Olympic Sailors: Don't Fall in Rio's Water," *New York Times*, May 18, 2014, www.nytimes.com/2014/05/19/world/americas/memo-to-olympic-sailors-in-rio-dont-touch-the-water. html?_r=0.
4. "Facts and Figures on Water Quality and Health," *Water Sanitation and Health*, World Health Organization, 2015, http://who.int/water_sanitation_health/facts_figures/en/ (site discontinued).
5. "EPA-Supported Scientists Find Average But Large Gulf Dead Zone," National Oceanic and Atmospheric Administration, August 4, 2014, www. noaanews.noaa.gov/stories2014/20140804_deadzone.html.
6. "Concentrated Feeding Operations: EPA Needs More Information and a Clearly Defined Strategy to Protect Air and Water Quality from Pollutants of Concern," US General Accounting Office Report to Congressional Requestors, September 2008, www.gao.gov/assets/290/280229.pdf, 5.
7. US Environmental Protection Agency, "EPA Priority Pollutant List," December 2014, www.epa.gov/sites/production/files/2015-09/documents/priority-pollutant-list-epa.pdf.
8. European Commission, "Priority Substances and Certain Other Pollutants according to Annex II of Directive 2008/105/EC," last modified August 6, 2016, http://ec.europa.eu/environment/water/water-framework/priority_substances.htm.
9. "Factsheet: Polybrominated Diphenyl Ethers (PBDEs) and Polybrominated Biphenyls (PBBs)," Centers for Disease Control and Prevention, last modified July 23, 2013, www.cdc.gov/biomonitoring/PBDEs_FactSheet.html.
10. EPA New England, "Clean Water Act NPDES Determinations for Thermal Discharge and Cooling Intake from Brayton Point Station in Somerset, MA (NPDES Permit No. MA 0003654)," Chapter 2.6, July 22, 2002.
11. "Access to Sanitation," *Water for Life 2005–2015*, United Nations Department of Economic and Social Affairs, last modified October 23, 2014, www. un.org/waterforlifedecade/sanitation.shtml.

12. Christine Dell'Amore, "Antarctica May Contain 'Oasis of Life,'" *National Geographic News*, December 27, 2007, http://news.nationalgeographic.com/news/2007/12/071227-antarctica-wetland.html.

13. Felicity Barringer, "Michigan Landowner who Filled Wetlands Faces Prison," *New York Times*, May 18, 2004, www.nytimes.com/2004/05/18/us/michigan-landowner-who-filled-wetlands-faces-prison.html.

14. 40 C.F.R. 230.4 (t).

15. US Environmental Protection Agency, "Wetlands & West Nile Virus," 2003, nepis.epa.gov.

16. "Habitat Conservation," National Oceanic and Atmospheric Administration, November 21, 2013, www.habitat.noaa.gov/highlights/coastalwetlandsreport.html.

17. United Nations, "Global Issues: Water," last accessed September 30, 2016, www.un.org/en/globalissues/water/.

18. Scott Friedman, "EPA Tests Show 'High' Percentage of Airplanes Still Have Bacteria in Water Served On-Board," NBC 5 Investigates, October 29, 2013, www.nbcdfw.com/investigations/EPA-Tests-Show-High-Percentage-of-Airplanes-Still-Have-Bacteria-in-Water-Served-On-Board-226813491.html.

CHAPTER 6

1. World Health Organization, "7 Million Premature Deaths Linked to Air Pollution," March 24, 2014, www.who.int/mediacentre/news/releases/2014/air-pollution/en/.

2. Jennifer Chu, "Study: Air Pollution Causes 200,000 Early Deaths Each Year in the U.S.," *MIT News*, August 29, 2013, http://newsoffice.mit.edu/2013/study-air-pollution-causes-200000-early-deaths-each-year-in-the-us-0829.

3. US Environmental Protection Agency, Air Pollutants, last modified October 26, 2015, www.epa.gov/learn-issues/learn-about-air.

4. "A Treaty that Inspires Global Action," The World Bank, September 19, 2012, www.worldbank.org/en/news/feature/2012/09/19/treaty-inspires-global-action.

5. World Health Organization, "Ambient Air Pollution," last accessed September 30, 2016, www.who.int/gho/phe/outdoor_air_pollution/en/.

6. US Environmental Protection Agency, "Visibility, Basic Information," last modified September 26, 2016, www.epa.gov/visibility/visibility-basic-information.

7. World Health Organization Media Center, "Asthma," Fact sheet No. 307, 2013, last modified November 2013, www.who.int/mediacentre/factsheets/fs307/en/.

8. US Environmental Protection Agency, "Nearly 26 Million Americans Continue to Live with Asthma, EPA Says," May 7, 2013, http://yosemite.epa.gov/opa/admpress.nsf/0c0affede4f840bc8525781f00436213/3b36ff39a3e4874985257b64004bc30d!OpenDocument.

9. http://www.lung.org/lung-health-and-diseases/lung-disease-lookup/asthma/learn-about-asthma/asthma-children-facts-sheet.html?referrer=https://www.google.com/.

10. US Environmental Protection Agency, "What Are Hazardous Air Pollutants?" www.epa.gov/haps/what-are-hazardous-air-pollutants.

11. World Health Organization, "Radon," last accessed October 1, 2016, www. who.int/ionizing_radiation/env/radon/en/.

12. American Academy of Pediatrics Policy Statement, "Ambient Air Pollution: Health Hazards to Children," *Pediatrics* 114 (2004): 1699–1707, doi: 10.1542/ peds. 2004-2166, p. 5, http://pediatrics.aappublications.org/content/114/6/ 1699.full.

13. US General Accounting Office, "Information on Tall Smokestacks and their Contribution to Interstate Transport of Air Pollution," GAO-11-473, June 10, 2011, www.gao.gov/products/GAO-11-473.

14. US Environmental Protection Agency, "Cross-State Air Pollution Rule," last modified September 7, 2016, www3.epa.gov/airtransport/CSAPR/.

15. US Environmental Protection Agency, "Air Quality Trends," last modified July 21, 2016, www.epa.gov/air-trends/air-quality-national-summary.

16. US Environmental Protection Agency, "Highlights from the Clean Air Act 40th Anniversary Celebration," last modified August 8, 2016, www.epa.gov/clean-air-act-overview/highlights-clean-air-act-40th-anniversary-celebration.

17. American Lung Association, "Millions of Americans Breathing Unhealthy, Polluted Air, Finds American Lung Association's 2015 'State of the Air' Report," April 29, 2015, www.lung.org/about-us/media/press-releases/ 2015-stateoftheair.html?referrer=https://www.google.com/.

18. US Environmental Protection Agency, Air Quality Index, last modified August 31, 2016, http://airnow.gov/index.cfm?action=aqibasics.aqi.

19. www.airqualitynow.eu/comparing_home.php (last accessed October 1, 2016).

20. World Air Quality Index, Real time, https://waqi.info/.

CHAPTER 7

1. Rachel Carson, *Silent Spring* (New York: Houghton Mifflin, 1962), 189.

2. Barry Commoner, *The Closing Circle: Nature, Man, and Technology* (New York: Knopf, 1971), 33.

3. Millennium Ecosystem Assessment 2005, *Ecosystems and Human Wellbeing Synthesis* (Washington, DC: Island Press, 2005), www.millenniumassessment.org/documents/document.356.aspx.pdf, 1.

4. EPA, "Terminology Services, Terms and Acronyms," last modified September 1, 2015, http://iaspub.epa.gov/sor_internet/registry/termreg/searchandretrieve/termsandacronyms/search.do.

5. Camilio Mora, Derek P. Tittensor, Sina Adl, Alaastair G. B. Simpson, and Boris Worm, "How Many Species Are There on Earth and in the Ocean?," August 23, 2011, *PLOS Biology* (8): e1001127, doi: 10.1371/journal.pbio.1001127, http:// journals.plos.org/plosbiology/article?id=10.1371/journal.pbio.1001127.

6. Robert May, "Tropical Arthropod Species, More or Less?," *Science*, July 2, 2010: 41, doi: 1126/science.1191058.

7. Convention on Biological Diversity, "Sustaining Life on Earth," Secretariat of the Convention on Biological Diversity, April 2000, p. 5, www.cbd.int/ doc/publications/cbd-sustain-en.pdf.

8. Subcommission on Quarternary Stratigraphy, International Commission on Stratigraphy, last modified May 5, 2015, quaternary.stratigraphy.org/ workinggroups/anthropocene/.

9. US National Institutes of Health, National Cancer Institute, "Success Story: Taxol (NSC 125973)," last accessed October 1, 2016, https://dtp.cancer. gov/timeline/flash/success_stories/S2_taxol.htm.

10. Ewen Callaway, "How Elephants Avoid Cancer," *Nature* (October 8, 2015), doi: 10.1038/nature.2015.18534, www.nature.com/news/how-elephants-avoid-cancer-1.18534.

11. John Seidensticker, "Ecological and Intellectual Baselines: Saving Lions, Tigers, and Rhinos in Asia," in *Foundations of Environmental Sustainability: The Coevolution of Science and Policy*, ed. Larry L. Lockwood, Ronald E. Stewart, and Thomas Dietz (New York: Oxford University Press, 2008), 100.

12. 42 USC § 1531 (a) (1), (2), (3), and (4).

13. US Fish and Wildlife Service, ECOS, Summary of Listed Populations and Recovery Plans, last accessed October 1, 2016, https://ecos.fws.gov/tess_public/pub/Boxscore.do.

14. IUCN 2016. *The IUCN Red List of Threatened Species. Version 2016–2*, last accessed October 1, 2016, http://www.iucnredlist.org.

15. European Commission, "Invasive and Alien Species," last modified September 20, 2016, http://ec.europa.eu/environment/nature/invasivealien/index_en.htm.

16. Worldwatch Institute, "Vision for a Sustainable World: Rising Number of Farm Animals Poses Environmental and Public Health Risks," 2012, www. worldwatch.org/rising-number-farm-animals-poses-environmental-and-public-health-risks.

17. John Muir, *The Yosemite* (Auckland, NZ: The Floating Press, 2012), https:// books.google.com/books?id=LImED8WgrWQC&pg=PA5&source=gbs_toc_r&cad=3#v=onepage&q&f=false, 6.

18. Millennium Ecosystem Assessment, *Ecosystems and Human Well-being: Synthesis* (Washington, DC: Island Press, 2005), www.millenniumassessment.org/documents/document.356.aspx.pdf, 6.

19. Millennium Ecosystem Assessment, *Ecosystems and Human Well-being: Synthesis* (Washington, DC: Island Press, 2005), www.millenniumassessment.org/documents/document.356.aspx.pdf, 6.

20. United Nations Decade on Biodiversity, "Strategic Goals and Targets for 2020," last accessed March 20, 2015, www.cbd.int/2011-2020/goals/.

CHAPTER 8

1. Robert Rohde, Richard A. Muller, Robert Jacobsen, Elizabeth Muller, Saul Perlmutter, Arthur Rosenfeld, Jonathan Wurtele, Donald Groom, and Charlotte Wickham, "A New Estimate of the Average Earth Surface Land Temperature Spanning 1753 to 2011," *Geoinformatics & Geostatistics: An Overview* 1, no. 1 (2013), www.scitechnol.com/new-estimate-of-the-average-earth-surface-land-temperature-spanning-to-1eCc.pdf.

2. IPCC, 2013, "Summary for Policymakers," in *Climate Change 2013: The Physical Science Basis. Contribution of Working Group I to the Fifth Assessment Report of the Intergovernmental Panel on Climate Change*, ed. T. F. Stocker and D. Qin (New York: Cambridge University Press, 2014), www.climatechange2013.org/images/report/WG1AR5_SPM_FINAL.pdf, 4.

3. US Environmental Protection Agency, "Future Climate Change," last updated September 29, 2016, www.epa.gov/climate-change-science/future-climate-change.
4. Intergovernmental Panel on Climate Change, "Climate Change 2014: Synthesis Report, Summary for Policymakers," 2014, www.ipcc.ch/pdf/assessment-report/ar5/syr/AR5_SYR_FINAL_SPM.pdf, 2.
5. Intergovernmental Panel on Climate Change, "The Physical Science Basis, Frequently Asked Questions 3.1," 2013, www.ipcc.ch/report/ar5/wg1/docs/WG1AR5_FAQbrochure_FINAL.pdf, 11.
6. Intergovernmental Panel on Climate Change, "The Physical Science Basis, Frequently Asked Questions 8.1," 2013, www.ipcc.ch/report/ar5/wg1/docs/WG1AR5_FAQbrochure_FINAL.pdf, 37, 38.
7. Apple Environmental Report, "iPhone 6s," September 2016, http://images.apple.com/environment/pdf/products/iphone/iPhone6s_PER_sept2016.pdf.
8. IPCC Fourth Assessment Report, "Climate Change 2007: Synthesis Report," 2007, www.ipcc.ch/publications_and_data/ar4/syr/en/spms1.html.
9. US Global Change Research Program, "National Climate Assessment," 2014, http://nca2014.globalchange.gov/highlights/overview/overview.
10. Brad Johnson, "Inhofe: God Says Global Warming is a Hoax," *Climateprogress*, March 9, 2012, http://thinkprogress.org/climate/2012/03/09/441515/inhofe-god-says-global-warming-is-a-hoax/.
11. Pope Francis (Pontifex), Twitter statement, April 21, 2015.
12. Coral Davenport and Laurie Goldstein, "Pope Francis Steps up Campaign on Climate Change, To Conservatives' Alarm," *New York Times*, April 27, 2015, www.nytimes.com/2015/04/28/world/europe/pope-francis-steps-up-campaign-on-climate-change-to-conservatives-alarm.html?_r=0.
13. Union of Concerned Scientists, "Smoke, Mirrors, and Hot Air: How ExxonMobil Uses Big Tobacco's Tactics to Manufacture Uncertainty on Climate Science," Union of Concerned Scientists, January 2007, www.ucsusa.org/sites/default/files/legacy/assets/documents/global_warming/exxon_report.pdf.
14. IPCC, "Summary for Policymakers," in *Climate Change 2014: Impacts, Adaptation, and Vulnerability. Part A: Global and Sectoral Aspects. Contribution of Working Group II to the Fifth Assessment Report of the Intergovernmental Panel on Climate Change*, ed. Christopher B. Field and Vicente R. Barros (New York: Cambridge University Press, 2014), 1–32.
15. David Abel, "Logan Airport Drafts Climate Change Plan," *Boston Globe*, May 4, 2015, www.bostonglobe.com/metro/2015/05/03/logan-plans-major-changes-address-climate-change/KXnlO6Q0DwqlqessI17d12H/story.html.
16. Kia Gregory and Marc Santora, "Bloomberg Outlines $ 20 Billion Storm Protection Plan," *New York Times*, June 11, 2013, www.nytimes.com/2013/06/12/nyregion/bloomberg-outlines-20-billion-plan-to-protect-city-from-future-storms.html.
17. Alan Harish, "New Law in North Carolina Bans Latest Scientific Predictions of Sea-Level Rise," *ABC News*, August 2, 2012, http://abcnews.go.com/US/north-carolina-bans-latest-science-rising-sea-level/story?id=16913782; N.C. Gen. Stat. § 113A-107.1.

18. IPCC, *Climate Change 2014: Mitigation of Climate Change. Contribution of Working Group III to the Fifth Assessment Report of the Intergovernmental Panel on Climate Change* (New York, Cambridge University Press, 2014).
19. US Environmental Protection Agency, "Assessment of the Potential Impacts of Hydraulic Fracturing for Oil and Gas on Drinking Water Resources," June 2015, www.epa.gov/hydraulicfracturing.
20. Columbia Law School, Sabin Center for Climate Change Law, "Climate Change Laws of the World," last accessed November 19, 2016, columbiaclimatelaw.com.
21. John Schwartz, "Ruling Says Netherlands Must Reduce Greenhouse Gas Emissions," *New York Times*, June 24, 2015, www.nytimes.com/2015/06/25/science/ruling-says-netherlands-must-reduce-greenhouse-gas-emissions.html?_r=0.
22. *Massachusetts v. EPA*, 549 US 497 (2007).
23. "UN Chief Hails New Climate Change Agreement as 'Monumental Triumph,'" *United Nations News Centre*, December 12, 2015, www.un.org/apps/news/story.asp?NewsID=52802#VnGs25MrKMI.
24. Paris Agreement, December 12, 2015, Article 2, 1 (a), https://unfccc.int/files/meetings/paris_nov_2015/application/pdf/paris_agreement_english_.pdf.
25. Paris Agreement, Article 4, 2.
26. Paris Agreement, Article 21, 1.
27. United Nations Framework Convention on Climate Change, United Nations 1992, Article 3, Principle 1.
28. United Nations Framework Convention on Climate Change, United Nations 1992, Article, 4, §§ 4 and 7.
29. Paris Agreement, preamble.
30. Coral Davenport, "Climate Change Deemed Growing Security Threat by Military Researchers, *New York Times*, May 13, 2014, www.nytimes.com/2014/05/14/us/politics/climate-change-deemed-growing-security-threat-by-military-researchers.html.
31. Coral Davenport, "Pentagon Signals Security Risks of Climate Change," *New York Times*, October 13, 2014, www.nytimes.com/2014/10/14/us/pentagon-says-global-warming-presents-immediate-security-threat.html.
32. Intergovernmental Panel on Climate Change, *Climate Change 2014: Synthesis Report*, Summary for Policymakers 2.3, last accessed October 1, 2016, www.ipcc.ch/pdf/assessment-report/ar5/syr/AR5_SYR_FINAL_SPM.pdf.

CHAPTER 9

1. Barry Commoner, *The Closing Circle: Nature, Man, and Technology* (New York: Knopf, 1971), 40.
2. United Nations Environment Programme, "Solid Waste Management," last accessed October 1, 2016, www.unep.org/resourceefficiency/Policy/ResourceEfficientCities/FocusAreas/SolidWasteManagement/tabid/101668/Default.aspx.
3. The World Bank, "Solid Waste Management," December 21, 2013, www.worldbank.org/en/topic/urbandevelopment/brief/solid-waste-management.
4. UN News Centre, "Biodegradable Plastics Are Not the Answer to Reducing Marine Litter, Says UN," November 17, 2015, www.un.org/newscentre/Default.aspx?DocumentID=26854&ArticleID=35564.

5. 42 USC § 6901 (a) and (b).
6. Eckhardt C. Beck, "The Love Canal Tragedy," *EPA Journal*, January 1979, last updated September 22, 2016, www.archive.epa.gov/aboutepa/love-canal-tragedy.html.
7. US Environmental Protection Agency, "Brownfield Overview and Definition," December 13, 2015, www.epa.gov/brownfields/brownfield-overview-and-definition.
8. Zoe Schlanger, "Millennials Not That Into 'Things' and That Goes for Cars Too," *Newsweek*, January 27, 2014, www.newsweek.com/millenials-just-not-things-and-goes-cars-too-227210.
9. World Bank, *What a Waste: A Global Review of Solid Waste Management*, 2012, http://siteresources.worldbank.org/INTURBANDEVELOPMENT/Resources/336387-1334852610766/What_a_Waste2012_Final.pdf, 27.

CHAPTER 10

1. David Owen, "Green Manhattan: Everywhere Should Be More Like New York," *The New Yorker*, October 18, 2004, 111.
2. US Environmental Protection Agency, "Heat Island Effect," last updated September 2, 2016, www.epa.gov/heat-islands.
3. Andrew Goudie, *The Human Impact on the Natural Environment*, 7th ed. (Oxford: Wiley-Blackwell, 2013), 161.
4. Jayne E. Daly, "A Glimpse of the Past—A Vision for the Future: Senator Henry M. Jackson and National Land Use Regulation," *The Urban Lawyer* 28, no. 1 (Winter 1996): 7, n. 1.
5. 42 USC § 4331 (b) (1).

CHAPTER 11

1. Commonwealth of Massachusetts, Environmental Justice Policy of the Executive Office of Environmental Affairs, October 9, 2002, Definitions, www.mass.gov/eea/docs/eea/ej/ej-policy-english.pdf.
2. US Environmental Protection Agency, "Environmental Justice," last modified September 14, 2016, www.epa.gov/environmentaljustice.
3. US General Accounting Office, "Siting of Hazardous Waste Landfills and their Correlation with Racial and Economic Status of Surrounding Communities," June 1, 1983, GAO/RCED 83–68, www.gao.gov/products/RCED-83-168.
4. Commission for Racial Justice, United Church of Christ, "Toxic Waste and Race in the United States: A National Report on Racial and Socioeconomic Characteristics of Communities with Hazardous Waste Sites," 1987, www.csu.edu/cerc/researchreports/documents/ToxicWasteandRace-TOXICWASTEANDRACE.pdf.
5. Exec. Order No.12898, 59 FR 7629, February 16, 1994.

CHAPTER 12

1. Millennium Ecosystem Assessment, *Ecosystems and Human Well-being: Biodiversity Synthesis* (Washington, DC: World Resources Institute, 2005), www.unep.org/maweb/documents/document.354.aspx.pdf, 6.
2. Lisa Heinzerling and Frank Ackerman, *Pricing the Priceless: Cost-Benefit Analysis of Environmental Protection* (Washington, DC: Georgetown Environmental Law

and Policy Institute, Georgetown University Law Center, 2002), www.ase.tufts. edu/gdae/publications/C-B%20pamphlet%20final.pdf, 4.

3. Adam Liptak and Coral Davenport, "Supreme Court Blocks Obama's Limits on Power Plants," *New York Times*, June 29, 2015.

CHAPTER 13

1. US Environmental Protection Agency, "Climate Change Impacts," last updated August 23, 2016, www3.epa.gov/climatechange/impacts/.

2. Jennifer A. Kingson, "Portland Will Still Be Cool, But Anchorage May Be the Place to Be: On a Warmer Planet, Which Cities will Be Safest," *New York Times*, September 22, 2014, www.nytimes.com/2014/09/23/science/on-a-warmer-planet-which-cities-will-be-safest.html.

3. Gardiner Harris, "Borrowed Time on Disappearing Land: Facing Rising Seas, Bangladesh Confronts the Consequences of Climate Change," *New York Times*, March 28, 2014, www.nytimes.com/2014/03/29/world/asia/facing-rising-seas-bangladesh-confronts-the-consequences-of-climate-change.html.

4. Porter Fox, "The End of Snow?'," *New York Times*, February 7, 2014, www.nytimes.com/2014/02/08/opinion/sunday/the-end-of-snow.html.

5. Gernot Wagner and Martin L. Weitzman, *Climate Shock: The Economic Consequences of a Hotter Planet* (Princeton, NJ: Princeton University Press, 2015), 53.

6. E. O. Wilson, *The Future of Life* (New York: Vintage, 2003), 39–40.

7. World Bank, *What a Waste: A Global Review of Solid Waste Management*, March 2012, http://siteresources.worldbank.org/INTURBANDEVELOPMENT/Resources/336387-1334852610766/What_a_Waste2012_Final.pdf, 3.

8. Susan Hanson, Robert Nicholls, and Nicola Ranger, "A Global Ranking of Port Cities with High Exposure to Climate Extremes," *Climate Change* 104 (1) (2011): 89–111: 99, www.researchgate.net/publication/225826456_A_global_ranking_of_port_cities_with_high_exposure_to_climate_extremes.

9. Nelson Mandela, "Beyond Freedom: Transforming 'Ngalamadami' into 'Sithi Sonke,'" address at the launch of Final Report of World Commission on Dams, November 16, 2000, www.mandela.gov.za/mandela_speeches/2000/001116_wcd.htm.

10. CNBC: "Woah! 1.7 Billion Cars on the Road by 2035," November 12, 2012, www.cnbc.com/id/49796736.

FURTHER READING

Bodansky, Daniel, Jutta Brunnee, and Ellen Hay, eds. *The Oxford Handbook of International Environmental Law*. New York: Oxford University Press, 2007.

Brennan, Andrew, and Yeuk-Sze Lo. "Environmental Ethics." In *The Stanford Encyclopedia of Philosophy* (Winter 2015 Edition), edited by Edward N. Zalta. http://plato.stanford.edu/archives/win2015/entries/ethics-environmental/.

Bullard, Robert D., ed. *The Quest for Environmental Justice: Human Rights and the Politics of Pollution*. San Francisco: Sierra Club Books, 2005.

Carson, Rachel. *Silent Spring*. New York: Houghton Mifflin, 1962. With a new introduction by Al Gore, copyright 1994.

Commoner, Barry. *The Closing Circle*. New York: Knopf, 1971.

Farber, Daniel A., and Roger W. Findley. *Environmental Law in a Nutshell*. 9th ed. St. Paul, MN: West, 2014.

Gore, Al. *Earth in the Balance*. New York: Rodale, 1992.

Gore, Al. *The Future: Six Drivers of Global Change*. New York: Random House, 2013.

Goudie, Andrew. *The Human Impact on the Natural Environment: Past, Present, and Future*. 7th ed. West Sussex: Wiley-Blackwell, 2013.

Graham, Mary. *The Morning after Earth Day: Practical Environmental Politics*. Washington, DC: The Brookings Institution, 1999.

Jacobs, Jane. *The Death and Life of Great American Cities*. New York: Vintage Books edition, 1992. First published 1961 by Random House.

Kriebel, David, Joel Tickner, Paul Epstein, John Lemons, Richard Levins, Edward C. Loechler, Margaret Quinn, Ruthann Rudel, Ted Schettler, and Michael Stoto. "The Precautionary Principle in Environmental Science." *Environmental Health Perspectives* 109 (2001): 871–76.

Maslin, Mark. *Climate Change: A Very Short Introduction*. 3rd ed. Oxford: Oxford University Press, 2014.

Percival, Robert V., Christopher H. Schroeder, Alan S. Miller, and James P. Leape. *Environmental Regulation: Law, Science, and Policy*. 7th ed. New York: Wolters Kluwer Law and Business, 2013.

Randers, Jorden. *2052: A Global Forecast for the Next Forty Years*. White River Junction, VT: Chelsea Green Publishing, 2012.

Revesz, Richard L. *Foundations of Environmental Law and Policy*. New York: Oxford University Press, 1997.

Rockwood, Larry L., Ronald E. Stewart, and Thomas Dietz, eds. *Foundations of Environmental Sustainability: The Coevolution of Science and Policy.* New York: Oxford University Press, 2008.

Sachs, Jeffrey D. *The Age of Sustainable Development.* New York: Columbia University Press, 2015.

Smith, Stephen. *Environmental Economics: A Very Short Introduction.* New York: Oxford University Press, 2011.

Susskind, Lawrence E., and Saleem H. Ali. *Environmental Diplomacy: Negotiating More Effective Global Agreements.* 2nd ed. New York: Oxford University Press, 2015.

Wagner, Gernot, and Martin L. Weitzman. *Climate Shock: The Economic Consequences of a Hotter Planet.* Princeton, NJ: Princeton University Press, 2015.

Weis, Judith S. *Marine Pollution: What Everyone Needs to Know.* New York: Oxford University Press, 2015.

Wilson, Edward O. *The Future of Life.* New York: Vintage, 2003.

ONLINE RESOURCES

General
For definitions of environmental terms: US Environmental Protection Agency, http://iaspub.epa.gov/sor_internet/registry/termreg/searchandretrieve/termsandacronyms/search.do; search on specific terms.

Environmental Laws
For US environmental laws and related materials: US Environmental Protection Agency, Laws & Regulations page, www.epa.gov/laws-regulations.
For Native American law and policy: US Department of the Interior, Indian Affairs FAQ page, www.bia.gov/FAQs.
For environmental laws and related materials in the United Kingdom: UK Government, Environment Agency page, www.gov.uk/government/organisations/environment-agency.
For Canadian environmental laws and related materials: Government of Canada, Environment and Climate Change page, www.ec.gc.ca/default.asp?lang=en&n=FD9B0E51-1.
For environmental laws and related materials from around the world: Practical Law, Global.practicallaw.com; search on "environmental law."
For European Union legislation, directives, and related materials: European Commission, Environment page, http://ec.europa.eu/environment/index_en.htm.

Environmental Protection and the Global Community
For general information on the United Nations Environment Programme: www.unep.org.
For United Nations environmental treaties, conventions, protocols, and related materials: United Nations Treaty Collection, Multilateral Treaties Deposited with the Secretary-General page, https://treaties.un.org/pages/Treaties.aspx?id=27&subid=A&lang=en.

Water
For water-related information with a US focus: US Environmental Protection Agency, Learn About Water page, http://water.epa.gov.
For global information: Global Issues, Water page, www.un.org/en/sections/issues-depth/water/index.html.

Air
For air-related information with a US focus: US Environmental Protection Agency, Learn About Air page, https://www.epa.gov/learn-issues/learn-about-air.

Ecosystems
For global information: Millennium Ecosystem Assessment, Guide to the Millennium Assessment Reports page, www.millenniumassessment.org/en/reports.html.
For US species-related information: US Fish & Wildlife Service, Endangered Species page, www.fws.gov/endangered.

Climate Change
For IPCC reports, summaries, and frequently asked questions: Intergovernmental Panel on Climate Change Reports page, http://ipcc.ch/publications_and_data/publications_and_data_reports.shtml.
For climate-related topics with a US focus: US Environmental Protection Agency, Climate Change page, www.epa.gov/climatechange.

Waste
For general information on waste in the United States: US Environmental Protection Agency, Learn About Waste page, www.epa.gov/learn-issues/learn-about-waste; US Environmental Protection Agency, Advancing Sustainable Materials Management page, www.epa.gov/smm/advancing-sustainable-materials-management-facts-and-figures.
For global information: The World Bank, What a Waste page, siteresources.worldbank.org/INTURBANDEVELOPMENT/Resources/336387-1334852610766/What_a_Waste2012_Final.pdf.

The Built Environment
For information about smart growth: US Environmental Protection Agency, Smart Growth page, www.epa.gov/smartgrowth/about-smart-growth.

Environmental Justice
For general information about environmental justice in the United States: US Environmental Protection Agency, Environmental Justice page, www.epa.gov/environmentaljustice.

INDEX